EDL WORD CLUES ™.

J

Senior Author

Helen Frackenpohl Morris
Educational Developmental Laboratories

Consultant

Arthur S. McDonald
Nova Scotia Department of Education

Lesson Authors

Nancy Joline
Alan Petraske

Test Author

Elinor H. Kinney
Rumson-Fair Haven (N.J.) Regional High School

INTRODUCTION

What do you do when you encounter a word that is not familiar? Do you stop to look it up, do you try to analyze its parts, or do you look for clues in the way the word is used in its setting or surroundings?

There are several methods that may be used in unlocking the meaning of unfamiliar words. But the quickest and most practical approach is knowing how to use the context, or the words around the unknown word, to unlock its meaning. This method is called using context clues or "word clues."

You may say, "Why not look up all unknown words in a dictionary?" The dictionary is, of course, one of our most valuable tools in meeting and dealing with new words. You can't get by without it. But there are many times a dictionary will not be available. Even if you're reading with a dictionary near at hand, you don't want to stop every few minutes to look up a word. The chain of thought would be interrupted so often that you would lose much of the pleasure and profit in your reading.

Let's look at some of the ways we can get the meaning of a word from context without looking it up in the dictionary.

1. One way to use context clues is to look for a *synonym*, or a word that has the same meaning. Sometimes a writer or a speaker will give a synonym for an unfamiliar word just to make sure that we understand it. For example, look at this sentence:

   "When an atom undergoes fission, or splitting, a tremendous amount of energy is released."

   In this case, the author thought that you might not know the meaning of *fission*, so he or she provided a synonym—*splitting*.

2. Another context clue is a definition or explanation that precedes or follows a difficult word. For example, you might not know what the word *quandary* means, but by studying its use in the context of this sentence, you could find its meaning:

   "When a person cannot choose between two solutions to a difficult problem, this is called being in a quandary."

   This sentence makes it very clear that *quandary* means a state of perplexity or uncertainty.

3. At other times, the context may give us a fairly good meaning of a word by telling what it is like or even what it is not like. We might call these clues of similarities or differences. Do you know what *opacity* means? See if you can figure out its meaning from these two sentences:

   "The opacity of various materials differs greatly. We know, for example, that transparent substances, such as air, glass, and water, have almost no opacity. Light passes directly through them."

   Now you know that *opacity* means something that is different from air, glass, and water, or something that is not clear or transparent. When materials are clear or transparent and light passes through them easily, they are said to have no *opacity*. Therefore, you can reason that *opacity* must mean "a blocking of light."

4. Another way to use context clues is to notice the circumstances in which the word appears. When you are aware of information given in connection with a word, you can "put two and two together" and guess its meaning. Read this sentence in which the word *feasible* is used:

   "The mountain climbers searched desperately for a feasible means of rescuing the injured man. They finally decided that the only way they could reach him was by lowering another man on a rope."

   It is not difficult to see that *feasible* has to do with being able to effect, or accomplish, something. *Feasible*, therefore, means "capable of being done."

There will be times when none of these four approaches will work. When you cannot use context clues, you must use the dictionary. But even then, you will need to use context clues in order to select the appropriate dictionary definition. The dictionary might give you the generally accepted meaning or perhaps a number of different meanings. It is up to you to choose the correct meaning and adapt it to the context with which you are working.

The WORD CLUES series will help you use context clues to discover the meanings of unfamiliar words. This series consists of seven books on a variety of reading levels. One way to find your starting level is to use the *EDL Word Clues Self-Placement Guide*.* It will help you find the WORD CLUES book with which you should start.

*EDL Word Clues Self-Placement Guide. Copyright© 1975 Educational Developmental Laboratories, Inc.

ISBN 1-55855-806-3

11 12 13 14 15 PO 00 99 98 97 96

HOW TO USE THIS BOOK

WORD CLUES is a programmed book. It teaches you in a step-by-step fashion and tells you immediately whether you are right or wrong.

You don't read the pages in this book in the usual way. You have probably noticed that the pages are divided into bands of white and gray. Each of these bands is called a frame, and all of the frames are numbered. You work through the book "by the numbers," turning the page for each new frame, and **working only on the right-hand pages**. After starting with frame 1, you go on to 1a, 1b, 1c, 2a, 2b, 2c, etc.

Each of the 30 lessons in the book starts with the beginning of a story. You then complete 30 frames to help you master ten words. The three frames for each word are labeled *a*, *b*, and *c*.

The *a* frame Here the word is introduced. It is divided into syllables and its pronunciation is given. Say the word to yourself. This may help you think of its meaning. If you are not sure of the pronunciation, refer to the pronunciation key on the inside back cover. Then read the sentence or sentences in which the word is used. Looking at the way the word is used, write a definition or synonym in the space provided. If you are not sure, guess. This is not a test but rather a way to help you find out how well you know the word's meaning.

The *b* frame The word is used again. This time, the setting contains more clues to the meaning of the word. Find these clues and use them to complete the meaning, or synonym, exercise in this frame. Then check to see if you were correct by turning the page and looking at the extreme left of the *c* frame. If you were wrong, circle the correct meaning, and then read the sentences again with this meaning in mind.

The *c* frame The dictionary entry* appears at the left. When a word has multiple meanings, study all of them. Also notice if the word can be used as several parts of speech. If other forms of the word are given, study these too. Notice any pronunciation changes.

The right side of the *c* frame gives you a chance to see if you understand how the word can be used. You will find two kinds of exercises: usage exercises and analogies. For some of the usage exercises you will need to refer to the dictionary entry. Other times, you will have to rely on your experience.

The analogy exercises deal with relationships between pairs of words. A definition of analogy is "likeness in some ways between things that are otherwise different."

To complete an analogy exercise, you need to figure out how two words are related, and then apply this knowledge to another pair of words.

Here is one type of analogy:

> **Winter** is to **summer** as **day** is to
> a. light
> b. night
> c. cold
> d. warm

Winter and summer are opposites. To complete the analogy, you select the word that is the opposite of day. The answer is, of course, choice c—night.

Sometimes analogies deal with synonyms, as in this example:

> **Rough** is to **crude** as
> a. coarse is to smooth
> b. bark is to tree
> c. tender is to gentle
> d. cruel is to kind

Here you look for a choice in which the words are synonyms. The answer is choice c, because tender and gentle are synonyms.

Notice the difference between the two examples given so far. In the first, you looked for *one word* to complete the analogy. In the second, you looked for a *pair of words* that bare related in the same way as the words in the first pair.

Here are some additional kinds of analogies:
PART-WHOLE: **Leaf** is to **plant** as **page** is to **book**.
FUNCTION: **Write** is to **pencil** as **paint** is to **brush**.
QUALITY: **Smooth** is to **satin** as **coarse** is to **burlap**.
You will encounter other kinds of analogies as you work through the lessons in this book.

A special kind of punctuation is used to express analogies. It looks like this:
Smile : cheer :: frown : worry
This would be read as:
Smile *is to* cheer *as* frown *is to* worry. This special punctuation is used in all of the analogy exercises in this book.

When you have finished the *c* exercise, check your answers by turning the page and looking to the left of the next frame. If you were wrong, circle the correct meaning and then reread the exercise to see why you were wrong. You are then ready to proceed to the next *a* frame.

Whenever you use WORD CLUES, be ready to give it your complete attention. Never leave a word until you are sure you understand its meaning or meanings.

Now you are ready to start on frame 1.

---

*Dictionary entries are taken from SCOTT, FORESMAN ADVANCED DICTIONARY by E. L. Thorndike and Clarence L. Barnhart. Copyright © 1979, 1974 by Scott, Foresman and Company.

BOOK J
ANSWER KEY FOR MASTERY TESTS

Lesson 1	Lesson 6	Lesson 11	Lesson 16	Lesson 21	Lesson 26
1. b	51. b	101. d	151. c	201. c	251. e
2. b	52. c	102. c	152. e	202. b	252. d
3. d	53. d	103. b	153. d	203. d	253. e
4. e	54. e	104. e	154. c	204. a	254. b
5. d	55. a	105. d	155. b	205. b	255. c
6. a	56. c	106. b	156. e	206. c	256. d
7. a	57. d	107. c	157. e	207. e	257. e
8. e	58. a	108. c	158. a	208. c	258. d
9. c	59. d	109. b	159. b	209. c	259. a
10. b	60. e	110. d	160. e	210. e	260. b
Lesson 2	**Lesson 7**	**Lesson 12**	**Lesson 17**	**Lesson 22**	**Lesson 27**
11. a	61. e	111. e	161. d	211. a	261. b
12. d	62. b	112. c	162. b	212. b	262. c
13. b	63. c	113. a	163. c	213. a	263. a
14. c	64. d	114. b	164. a	214. b	264. e
15. e	65. d	115. a	165. d	215. c	265. c
16. c	66. e	116. e	166. c	216. e	266. b
17. e	67. a	117. d	167. e	217. e	267. d
18. d	68. b	118. e	168. b	218. c	268. a
19. a	69. d	119. b	169. a	219. b	269. c
20. b	70. c	120. c	170. e	220. e	270. d
Lesson 3	**Lesson 8**	**Lesson 13**	**Lesson 18**	**Lesson 23**	**Lesson 28**
21. a	71. e	121. d	171. e	221. d	271. e
22. b	72. d	122. a	172. c	222. a	272. d
23. b	73. a	123. d	173. a	223. b	273. c
24. e	74. e	124. e	174. b	224. d	274. e
25. c	75. c	125. e	175. c	225. a	275. a
26. e	76. b	126. b	176. d	226. e	276. b
27. d	77. d	127. c	177. e	227. c	277. a
28. c	78. a	128. a	178. b	228. c	278. b
29. d	79. b	129. e	179. d	229. d	279. c
30. a	80. c	130. d	180. c	230. c	280. e
Lesson 4	**Lesson 9**	**Lesson 14**	**Lesson 19**	**Lesson 24**	**Lesson 29**
31. b	81. c	131. d	181. e	231. e	281. d
32. d	82. e	132. a	182. b	232. b	282. c
33. e	83. b	133. a	183. d	233. d	283. a
34. a	84. a	134. b	184. e	234. b	284. e
35. c	85. a	135. c	185. b	235. e	285. b
36. a	86. e	136. d	186. c	236. b	286. e
37. d	87. c	137. a	187. d	237. c	287. d
38. c	88. e	138. e	188. a	238. d	288. a
39. e	89. d	139. c	189. e	239. e	289. b
40. b	90. c	140. b	190. d	240. b	290. d
Lesson 5	**Lesson 10**	**Lesson 15**	**Lesson 20**	**Lesson 25**	**Lesson 30**
41. a	91. a	141. b	191. a	241. a	291. a
42. c	92. e	142. c	192. e	242. b	292. d
43. d	93. c	143. a	193. c	243. a	293. e
44. b	94. b	144. b	194. d	244. c	294. b
45. e	95. e	145. e	195. e	245. d	295. c
46. c	96. d	146. d	196. d	246. e	296. c
47. c	97. a	147. c	197. a	247. b	297. d
48. d	98. b	148. e	198. b	248. c	298. b
49. e	99. d	149. a	199. c	249. d	299. e
50. b	100. a	150. b	200. d	250. e	300. c

ANSWER KEY FOR BOOK J POSTTEST

1. b 2. a 3. c 4. a 5. a 6. d 7. c 8. a 9. d 10. a 11. d 12. a 13. b 14. a 15. d 16. d 17. c 18. a 19. c 20. a 21. d 22. b 23. b 24. b 25. c

LESSON

1

The Friends of the Sea

The oceans of the world are our last frontier, and we're in danger of spoiling them by pollution. That's what Sally Kendall believed. After working with concerned groups and individuals across America, Sally decided to move to Washington, D.C. Her next step was to push for laws to protect the oceans. She knew that her main opponent would be Congressman Rupert Jamison.

26a

fal la cy (fal′ ə sē)

Frank Ferter went over Connie's testimony again and again, looking for a **fallacy** in her story.

Write a definition or synonym:

51a

bi ol o gy (bī ol′ ə jē)

Tom and Peggy obtained permission to visit Dr. Thornbill's **biology** lab. Dr. Thornbill greeted them at the door and immediately began to explain his work.

Write a definition or synonym:

76b

Even today, however, many people are deceived by **humbugs** who claim to possess supernatural powers.

The meaning of **humbug** is:
__**a.** fraud
__**b.** performer
__**c.** palm reader
__**d.** magician

101b

Lady Pamela sat on deck in the morning. The air was less **torrid** then because the sun was low and there was a slight breeze.

Torrid means:
__**a.** humid
__**b.** sluggish
__**c.** quiet
__**d.** hot

126c

sil hou ette (sil′ü et′), *n., v.,* **-et ted, -et ting.** —*n.* 1 an outline portrait, especially in profile, cut out of a black paper or drawn and filled in with some single color. 2 a dark image outlined against a lighter background. 3 contour of a garment, figure, etc. —*v.t.* show in outline: *The mountain was silhouetted against the sky.* [< Étienne de *Silhouette,* 1709-1767, French finance minister]

Check the qualities that are characteristic of a **silhouette.**
__**a.** contrasts with background
__**b.** is dark
__**c.** has a definite shape
__**d.** is always moving
__**e.** has fuzzy edges

1

176b

Most dealers will give you exactly what you pay for. Occasionally, however, you may meet one who is not **ethical**. Such a dealer is interested only in the money he can make.

Another word for **ethical** is:
_a. eternal _c. polite
_b. moral _d. sly

Go back to page 154 and continue on frame 176c.

201a

au ra (ôr′ ə)

There is an **aura** about New York which no other city in the world has.

Write a definition or synonym:

Go back to page 154 and continue on frame 201b.

226a

b, d, f

hy drau lic (hī drô′ lik)

When asked how the huge segments of the bridge are being joined together, John answered in two words: "**hydraulic** crane."

Write a definition or synonym:

Go back to page 154 and continue on frame 226b.

a, b, d

LESSON  | That's Why the Lady Is a Spy!

You can call her Maria. It's not her real name, but you're not going to learn her real name—not if she wants to stay alive. Maria has been a field agent for a branch of the government for almost seven years. Maria's life is one of constant, almost unbearable danger.

Go back to page 154 and continue on frame 251a.

275c

b

gen teel (jen tēl′), *adj.* 1 belonging or suited to polite society. 2 polite; well-bred; fashionable; elegant. 3 artificially polite and courteous. [< Middle French *gentil* < Latin *gentilis.* Doublet of GENTILE, GENTLE, JAUNTY.] —**gen teel′ly,** *adv.* —**genteel′ness,** *n.*

Check the item(s) which can correctly describe a **genteel** person.
_a. well-mannered
_b. affected
_c. thoroughbred
_d. stylish
_e. extravagant
_f. refined

Go back to page 154 and continue on frame 276a.

300c

d

sear (sir), *v.t.* 1 burn or char the surface of: *sear a roast.* See **burn** for synonym study. 2 make hard or unfeeling: *That cruel man must have a seared conscience.* 3 dry up; wither: *The hot summer sun seared the grain.* —*v.i.* become dry, burned, or hard. See **burn** for synonym study. —*n.* mark made by searing. —*adj.* sere. [Old English *sēarian* < *sēar,* adjective]

Check the sentence(s) in which **sear** or **seared** can be correctly substituted for the italicized word.
_a. The fire will *burn* better with dry wood.
_b. Misfortune had *hardened* his once gentle nature.
_c. The brand of the ranch was *burned* into the steer's hide.

The End

2

1a

seethe (sēᴛʜ)

If you could have seen inside the mind of Sally Kendall before her fight with Congressman Rupert Jamison, you would have found it **seething** with activity.

Write a definition or synonym:

26b

According to Connie, she had forgiven her husband for running away, she had agreed to take him back again, and she had promised to do everything he wanted. Now where was the **fallacy** in that story? Surely there must be a mistake or a falsity there someplace!

Another word for **fallacy** is:
— **a.** weakness
— **b.** prejudice
— **c.** trick
— **d.** error

51b

"In the study of **biology**," Thornbill explained, "we learn about the lower forms of plant and animal life. We also investigate more advanced forms of life, like this creature. It seems to be a new life-form."

Biology is the science of:
— **a.** animals
— **b.** plants
— **c.** life
— **d.** the earth

76c

a

hum bug (hum′bug′), *n., v.,* **-bugged, -bug ging.** —*n.* 1 person who pretends to be what he is not; fraud; impostor. 2 cheat; sham. 3 nonsense or pretense. —*v.t.* deceive with a sham; cheat. [origin unknown]

ANALOGY humbug : sham :: strength :
— **a.** witchcraft
— **b.** truth
— **c.** supernatural
— **d.** trick
— **e.** power

101c

d

tor rid (tôr′id, tor′id), *adj.* 1 very hot; burning; scorching: *torrid weather.* 2 exposed or subject to great heat: *torrid deserts.* 3 very ardent; passionate: *a torrid love scene.* [< Latin *torridus* < *torrere* to parch] —**tor′rid ly,** *adv.* —**tor′rid ness,** *n.*

If you were taking a trip to a **torrid** country, which of the following should you pack?
— **a.** water container
— **b.** sunglasses
— **c.** ice skates
— **d.** parka
— **e.** head covering

127a

a,b,c

frus trate (frus′ trāt)

Because of Lou's mishap, the guerrilla's mission against the enemy was **frustrated**.

Write a definition or synonym:

176a

eth i cal (eth′ ə kəl)

It is not **ethical** to deal in bogus stamps.

Write a definition or synonym:

LESSON 21

The Big Apple!

One of my favorite cities is New York. I have visited this great, exciting city several times. There is always something new to see: the shops and art galleries of Soho and Greenwich Village, Central Park, the stores on Fifth Avenue, the museums, churches, and theaters. . .

225c

b

la bo ri ous (lə bôr′ē əs, lə bōr′ē əs), *adj.* 1 requiring much work; requiring hard work: *Climbing a mountain is laborious.* 2 showing signs of effort; not easy; labored: *laborious excuses for being late.* 3 hard-working; industrious: *Bees and ants are laborious insects.* —**la bo′ri ous ly,** *adv.*

Which of the following words mean the *opposite* of **laborious**?
—**a.** wearisome
—**b.** simple
—**c.** energetic
—**d.** idle
—**e.** uphill
—**f.** slothful

250c

a

prov i dent (prov′ə dənt), *adj.* 1 having or showing foresight; careful in providing for the future; prudent. 2 economical; frugal. —**prov′i dent ly,** *adv.*

Check the sentence(s) that illustrate(s) the meaning of **provident**.
—**a.** "A stitch in time saves nine."
—**b.** "Waste not, want not."
—**c.** "A new broom sweeps clean."
—**d.** "A penny saved is a penny earned."
—**e.** "Don't cry over spilt milk."

275b

The **genteel** upper classes are usually the only ones who have both the money and the interest for such a long, leisurely voyage.

The meaning of **genteel** is:
—**a.** traveling about
—**b.** well-bred
—**c.** gentle
—**d.** young

300b

I tried to grow some plants I had brought from home, but they quickly became brown and **seared** from the heat of the sun. If it had been any hotter, I think the leaves would have burst into flames!

A synonym for **sear** is:
—**a.** droop
—**b.** cut
—**c.** invigorate
—**d.** burn

1b

Meetings between Sally and the Congressman were outwardly calm and friendly. Inside, however, both people were **seething** with rage.

Another word for **seethe** is:
___a. blush
___b. act
___c. boil
___d. talk

26c

d

fal la cy (fal/ə sē), *n., pl.* **-cies.** 1 a false idea; mistaken belief; error: *It is a fallacy to suppose that riches always bring happiness.* 2 mistake in reasoning; misleading or unsound argument. [< Latin *fallacia* < *falla-cem* deceptive < *fallere* deceive]

Which of the following is **a fallacy**?
___a. Fiction is real.
___b. Truth is often stranger than fiction.
___c. All people love insects.
___d. Spiders trap other insects.
___e. A dictionary is filled with words.

51c

c

bi ol o gy (bī ol/ə jē), *n.* 1 the scientific study of plant and animal life, including its origin, structure, activities, and distribution. Botany, zoology, and ecology are branches of biology. 2 the plant and animal life of a particular area or region. 3 the biological facts about a particular plant or animal.

A **biologist** might study:
___a. desert plants
___b. floral arrangements
___c. rodents
___d. carnivorous animals
___e. rocks

77a

b

froth (frôth, froth)

As the peasant women knelt before their lady, one of them suddenly began to **froth** at the mouth.

Write a definition or synonym:

102a

a,b,e

stu pe fy (stü′ pə fī, styü′ pə fī)

Unfortunately, disaster struck during the noon hour when the heat was most **stupefying**.

Write a definition or synonym:

127b

Although the guerrilla attack had been **frustrated** for that night, Costas promised to make another try two nights later. The men called it a postponement rather than a defeat.

A synonym for **frustrate** is:
___a. lose
___b. encourage
___c. foil
___d. postpone

175c

d

bo gus (bō′gəs), *adj.* U.S. not genuine; counterfeit; sham. [origin unknown]

ANALOGY bogus : artificial :: genuine :
— **a.** real
— **b.** formal
— **c.** flavor
— **d.** leather
— **e.** died

200c

a

tran scribe (tran skrib′), *v.,* -scribed, -scrib ing. —*v.t.* 1 copy in writing or in typewriting: *The account of the trial was transcribed from the stenographer's shorthand notes.* 2 set down in writing or print: *a speech transcribed in the newspapers, word for word.* 3 arrange (a piece of music) for a different instrument or voice.* 4 make a recording or phonograph record of (a program, music, etc.) for playing back or broadcasting. 5 represent (a speech sound) by a phonetic symbol. —*v.i.* broadcast a phonograph record. [< Latin *transcribere* < *trans-* over + *scribere* write] —**tran scrib′er,** *n.*

Check the sentence(s) in which a form of **transcribe** is used correctly.
— **a.** We spent a quiet evening gazing into the fire and transcribing phonograph records.
— **b.** He transcribed my piano lesson book for his accordion.
— **c.** I transcribed a postcard to my friend.
— **d.** The secretary had difficulty transcribing her notes.

225b

Bridge-building is a complex job that requires the **laborious** efforts of a great many men. Each step of construction may take months of toil to complete.

Laborious means:
— **a.** easy
— **b.** hard-working
— **c.** lazy
— **d.** united

250b

The **provident** farm families grew their own food and kept cows, pigs, and chickens. They made use of everything and wasted nothing.

Provident means:
— **a.** prudent
— **b.** lucky
— **c.** extravagant
— **d.** intelligent

275a

c

gen teel (jen tēl′)

Rhoda's aunt and most of her fellow passengers were very **genteel**.

Write a definition or synonym:

300a

e

sear (sir)

By the time we reached the company headquarters and settled down in our new home, I had learned one thing that was never mentioned in the *Arabian Nights:* the desert heat is **searing**.

Write a definition or synonym:

1c

seethe (sēTH), *v.*, **seethed, seeth ing.** —*v.i.*
1 be excited; be disturbed: *seethe with discontent.* See **boil**[1] for synonym study.
2 bubble and foam: *Water seethed under the
falls.* 3 ARCHAIC. boil. —*v.t.* 1 soak; steep.
2 boil. [Old English *sēothan*]

Syn. *v.i., v.t.* 6 **Boil, simmer, seethe,** when
used figuratively, mean to be emotionally
excited. **Boil** suggests being so stirred up by
emotion, usually anger, that one's feelings
are thought of as bubbling over: *Resentment
was boiling in my breast.* **Simmer** suggests
less intense emotion or greater control, so
that one's feelings are just below the boiling
point: *I was simmering with laughter.* **Seethe**
suggests being violently stirred up, so that a
person or a group of people is thought of as
boiling and foaming: *The people seethed with
discontent.*

Check the sentence(s) in which a form of **seethe** is used correctly.

__a. Please seethe the water for coffee.

__b. The trees were seething in the breeze.

__c. The water seethed as the waves broke on the rocks.

__d. The farmer asked me to seethe the field.

27a

a, c

glib (glib)

As Berry listened to his client's testimony, he, too, felt Connie was a little too **glib**.

Write a definition or synonym:

52a

a, c, d

dis sect (di sekt′, dī sekt′)

A team of biologists with very strong stomachs were preparing to **dissect** the slimy creature.

Write a definition or synonym:

77b

The other women ran away. They knew that the **froth**, pouring like soapsuds from the woman's mouth, meant she had also been stricken by the malady.

Another word for **froth** is:

__a. cleanser

__b. bubble

__c. saliva

__d. foam

102b

As usual, Lord Stanley kept the crew at work even though the intense noonday heat dulled the senses. The men were so **stupefied** by the heat, their wits were slow. No one saw the logs floating just under the water until the logs rammed the boat and broke the propeller.

The meaning of **stupefy** is:

__a. alert

__b. make dull

__c. melt; soften

__d. relax

127c

c

frus trate (frus′trāt), *v.t.*, **-trat ed
-trat ing.** 1 make useless or worthless; bring
to nothing; foil; defeat. 2 prevent from accomplishing; thwart; oppose: *frustrated in
one's ambition.* See synonym study below.
[< Latin *frustratum* disappointed < *frustra*
in vain]
Syn. 2 **Frustrate, thwart, baffle** mean to
keep from accomplishing some purpose.

Frustrate implies making a person's efforts
and plans seem useless: *The police frustrated
the bandits' attempt to rob the bank.* **Thwart**
implies blocking his efforts: *The sudden
storm thwarted the men trying to reach the
wrecked plane.* **Baffle** implies confusing or
bewildering him so that he can proceed no
further: *The absence of clues baffled the
police.*

Check the sentence(s) in which a form of **frustrate** is used correctly.

__a. Management frustrated the workers' strike.

__b. The ten-dollar bill was counterfeit and therefore was frustrated.

__c. He was frustrated at losing the game.

175b

A collector may treasure a **bogus** stamp under the illusion that he possesses a valuable specimen.

Another word for **bogus** is:
- _a. worthless
- _b. irreplaceable
- _c. colorful
- _d. counterfeit

200b

After the concert is **transcribed** on tape, our director will have the tapes used to make a record album. This will give more people a chance to hear us and will allow us to hear ourselves in order to further improve our performances.

A synonym for **transcribe** is:
- _a. record
- _b. televise
- _c. preserve
- _d. broadcast

225a

e

la bo ri ous (lə bôr′ ē əs, lə bōr′ ē əs)

John didn't say so, but we all know that building a bridge is a **laborious** task.

Write a definition or synonym:

250a

d

prov i dent (prov′ ə dənt)

In one section of town everyone dressed the way people did one hundred years ago. There was a display of a farm kitchen and workshop which showed how **provident** the early farmers were.

Write a definition or synonym:

274c

c

in fi del (in′fə dəl), *n.* 1 person who does not believe in religion. 2 person who does not accept a particular faith. During the Crusades, Moslems called Christians infidels. 3 person who does not accept Christianity. —*adj.* not believing in religion. [< Latin *infidelis* unfaithful < *in-* not < *fides* faith]

ANALOGY infidel : saint :: villain :
- _a. minister
- _b. deity
- _c. hero
- _d. confession
- _e. congregation

299c

d

in fer nal (in fer′nl), *adj.* 1 of or having to do with hell. 2 of the lower world which the ancient Greeks and Romans thought of as the abode of the dead. 3 fit to have come from hell; hellish; diabolical: *infernal cruelty.* 4 INFORMAL. abominable; outrageous. [< Late Latin *infernalis* < *infernus* hell < Latin, lower < *inferus* situated below] —**in fer′nal ly,** *adv.*

ANALOGY infernal : flames :: heavenly :
- _a. host
- _b. sincere
- _c. taste
- _d. dress
- _e. angels

8

2a

c

re or gan ize (rē ôr′ gən īz)

Sally began to **reorganize** a citizen's committee called The Friends of the Sea.

Write a definition or synonym:

27b

Connie Craven seemed to have a **glib** answer ready for every question. Because each answer came so easily and so neatly, her story sounded too perfect. Would the jury believe her?

A synonym for **glib** is:
__**a.** smooth-talking
__**b.** insincere
__**c.** deceptive
__**d.** quick-acting

52b

After they had **dissected** the creature using special knives, they would examine each part, in hopes of discovering its species.

Dissect means:
__**a.** to dissolve
__**b.** to change to
__**c.** to remove the skin of
__**d.** to divide into parts

77c

d

froth (frôth, froth), *n.* 1 foam. 2 foaming saliva coming from the mouth, caused by disease, exertion, etc. 3 something light or trifling; trivial notions, talk, etc. —*v.i.* give out froth; foam. —*v.t.* 1 cover with foam. 2 cause to foam by beating, pouring, etc. [Middle English *frothe* < Scandinavian (Old Icelandic) *frotha*]

Which of the following might show **froth**?
__**a.** a pig eating at a trough
__**b.** a tired horse
__**c.** beaten egg whites
__**d.** a stagnant pond
__**e.** an ocean wave
__**f.** the wake of a boat

102c

b

stu pe fy (stü′pə fī, styü′pə fī), *v.t.*, **-fied**, **-fy ing.** 1 make stupid, dull, or senseless. 2 overwhelm with shock or amazement; astound: *They were stupefied by the calamity.* [< Latin *stupefacere* < *stupere* be amazed + *facere* to make] —**stu′pe fi′er**, *n.*

If you were **stupefied** you could be:
__**a.** "all agog"
__**b.** "full of wonder"
__**c.** "out cold"
__**d.** "bright as a new penny"
__**e.** "bowled over"

128a

a,c

dem o li tion (dem′ ə lish′ ən, dē′ mə lish′ ən)

Even though he had a chance to return to the U.S. lines, Lou decided to stay with Costas and his guerrillas. He knew the objective of the next raid was the **demolition** of an important railroad bridge.

Write a definition or synonym:

9

175a

a

bo gus (bō′ gəs)

Since rare stamps can bring such high prices, there are always some **bogus** stamps in circulation.

Write a definition or synonym:

200a

. c, d, e
. finally
final
finale

tran scribe (tran skrīb′)

Our director has promised to **transcribe** our next concert.

Write a definition or synonym:

224c

c

seg ment (seg′mənt), *n.* 1 piece or part cut, marked, or broken off; division; section: *A tangerine is easily pulled apart into its segments.* 2 in geometry: **a** part of a circle, etc., cut off by a line, especially a part bounded by an arc and its chord. **b** part of a sphere cut off by two parallel planes. **c** line segment. —*v.t., v.i.* divide into segments. [< Latin *segmentum* < *secare* to cut]

ANALOGY segment : whole :: rung :
    __**a.** cube
    __**b.** ball
    __**c.** foot
    __**d.** plane
    __**e.** ladder

249c

d

mon o logue (mon′l ôg, mon′l og), *n.* 1 a long speech by one person in a group; speech that monopolizes conversation. 2 entertainment by a single speaker. 3 a play for a single actor. 4 part of a play in which a single actor speaks alone. 5 poem or other literary composition in the form of a soliloquy. Also, **monolog.** [< French < *mono-* + *(dia)logue*]

ANALOGY monologue : dialogue :: single :
    __**a.** speaker
    __**b.** printer
    __**c.** entertainer
    __**d.** double
    __**e.** crowd

274b

Of course, to the Turks, the Christian invaders had also been **infidels** because they did not embrace the Islamic religion of the Turks.

An **infidel** is:
    __**a.** a believer
    __**b.** a faithful person
    __**c.** a nonbeliever
    __**d.** an enemy

299b

Every morning we had to shake our shoes in case scorpions had crept inside. These **infernal** creatures are not only hideous in appearance, but have a deadly sting as well.

The meaning of **infernal** is:
    __**a.** immense
    __**b.** fertile
    __**c.** living in desert regions
    __**d.** abominable

2b

Sally thought the existing committee would be more effective if it were **reorganized**. She planned to form two subcommittees: one to gather research and the other to work with Congress.

Reorganize means:
- __a. open again
- __b. rearrange
- __c. recruit
- __d. inspire

27c

a

glib (glib), *adj.,* **glib ber, glib best.** speaking or spoken too smoothly and easily to be believed: *a glib sales talk. No one believed his glib excuses.* See **fluent** for synonym study. [probably < Frisian *glibberig* slippery] **—glib′ly,** *adv.* **—glib′ness,** *n.*

ANALOGY glib : tongue-tied ::
- __a. smart : bright
- __b. horrible : terrible
- __c. bold : shy
- __d. red : orange
- __e. beast : monster

52c

d

dis sect (di sekt′, dī sekt′), *v.t.* **1** cut apart (an animal, plant, etc.) in order to examine or study the structure. **2** examine carefully part by part; criticize in detail; analyze. [< Latin *dissectum* cut apart < *dis-* + *secare* to cut] **—dis sec′tor,** *n.*

Check the sentence(s) in which a form of **dissect** is used correctly.
- __a. The critic dissected the play to show its poor construction.
- __b. She dissected the light by pulling out the plug.
- __c. The doctor dissected her new theory.
- __d. He dissected the engine to try to find why it would not run.

78a

b, c, e, f

ire (īr)

Nobody knew whether Wanda really was a witch. But it looked as though she had caused the peasant woman to fall sick. It would be difficult for Wanda to convince her husband of her innocence. And Wanda, like everyone else at the manor, was deathly afraid of his ire.

Write a definition or synonym:

103a

a, b, c, e

sloth ful (slōth′ fəl, slôth′ fəl)

The men struggled to repair the damage, but the intense heat made it difficult to work. Lady Stanley screamed at the men and called them **slothful**.

Write a definition or synonym:

128b

All the enemy's supply trains had to cross this one steel bridge. Its **demolition** would stop the flow of supplies to the enemy and cause them great hardship.

Demolition means:
- __a. loss
- __b. destruction
- __c. impairment
- __d. explosion

11

174c

a

de pre ci ate (di prē′shē āt), *v.,* **-at ed, -at ing.** —*v.t.* 1 lessen the value or price of. 2 speak slightingly of; belittle: *Some people depreciate the value of exercise.* —*v.i.* lessen in value: *The longer an automobile is driven the more it depreciates.* [< Latin *depretiatum* lessened in price < *de-* + *pretium* price]

ANALOGY depreciate : decrease in value :: appreciate :
- __a. grow in value
- __b. enjoy to the fullest
- __c. decline in worth
- __d. criticize unfairly
- __e. praise highly

199c

c

fi na le (fə nä′lē, fi nal′ē), *n.* 1 the concluding part of a piece of music or a play. 2 the last part; end. [< Italian]

1. Check the word(s) that mean(s) about the *opposite* of **finale**.
   - __a. termination   __d. commencement
   - __b. finish   __e. inauguration
   - __c. overture   __f. conclusion
2. Place these words in the proper slots in the sentence below: **final, finale, finally.**
   We _____ came to the _____ note in the _____.

224b

The **segments** are being lifted up and joined until they span the entire width of the river.

Segment means:
- __a. partition
- __b. flat piece
- __c. section
- __d. link

249b

A **monologue** is a difficult feat because the performer has no one with whom to share the task of keeping the audience entertained.

A **monologue** is:
- __a. a lecture on a single subject
- __b. saying whatever one pleases
- __c. talking "off the top of one's head"
- __d. entertainment by a single speaker

274a

c

in fi del (in′ fə dəl)

When they docked for a visit to Istanbul, Rhoda found it hard to remember that these friendly Turks had been the **infidels** of the Crusades.

Write a definition or synonym:

299a

a, c, d

in fer nal (in fėr′ nl)

We were frightened by the **infernal** appearance of some desert creatures.

Write a definition or synonym:

2c

b

re or gan ize (rē ôr′gə nīz), v.t., v.i., -ized,
-iz ing. 1 organize anew; form again; arrange in a new way. 2 form a new company
to operate (a business in the hands of a
receiver). —re or′gan iz′er, n.

Check the word(s) or expression(s) that mean(s) the *opposite* of **reorganize**.
__a. remodel
__b. make do
__c. retain
__d. antagonize

28a

c

plau si ble (plô′ zə bəl)

When Berry Amazing stood up to address the jury, he
said: "Ladies and gentlemen, I will show you that the
accused, Connie Craven, has given you a perfectly
plausible account of what happened."

Write a definition or synonym:

53a

a,c

col league (kol′ ēg′)

Thornbill's **colleague**, Dr. Alice Legrand, was a little
worried about the project.

Write a definition or synonym:

78b

Wanda knew the slightest mistake stirred her
husband's **ire**. His wrath would be even stronger now
because the sick peasants could not work their fields
or pay their rent.

Ire means:
__a. displeasure
__b. anger
__c. lash
__d. curiosity

103b

The apparently **slothful** performance of the men did
not result from lack of desire to work. Rather, the
intense heat and high humidity made work almost
impossible. What looked like laziness was really heat
exhaustion!

Slothful means:
__a. tired
__b. forgetful
__c. lazy
__d. stubborn

128c

b

dem o li tion (dem′ə lish′ən,   dē′mə-
lish′ən), n. a demolishing; destruction.

Which of the following words mean about the *opposite*
of **demolition**?
__a. destruction
__b. eruption
__c. creation
__d. construction

298c

rift (rift), *n.* 1 cleft or fissure in the earth, a rock, etc. 2 an opening or break in clouds or mist. 3 crack, rent, or chink in any object. 4 breach in relations; *a rift in a friendship.* —*v.t.* cause or form a rift; split; cleave. —*v.i.,* cause or form a rift; split; cleave.
[< Scandinavian (Old Icelandic) *ript*]

Check the word(s) that mean(s) the *opposite* of **rift**.
__a. union
__b. incision
__c. attachment
__d. joining
__e. fracture

b

273c

dis il lu sion (dis'il iu/zhən), *v.t.* set free from illusion; disenchant. —*n.* freedom from illusion. —dis il lu sion ment, *n.*

ANALOGY disillusion : enchant ::
__a. magic : science
__b. ocean : sea
__c. damage : repair
__d. forbid : prevent
__e. trick : fool

d

249a

mon o logue (mon' l ŏg, mon' l og)

For the centennial, he delivered a lengthy **monologue** which reviewed the history of the entire town.

Write a definition or synonym:

b, c

224a

seg ment (seg' mant)

John told us that the Southport Bay Bridge, like most bridges, is being built in **segments**.

Write a definition or synonym:

a, b, c

199b

Toward the end of every concert, the chorus and orchestra alike put forth a burst of effort for the **finale**.

Another word for **finale** is:
__a. apex
__b. pinnacle
__c. conclusion
__d. climax

174b

A collection that contains many rare stamps will be worth a great deal of money. These stamps will never **depreciate** and may even continue to grow in value.

The meaning of **depreciate** is:
__a. lessen in value
__b. break into pieces
__c. fade in color
__d. increase in value

3a

b, c

dy nam ic (dī nam′ ik)

Sally was a **dynamic** young woman who believed in protecting the natural resources in the sea. She was against Rupert Jamison and the business interests he represented.

Write a definition or synonym:

28b

"If you will remember that Connie is really as sweet and kind and as dumb as she seems, her actions on the night of the murder will seem **plausible**. Connie's story could easily be the truth, even though there are no witnesses to back her up."

Another word for **plausible** is:
__a. true
__b. natural
__c. honest
__d. reasonable

53b

Not all Thornbill's **colleagues** in the biology lab shared his interest in loathesome life-forms. Many of his fellow workers, in fact, were in favor of shipping the creature straight to Hollywood. It would be a great model for a horror movie!

Another word for **colleague** is:
__a. twin
__b. alternate
__c. associate
__d. friend

78c

b

ire (īr), *n.* anger; wrath. [< Old French
< Latin *ira*]

Which of the following situations might cause **ire**?
__a. a boy finding a dollar in a drawer
__b. a successful space shot
__c. being punched in the nose
__d. having your car smashed

103c

c

sloth ful (slôth′fəl, slōth′fəl), *adj.* unwilling
to work or exert oneself; lazy; idle.
—**sloth′ful ly,** *adv.* —**sloth′ful ness,** *n.*

Check the word(s) that mean(s) the *opposite* of **slothful**.
__a. indulgent
__b. energetic
__c. lively
__d. strong
__e. active
__f. listless

129a

c, d

sal ly (sal′ ē)

The first **sally** against the bridge was successful.

Write a definition or synonym:

299b

We were completely dependent upon our guides. If there were a **rift** in our friendship, they might ride off and desert us.

A synonym for **rift** is:
__**a.** pleasure
__**b.** break
__**c.** dislike
__**d.** Arab

273b

She had been expecting adventure and excitement on board the ocean liner. When one day began to feel very much like the next, Rhoda became **disillusioned**.

The meaning of **disillusion** is:
__**a.** excite
__**b.** upset
__**c.** become monotonous
__**d.** disenchant

248c

b

droll (drōl), *adj.* odd and amusing; quaint and laughable: *a monkey's droll tricks.* [< French *drôle*] —**droll'ness,** *n.*

Check the sentence(s) in which **droll** can be correctly substituted for the italicized word.
__**a.** There was a *funny* smell in the basement.
__**b.** The seven dwarfs were *comical* little men.
__**c.** Her sense of humor was delightfully *odd.*

223c

b

sta·bil·i·ty (stə bil'ə tē), *n., pl.* **-ties.** 1 a being fixed in position; firmness. 2 permanence. 3 steadfastness of character, purpose, etc. 4 ability of an object to maintain or to return to its original position.

Which of the following usually lack **stability**?
__**a.** a demented person
__**b.** a nomad
__**c.** a weightless object
__**d.** a large building
__**e.** president of a corporation

199a

a,b,d

fi na le (fə nä' lē, fi nal' ē)

Somehow, before I know it, we are singing the **finale.**

Write a definition or synonym:

174a

a, b

de pre ci ate (di prē' shē āt)

A valuable stamp will not **depreciate.**

Write a definition or synonym:

3b

Sally, like most **dynamic** people, was almost always active and in motion. She devoted all her energy to saving the environment.

A synonym for **dynamic** is:
- __a. powerless
- __b. forceful
- __c. athletic
- __d. pleasing

28c

d

plau si ble (plô′zə bəl), *adj.* 1 appearing true, reasonable, or fair. 2 apparently worthy of confidence but often not really so: *a plausible liar.* [< Latin *plausibilis* deserving applause, pleasing < *plaudere* applaud] —**plau′si bly,** *adv.*

Which of the following might be **plausible**?
- __a. a story
- __b. a newspaper
- __c. a sales appeal
- __d. a science fiction novel
- __e. a lie

53c

c

col league (kol′ēg′), *n.* fellow worker; fellow member of a profession, organization, etc.; associate. [< Middle French *collègue* < Latin *collega* < *com*- together + *legare* to delegate]

Which of the following words mean about the same as **colleague**?
- __a. superintendent
- __b. servant
- __c. partner
- __d. employee
- __e. co-worker

79a

c, d

flail (flāl)

Wanda ran out to the fields with her maid servants and a few soldiers who had sworn to protect her. If they were caught, Wanda's husband would **flail** them.

Write a definition or synonym:

104a

b, c, e

trib u tar y (trib′ yə ter′ ē)

Since the engine couldn't be repaired, Lord Stanley ordered the men to pole the boat along one of the Amazon's **tributaries**.

Write a definition or synonym:

129b

The **sally** caught the enemy by surprise. Costas and his men rushed forth from the underbrush beneath the bridge and planted the explosives. They were gone again before the enemy knew what hit them.

Another word for **sally** is:
- __a. attempt
- __b. battle
- __c. retreat
- __d. excursion

298a

rift (rift)

We hoped that our friendly relations with our guides would continue without a rift.

1. b 2. a

Write a definition or synonym:

273a

dis il lu sion (dis' i lu' zhan)

Rhoda was rather disillusioned after spending two weeks crossing the Atlantic Ocean.

c, e

Write a definition or synonym:

248b

He was a local doctor, whose daily manner was in no way unusual. On stage, however, his droll manner provoked many smiles and chuckles of pleasure.

The meaning of droll is:
__a. half serious
__b. quaintly amusing
__c. oddly mocking
__d. sarcastic

223b

John is like a house built on a stone foundation—he has real stability. John is known far and wide for being fair, firm, and completely unflappable.

A synonym for stability is:
__a. one-sidedness
__b. steadfastness
__c. foundation
__d. diversity

198c

d

qualm (kwäm, kwälm), n. 1 a sudden disturbing feeling in the mind; uneasiness; misgiving; doubt: I tried the test with some qualms. 2 disturbance or scruple of conscience: She felt some qualms about staying away from church. 3 a feeling of faintness or sickness, especially of nausea, that lasts for just a moment. [origin unknown]

In which of the following situations would you be likely to feel qualms?
__a. telling a white lie
__b. looking down from a great height
__c. getting an examination question on something you know
__d. suspecting you forgot something
__e. getting a reward you earned

173c

a

ca ter (kā'tər), v.i. 1 provide food, supplies, and sometimes service: They run a restaurant and also cater for weddings and parties. 2 provide what is needed or wanted: The new magazine caters to boys by printing stories about aviation, athletics, and camping. [verbal use of cater buyer of provisions < Old North French acateor < acater buy]

Check the sentences in which a form of the word cater is used correctly.
__a. The bride's parents had the wedding catered.
__b. The coach does not cater to the star quarterback's need for excessive praise.
__c. Three cats catered on the back fence.

3c

dy nam ic (dī nam′ik), *adj.* **1** having to do with energy or force in motion. **2** having to do with dynamics. **3** active; energetic: *a dynamic personality.* [< Greek *dynamikos* < *dynamis* power < *dynasthai* be powerful]
—**dy nam′i cal ly,** *adv.*

1. Check the phrase(s) in which **dynamic** is used correctly.
   —**a.** a dynamic vegetable
   —**b.** a dynamic society
2. If the prefix **astro-** pertains to the stars, then the science of **astrodynamics** would investigate:
   —**a.** the motion of bodies in space
   —**b.** the making of telescopes

29a

a, c,
d, e

glean (glēn)

"What hard evidence has the prosecutor **gleaned** against Connie Craven?" Berry Amazing demanded.

Write a definition or synonym:

54a

c, e

in ci sion (in sizh′ ən)

Nevertheless, Alice Legrand volunteered to make the first **incision.**

Write a definition or synonym:

79b

If the mysterious malady did not strike them, Wanda's husband surely would. He had been known to **flail** a man so cruelly that his battered body had to be carried away.

Flail means:
—**a.** stab
—**b.** wrestle
—**c.** burn
—**d.** thrash

104b

The Amazon River is fed by over two hundred **tributaries** and carries more water than the Nile, Mississippi, and Yangtze Rivers put together. Each of these streams empties its load of water, mud, and debris into the main riverbed.

A **tributary** is a:
—**a.** seasonal rainstorm
—**b.** stream that flows into a larger body of water
—**c.** jungle waterfall
—**d.** three-sided deposit of earth at the mouth of a river

129c

d

sal ly (sal′ē), *v.,* **-lied, -ly ing,** *n., pl.* **-lies.**
—*v.i.* **1** go suddenly from a defensive position to attack an enemy. **2** rush forth suddenly; go out. **3** set out briskly or boldly. **4** go on an excursion or trip. **5** (of things) issue forth.
—*n.* **1** a sudden attack on an enemy made from a defensive position; sortie. **2** a sudden rushing forth. **3** a going forth; trip; excursion. **4** a sudden start into activity. **5** outburst. **6** a witty remark. [< Old French *saillie* a rushing forth < *saillir* to leap < Latin *salire*]

Check the sentence(s) in which a form of **sally** is used *incorrectly.*
—**a.** She liked to make sarcastic sallies at his expense.
—**b.** I enjoy sallying beside a quiet lake.
—**c.** The Indians sallied forth to attack.
—**d.** The train sallied down the railroad tracks.

297c

c dote (dōt), v.i., dot·ed, dot·ing. 1 be weak-minded and childish because of old age. 2 dote on or dote upon, be foolishly fond of: be too fond of. [Middle English doten] —dot'er, n.

1. Which of the following would you be likely to dote on?
—a. a good book
—b. a pet dog

2. Which of the following can be described as doting?
—a. an aged grandfather
—b. a spoiled child

272c

c a stray (ə strā'), adj., adv. 1 out of the right way; off. 2 in or into error.

Which of the following expressions have the same meaning as astray?
—a. "at one's beck and call"
—b. "on the straight and narrow"
—c. "on the wrong track"
—d. "straight as a die"
—e. "wrong-way Corrigan"

248a

c, d, e droll (drōl)

There was one droll fellow who always performed at ceremonies.

Write a definition or synonym:

223a

a, c, g sta bil i ty (stə bil' ə tē)

John Aponovich himself is well known for his honesty and his stability.

Write a definition or synonym:

198b

I always have qualms about our ability to put on a professional performance. I wonder whether we have rehearsed enough and how the audience will receive our selection.

A synonym for qualm is:
—a. chill
—b. daydream
—c. fear
—d. doubt

173b

Stamp dealers who cater to the big collectors handle stamps worth thousands of dollars. Because my purchases are small, I cannot usually obtain the services of these larger dealers.

Cater means:
—a. supply
—b. sell
—c. pass
—d. trade

4a

1. b
2. a

ren o vate (ren′ ə vāt)

The Friends of the Sea grew so large that more space was needed for offices. They decided to move to a building that was being **renovated**.

Write a definition or synonym:

29b

Berry went on, "Frank Ferter has spent hours and hours examining every scrap of information that would make her look bad. But he has **gleaned** nothing that casts doubt on her story."

Glean means:
__a. reap
__b. acquire rapidly
__c. take notes
__d. gather slowly

54b

Alice knew that if she did not make a neat **incision** with her dissecting knife, she might damage the specimen. However, Thornbill said her incision was as clean as it could be.

Another word for **incision** is:
__a. mark
__b. cut
__c. bore
__d. scrape

79c

d

flail (flāl), *n.* instrument for threshing grain by hand, consisting of a wooden handle at the end of which a stouter and shorter pole or club is fastened so as to swing freely. —*v.t.* 1 strike with a flail. 2 beat; thrash. [< Old French *flaiel* < Latin *flagellum* whip]

Check the sentence(s) in which a form of **flail** is used correctly.
__a. There is no use flailing a tired horse.
__b. She showed an early flail for music.
__c. His arms and legs flailed about wildly in the water.
__d. She flailed all the other contestants in the chess match.
__e. Some farmers still use flails to thresh their fields.

104c

b

trib u tar y (trib′yə ter′ē), *n., pl.* **-tar ies,** *adj.* —*n.* 1 stream that flows into a larger stream or body of water: *The Ohio River is a tributary of the Mississippi River.* 2 person or country that pays tribute. —*adj.* 1 flowing into a larger stream or body of water. 2 paying tribute; required to pay tribute. 3 paid as tribute; of the nature of tribute. 4 contributing; helping.

Check the sentence(s) in which a form of **tributary** is used correctly.
__a. They laid tributary bouquets on the graves.
__b. We came to the river by way of one of its tributaries.
__c. Once many nations were tributary to Rome.
__d. His oration was a tributary to the workers.

130a

b, d

dev as tate (dev′ ə stāt)

The bridge and the surrounding area were **devastated**.

Write a definition or synonym:

21

297b

He **doted** on the boy, watching over him and worrying about him constantly. The poor child was never left to play in peace.

Dote means:

—**a.** keep one's eyes fixed upon
—**b.** be concerned about
—**c.** be too fond of
—**d.** treat kindly

272b

When her passport was late in arriving, Rhoda began to think she had written the return address incorrectly. Or perhaps someone had stolen it! She had convinced herself that her passport had gone **astray**, when it suddenly arrived, just in time for her departure.

The meaning of **astray** is:

—**a.** out to sea
—**b.** into the refuse heap
—**c.** out of the right way
—**d.** missing, absent

247c

dor mant (dôr′mənt), *adj.* 1 lying asleep; sleeping or apparently sleeping: *Bears and other animals that hibernate are dormant during the winter.* 2 in a state of rest or inactivity; not in motion, action, or operation; quiescent: *a dormant volcano.* See **inactive** for synonym study. 3 (of plants, bulbs, seeds, etc.) with development suspended; not growing. 4 used during a dormant period; *a dormant spray.* [< Old French, present participle of *dormir* to sleep < Latin *dormire*]

d

Which of the following correctly describe(s) a **dormant** animal?

—**a.** active
—**b.** restless
—**c.** hibernating
—**d.** still
—**e.** slumbering
—**f.** agitated

222c

rep u ta ble (rep′yə tə bəl), *adj.* having a good reputation; well thought of; in good repute. —**rep′u ta bly,** *adv.*

d

Check the expression(s) that best describe(s) a **reputable** person.

—**a.** "honest as the day is long"
—**b.** "cuts a sorry figure"
—**c.** "a straight shooter"
—**d.** "on the double"
—**e.** "double-crosser"
—**f.** "double-dealing"
—**g.** "a man of principles"

198a

qualm (kwäm, kwälm)

d, f

Always before the curtain goes up on a concert evening, I have some **qualms**.

Write a definition or synonym:

173a

ca ter (kā′ tәr)

a, b

There are many dealers who **cater** to small collectors like me.

Write a definition or synonym:

4b

After it was **renovated**, the old building would contain modern offices, a new library, and large meeting rooms.

Another word for **renovate** is:
_a. rent
_b. rebuild
_c. paint
_d. modernize

29c

d

glean (glēn), *v.t.* 1 gather (grain) left on a field by reapers. 2 gather little by little: *glean information.* —*v.i.* gather grain left on a field by reapers. [< Old French *glener* < Late Latin *glennare*] —**glean′er**, *n.*

Check the sentence(s) in which a form of **glean** is used correctly.
_a. Gleaning a field was formerly done by hand.
_b. That man gleaned a fortune in less than a year.
_c. During the summer the squirrel gleaned a food supply for winter.
_d. The teacher gleaned hard at me to see if I was listening.

54c

b

in ci sion (in sizh′ən), *n.* 1 cut made in something; gash: *The doctor made a tiny incision to take out the splinter in my hand.* 2 act of incising. 3 incisive quality.

ANALOGY incision : knife :: bruise :
_a. fork
_b. nurse
_c. fist
_d. wounded
_e. blood

80a

a, c, e

in quis i tive (in kwiz′ ə tiv)

As she hurried toward the dark forest, Wanda saw a small plant with dark, pointed leaves and bright blue flowers. She stopped to study it. Everyone seemed to be **inquisitive** about the plant.

Write a definition or synonym:

105a

a, b, c

bau ble (bô′ bəl)

Lady Stanley ordered one of the men to retrieve a **bauble** floating past the boat in a clump of tangled reeds. Carlos protested that the river was full of crocodiles, but she shoved him overboard just the same.

Write a definition or synonym:

130b

The area was so completely **devastated** that there was no chance of rebuilding the bridge in the near future.

Devastate means:
_a. bomb
_b. fire
_c. destroy
_d. uproot

172c

fer·ret (fer'it), n. 1 a white or yellowish-white domesticated form of the European polecat, used for killing rats and driving rabbits from their holes. 2 species of weasel of western North America with black feet. —v.t. 1 hunt with ferrets. 2 drive from, off, or out of a place. 3 hunt; search: *The detectives ferreted out new evidence.* —v.i. 1 hunt with ferrets. 2 search about; rummage. [< Old French *furet*, ultimately < Latin *fur* thief] —fer'-ret·er, n.

Check the sentence(s) in which a form of **ferret** is used correctly.
- __a. A ferret is a carnivorous animal.
- __b. I ferreted out an old hat to dress up in.
- __c. A ferret resembles a giraffe.
- __d. I ferreted the horses out of the barn.

197c

sub·side (səb sīd'), v.i., -sid·ed, -sid·ing. 1 grow less; die down; become less active; abate: *The storm finally subsided.* 2 sink to a lower level: *After the rain stopped, the flood waters subsided.* 3 sink or fall to the bottom; settle. [< Latin *subsidere* < *sub-* down + *sidere* settle]

Check the word(s) that mean(s) the *opposite* of **subside**.
- __a. sink
- __b. diminish
- __c. rise
- __d. strengthen
- __e. dwindle
- __f. ascend

222b

However, John knew of contractors who made a practice of bidding extremely low in order to get lots of jobs. Then they used shoddy materials to save money. Once this practice becomes known, they are no longer considered **reputable**.

Another word for **reputable** is:
- __a. respectful
- __b. well-known
- __c. honest
- __d. well-thought-of

247b

Sometimes a talent may lie **dormant** for years before it is awakened. Putting such a talent to use is like discovering unknown riches.

The meaning of **dormant** is:
- __a. in a window
- __b. awake
- __c. forgotten
- __d. inactive

272a

a **stray** (ə strā')

Rhoda began to think her passport had gone **astray** in the mails.

Write a definition or synonym:

297a

dote (dōt)

The man who was guiding us obviously **doted** on his young son.

Write a definition or synonym:

4c

d

ren o vate (ren′ə vāt), *v.t.*, **-vat ed,**
-vat ing. make new again; make like new;
restore to good condition. See **renew** for
synonym study. [< Latin *renovatum* made
new < *re-* again + *novus* new] **—ren′o-**
va′tion, *n.* **—ren′o va′tor,** *n.*

ANALOGY renovate : house ::
- __a. polish : silver
- __b. build : chair
- __c. destroy : table
- __d. rent : apartment
- __e. fix : happen

30a

a, c

per ti nent (pėrt′ n ənt)

"In all the testimony you have heard," Berry Amazing
continued, "there were only two **pertinent** facts.
Coward Craven had a weak heart. And Connie Craven
was an unusually nice person."

Write a definition or synonym:

55a

c

or gan ism (ôr′ gə niz′ əm)

It soon became clear that the creature from the
stagnant pond was a completely unknown type of
organism.

Write a definition or synonym:

80b

"Gather this plant quickly and boil the leaves to make
tea," Wanda commanded. "In my youth I was
inquisitive. By asking questions, I learned the nature
of this small plant. This alone can heal the evil
sickness."

"Surely you are a witch of wonderful goodness," the
maid answered. "I will do just as you say."

Inquisitive means:
- __a. curious
- __b. restless
- __c. thirsty
- __d. hungry

105b

When Carlos returned to the boat, Lady Stanley
looked with disgust at the bright colors and shiny
surface of the **bauble**.

"It's just a toy or some useless decoration," Lady
Stanley sniffed.

"It is a sign of the Brazos tribe," said Carlos. "This
sign means death."

A **bauble** is:
- __a. a showy trifle
- __b. a precious stone
- __c. an article of clothing
- __d. a simple toy

130c

c

dev as tate (dev′ə stāt), *v.t.*, **-tat ed,**
-tat ing. make desolate; lay waste; destroy;
ravage: *A long war devastated the country.*
[< Latin *devastatum* laid waste *de-* + *vastus*
waste] **—dev′as tat′ing ly,** *adv.* **—dev′as-**
ta′tion, *n.* **—dev′as ta′tor,** *n.*

Check the synonym(s) for **devastate.**
- __a. damage
- __b. demolish
- __c. harm
- __d. wreck
- __e. burn

296c

a

name·sake (nām'sāk'), n. one having the same name as another, especially one named after another: *Theodore, namesake of President Theodore Roosevelt.*

Check the sentence(s) in which a form of **namesake** is used correctly.
—**a.** They namesaked their new baby after him.
—**b.** A president usually has many namesakes.
—**c.** The statue of Lincoln is a namesake of him.

271c

a

al·lure (ə lur'), v., -lured, -lur·ing, n. — v.t. tempt or attract very strongly; fascinate; charm: *City life allured her with its action and excitement.* See **charm.** —n. great charm; fascination. Syn. studies. [< Middle French *aluer* < *a-* to + *leurre* lure] —al·lur'er, n.

Check the sentence(s) in which a form of **allure** is used correctly.
—**a.** The allure of the beautiful woman was enhanced by her mysterious past.
—**b.** The beautiful scenery allures many people to Switzerland.
—**c.** The noise allured me to the window to see what was happening in the street.

247a

c, e

dor·mant (dôr'mant)

Many people discover **dormant** talents at such a time.

Write a definition or synonym:

222a

b, d

rep·u·ta·ble (rep'yə tə bəl)

John explained that most of the bids for building the bridge were made by **reputable** contractors like himself.

Write a definition or synonym:

197b

When the clapping has **subsided** and the hall becomes quiet, he is ready to conduct.

Another word for **subside** is:
—**a.** vanish
—**b.** abate
—**c.** increase
—**d.** continue

172b

My correspondents include most of the big stamp dealers. We have more than once successfully **ferreted** out a real collector's item. **Ferreting** out such a stamp often requires considerable time and research.

A synonym for **ferret** is:
—**a.** corral
—**b.** glean
—**c.** search
—**d.** discover

5a

a

des ig nate (*v.* dez′ ig nāt; *adj.* dez′ ig nit,
dez′ ig nāt)

Soon, the committee learned that Congress had
designated Rupert Jamison to head a special study
group on our natural resources.

Write a definition or synonym:

30b

After the jury heard all the evidence, they sifted out
the testimony **pertinent** to the case and discarded the
rest. On this basis, they came to their decision:
Coward Craven died of a weak heart. Connie's
kindness was just too much for him to take.

Another word for **pertinent** is:
__a. related
__b. pointed
__c. native
__d. ideal

55b

In biology, all living bodies having a certain structure
are grouped together according to type. But no one in
the lab had ever seen an **organism** of this type before.

The meaning of **organism** is:
__a. living body
__b. social group
__c. individual
__d. collection of parts

80c

a

in quis i tive (in kwiz′ə tiv), *adj.* 1 asking
many questions; curious. 2 prying into other
people's affairs; too curious. See **curious** for
synonym study. —**in quis′i tive ly,** *adv.*
—**in quis′i tive ness,** *n.*

Which of the following expressions may be used to
describe **inquisitiveness**?
__a. "craning one's neck"
__b. "busybody"
__c. "curiosity killed the cat"
__d. "caught napping"
__e. "nosey"
__f. "clean as a whistle"

105c

a

bau ble (bô′bəl), *n.* 1 a showy trifle of little
value; trinket. 2 a jester's staff. [< Old
French *babel, baubel* toy]

ANALOGY **bauble : trinket :: jewel :**
__a. diamond
__b. necklace
__c. value
__d. gem
__e. beads

b, d

LESSON | Operation Deep-Freeze

14

Time: 2110 A.D. Place: The Kremlin.
The USSR-USA Cooperative Space Commission has just made a long-awaited
announcement. Operation Deep-Freeze has begun.

172a

b, c

fer ret (fer′ it)

It is exciting to **ferret** out a rare stamp.

Write a definition or synonym:

197a

a, c,
d, e

sub side (səb sīd′)

The director waits for the applause to **subside**.

Write a definition or synonym:

221c

a

front age (frun′tij), *n.* 1 front of a building
or of a lot. 2 length of this front. 3 direction
that the front of a building or lot faces. 4 land
facing a street, river, etc. 5 land between a
building and a street, river, etc.

Check the sentence(s) in which **frontage** is used
correctly.
__a. Our frontage measured 200 feet front to back.
__b. Our frontage lay along the river, so we
  looked out of our windows at the boats.
__c. The house was surrounded by a large frontage
  full of trees.
__d. Frontage along a highway is very valuable.

246c

d

ar ti san (är′tə zən), *n.* a skilled worker in
some industry or trade; craftsman. Carpen-
ters, masons, plumbers, and electricians are
artisans. See **artist** for synonym study.
[< Middle French < Italian *artigiano* < *arte*
art < Latin *artem*]

Which of the following people are **artisans**?
__a. a business executive
__b. an insurance agent
__c. a metal worker
__d. an engineer
__e. a weaver
__f. a grocery clerk

271b

To Rhoda, the **allure** of travel posters lies in the way
they suggest the exciting sights and adventures which
await the traveler.

Allure means:
__a. fascination
__b. idea
__c. suggestion
__d. sensation

296b

The son's name was Hassam, as was the father's. In
families the world over, men and women like to
continue their names by having a **namesake**.

Namesake means:
__a. one having the same name as another
__b. a close relative
__c. one resembling another person
__d. one having a different name

5b

Congress had the authority to **designate** individuals like Jamison for special assignments. After they had been named, they could begin exercising their power.

Another word for **designate** is:
— **a.** appoint
— **b.** educate
— **c.** send
— **d.** elect

30c

a

per ti nent (pėrt′n ənt), *adj.* having to do with what is being considered; relating to the matter in hand; to the point. See synonym study below. [< Latin *pertinentem* pertaining] —**per′ti nent ly,** *adv.*
Syn. Pertinent, relevant mean relating to the matter in hand. **Pertinent** means relating directly to the point of the matter and helping to explain or clarify it: *A summary of the events leading up to this situation would be pertinent information.* **Relevant** means having some bearing on the matter or enough connection with it to have some meaning or importance: *Even incidents seeming unimportant in themselves might be relevant.*

Which of the following words mean the *opposite* of **pertinent**?
— **a.** impudent
— **b.** careless
— **c.** unrelated
— **d.** disrespectful
— **e.** irrelevant

55c

a

or gan ism (ôr′gə niz′əm), *n.* **1** a living body made up of separate parts, such as cells, tissues, and organs, which work together to carry on the various processes of life; an individual animal or plant. **2** any organized system similar to this; a whole made up of related parts that work together. Human society, or any community, may be spoken of as a social organism.

Which of the following are **organisms**?
— **a.** typewriter
— **b.** flea
— **c.** ant colony
— **d.** rose
— **e.** man
— **f.** jar of jelly

LESSON 9 | The Trouble with Mother Nature

a, b,
c, e

Laura Samuelson had raised four children successfully. She had worked as a bank teller for forty years. Now, at the age of sixty-five, Laura was looking for new worlds to conquer.

106a

d

dirge (dėrj)

As the boat rounded a bend in the river, the sound of a **dirge** floated over the water.

Write a definition or synonym:

131a

sat el lite (sat′ l īt)

The announcement coincided with the first step in the project: the launching of a **satellite**.

Write a definition or synonym:

171c

d

hum drum (hum′drum′), *adj.* without variety; commonplace; dull. —*n.* person or thing that is humdrum. [< *hum*, verb]

Which of the following would most likely be **humdrum**?
_a. a mystery on TV
_b. washing dishes
_c. a row of brown houses
_d. a circus
_e. a motorboat race

196c

d

port ly (pôrt′lē, pōrt′lē), *adj.,* -li er, -li est.
1 having a large body; stout; corpulent. See **fat** for synonym study. 2 stately; dignified. [< *port*⁴] —**port′li ness,** *n.*

Check the word(s) that mean(s) the *opposite* of **portly**.
_a. slender
_b. robust
_c. gaunt
_d. undignified
_e. slim

221b

A bridge cannot be built right next to another structure. There must be enough **frontage** to accommodate the access roads leading to and from the bridge.

Frontage is:
_a. land facing a street or river
_b. building material
_c. public funds
_d. money voted for a project

246b

Artisans were creating wooden bowls, ceramic plates, jewelry, and all manner of articles to sell at the centennial.

Another word for **artisan** is:
_a. apprentice
_b. factory
_c. painter
_d. craftsman

271a

al lure (ə lür′)

There is an **allure** about strange lands and people.

Write a definition or synonym:

296a

d

name sake (nām′ sāk′)

One of our guides brought his son on the journey. The boy was his **namesake**.

Write a definition or synonym:

5c

des ig nate (*v.* dez′ig nāt; *adj.* dez′ig nit, dez′ig nāt), *v.*, **-nat ed, -nat ing,** *adj.* —*v.t.* 1 mark out; point out; indicate definitely; show: *Red lines designate main roads on this map.* 2 name; entitle: *The ruler of Iran is designated Shah.* 3 select for duty, office, etc.; appoint: *The President designated her as ambassador to Italy.* —*adj.* appointed; selected: *the bishop designate.* —**des′ig na′tor,** *n.*

In which of the following sentences is a form of **designate** used correctly?
__**a.** The marshal designated an extra deputy.
__**b.** He has designates on that car.
__**c.** Her elegant robes designated her high rank.
__**d.** Jane was designated secretary of the club.

LESSON 4 | Crazy Legs

Horace "Legs" Diamond had been one of the best soccer players in the world. He might have been the best if his old knee injury had not started acting up last season. Legs refused to let a doctor look at the leg, even though he was obviously in pain. When finally he slipped and fell on the playing field, the coach decided to call in a medical specialist. When Legs met the specialist, Dr. Jennifer Cardiac, be began acting more like a scared little boy than a star athlete.

56a

ver te brate (ver′ tə brit, ver′ tə brāt)

For one thing, the slimy, shapeless creature was, in fact, a **vertebrate**.

Write a definition or synonym:

81a

hor ti cul ture (hôr′ tə kul′ chər)

When she retired from the bank, Mrs. Samuelson became interested in **horticulture**.

Write a definition or synonym:

106b

A funeral was in progress. The villagers, wearing their finest costumes, were singing a **dirge** for a dead warrior.

The meaning of **dirge** is:
__**a.** ballad
__**b.** funeral song
__**c.** tribute
__**d.** chant

131b

The **satellite** in question is the heaviest manufactured object to revolve around the earth. Instead of weapons or cameras, it carries a huge refrigerator! It will be an enormous flying icebox, travelling around and around the earth.

A **satellite** is:
__**a.** a ramjet-powered airplane
__**b.** an object launched into orbit
__**c.** an astronaut
__**d.** a meteor

295c

c

bran·dish (bran'dish), v.t. wave or shake threateningly; flourish. —n. a threatening shake; flourish. [< Old French brandiss-, a form of brandir to brand < brand sword]

295c ANALOGY brandish : conceal :: enjoy :

- __a. dispel
- __b. display
- __c. punish
- __d. dislike
- __e. torrid

LESSON 28   Around the World by Ocean Liner

b, e

Last year, Rhoda's elderly and very wealthy aunt asked her to accompany her on a world cruise. Rhoda was expected to stay with her aunt and help entertain her. Since these duties were light, Rhoda accepted eagerly.

246a

1, b, c
2, no

ar ti san (är' tə zan)

The local artisans were kept busy making souvenirs for almost a year before the celebration began.

Write a definition or synonym:

221a

front age (frun' tij)

Before plans for a bridge were made, the frontage was determined.

Write a definition or synonym:

196b

The director's natural portliness is emphasized by evening dress. He resembles a plump penguin.

Portly means:

- __a. formal
- __b. black and white
- __c. birdlike
- __d. stout

171b

Many an otherwise humdrum day has been made interesting by a letter from one of my foreign correspondents.

Another word for humdrum is:

- __a. rainy
- __b. quiet
- __c. stormy
- __d. dull

6a

a,c,d

as sess (ə ses′)

Sally's committee wanted Congress to tax those cities and companies that polluted the sea. Jamison's study group could influence the amount of tax that might be **assessed**.

Write a definition or synonym:

31a

im per a tive (im per′ ə tiv)

Dr. Cardiac said it was **imperative** that she operate immediately.

"How do I know you're telling the truth?" Legs demanded.

Write a definition or synonym:

56b

All four-legged animals are **vertebrates**. So are fish, frogs, and any creature having a backbone. But this monster had more than a dozen arms (or legs) attached to its backbone. They were all covered with the lumpy green ooze that was its skin.

Vertebrate means:
__**a.** having bones
__**b.** having arms and legs
__**c.** upright; walking on hind legs
__**d.** having a backbone

81b

She quickly learned all aspects of **horticulture**. She enjoyed the digging and weeding as much as the vegetables and flowers that she grew.

A synonym for **horticulture** is:
__**a.** agriculture
__**b.** farming
__**c.** flower arranging
__**d.** gardening

106c

b

dirge (dèrj), *n.* a funeral song or tune. [contraction of Latin *dirige* direct! (first word in office for the dead)]

You would most likely hear a **dirge** at a:
__**a.** wedding
__**b.** wake
__**c.** burial
__**d.** birthday party
__**e.** political rally

131c

b

sat el lite (sat′l it), *n.* 1 a heavenly body that revolves around a planet, especially around one of the nine major planets of the solar system. The moon is a satellite of the earth. 2 artificial satellite. 3 follower of or attendant upon a person of importance. 4 a subservient follower. 5 country nominally independent but actually controlled by a more powerful country, especially a country under the control of the Soviet Union. —*adj.* of, having to do with, or of the nature of a satellite. [< Latin *satellitem* attendant]

Which of the following are **satellites**?
__**a.** a puppet government
__**b.** a lady-in-waiting
__**c.** a chairwoman
__**d.** the moon
__**e.** a "yes-man"

295b

During our trip through the desert, a band of horsemen approached. Our guides **brandished** their rifles and the men hastily rode away.

Another word for **brandish** is:

—**a.** drag
—**b.** shoot
—**c.** wave
—**d.** hide

270c

be fall (bi fôl'), v., -fell, -fall en, -fall ing.
—v.t. happen to: *Be careful that no harm befalls you.* —v.i. happen.

Check the expression(s) that mean(s) the same as **befall.**

—**a.** "stitch in time"
—**b.** "come to pass"
—**c.** "in the wind"
—**d.** "in question"
—**e.** "turn up"

245c

o ra to ry (ôr'ə tôr'ē, ôr'ə tōr'ē; or'ə tôr'ē, or'ə tōr'ē), *n.* 1 skill in public speaking; eloquent speaking or language. 2 the art of public speaking. [< Latin (*ars*) *oratoria* oratorical (art) < *orare* speak formally, pray]

o ra to ry² (ôr'ə tôr'ē, ôr'ə tōr'ē; or'ə tôr'ē, or'ə tōr'ē), *n., pl.* -**ries.** a small chapel, room, or other place set apart for private prayer. [< Late Latin *oratorium* < Latin *orare* plead, pray. Doublet of ORATORIO.]

1. At which of the following can you expect to find **oratory?**

—**a.** a tennis match
—**b.** a political rally
—**c.** a session of Congress
—**d.** daily conversation
—**e.** a concert

2. **Would you be likely to hear a choir in an oratory?** Yes _____ No _____

LESSON 23

How to Build a Big Bridge

For as long as anyone in Southport can remember, there has been a ferryboat to transport people and cars from one side of the bay to the other. Now, John Aponovich and his construction crews are building a bridge that will replace the old ferryboat. John discussed the bridge-building project in an interview for the *Southport Chronicle.*

196a

portly (pôrt' lē, pōrt' lē)

Members of the chorus take their places after the orchestra has tuned up. Our **portly** director is the last to enter the auditorium.

Write a definition or synonym:

171a

hum drum (hum' drum')

On a **humdrum** day, I can take out my stamp collection and lose myself in another world.

Write a definition or synonym:

6b

Sally believed the tax should be **assessed** according to the amount of pollution caused. Jamison didn't believe anyone could measure the pollution or fix the exact amount of the tax.

The meaning of **assess** is:
_**a.** fix the amount of
_**b.** underestimate the value of
_**c.** judge to be
_**d.** demand a fine

31b

"With serious knee injuries," she explained, "it is not only advisable to operate right away, it is **imperative**. It simply must be done if you expect to play soccer again."

Imperative means:
_**a.** illegal
_**b.** compulsory
_**c.** urgent
_**d.** dangerous

56c

d

ver te brate (vėr′tə brit, vėr′tə brāt), *n.* animal that has a backbone; any of the large subphylum of chordates having a segmented spinal column and a brain case or cranium, including fishes, amphibians, reptiles, birds, and mammals. —*adj.* 1 having a backbone. 2 of or having to do with vertebrates.

Which of the following animals are **vertebrates**?
_**a.** chicken
_**b.** coral snake
_**c.** whale
_**d.** worm
_**e.** dolphin
_**f.** ant

81c

d

hor ti cul ture (hôr′tə kul′chər), *n.* 1 science or art of growing flowers, fruits, vegetables, and plants. 2 cultivation of a garden. [< Latin *hortus* garden + English *culture*]

Which of the following people are practicing **horticulture**?
_**a.** nursery worker
_**b.** biologist
_**c.** shepherd
_**d.** garden club member
_**e.** man pruning rosebushes
_**f.** stargazer

107a

b, c

be reaved (bi rēvd′)

Lord and Lady Stanley made fun of the costumes and manners of the **bereaved** family.

Write a definition or synonym:

132a

a, b,
d, e

com po nent (kəm pō′ nənt)

Flash! The launching will be delayed because two of the rocket's **components** are defective.

Write a definition or synonym:

LESSON 18 | Confessions of a Philatelist

a, c,
b, d

For many years I have been an enthusiastic stamp collector. I have acquired a large collection, and find my stamps a source of much pleasure. In addition, I now correspond with friends all over the world.

195c

b

a pex (ā/peks), *n., pl.* **a pex es** or **ap i ces.**
1 the highest point; tip: *the apex of a triangle.*
2 climax; peak: *the apex of her career.*
[< Latin]

ANALOGY **apex : pinnacle :: extent :**
—a. church
—b. pit
—c. bottom
—d. limit
—e. steeple

220c

b

hew (hyü), *v.,* **hewed** or **hewn,**
hew ing. —*v.t.* 1 cut with an ax, sword,
etc.; chop: *He hewed down the tree.* 2 cut into
shape; form by cutting with an ax, etc.: *hew
stone for building, hew logs into beams.* —*v.i.*
hold firmly (to); stick fast or cling (to): *hew to
the rules.* [Old English *hēawan*] —**hew/-
er,** *n.*

Which of the following would *not* be **hewn?**
—a. a pattern for a dress
—b. a garden in a wilderness
—c. a ceramic dish
—d. a jungle trail
—e. stone pillars

245b

While most of the speakers would be boring, the few who were skilled in **oratory** would be enjoyable to hear.

Oratory means:
—a. artistic ability
—b. public speaking
—c. dramatic acting
—d. telling jokes

270b

These people are doing their best to see that the worst does not **befall** the African game animals and that they are not exterminated by game hunters and poachers.

A synonym for **befall** is:
—a. upset
—b. befit
—c. knock down
—d. happen to

295a

b, c

bran dish (bran' dish)
Our Arab guide **brandished** a rifle when we first met him. My husband said he hoped it was a way of saying "hello."

Write a definition or synonym:

6c

a

as sess (ə ses′), *v.t.* 1 estimate the value of (property or income) for taxation; value: *The town clerk has assessed our house at $20,000.* 2 fix the amount of (a tax, fine, damages, etc.). 3 put a tax on (a person, property, etc.). 4 determine the shares to be contributed by each of several persons toward a common object. 5 examine critically and estimate the merit, significance, value, etc., of: *The committee met to assess the idea of establishing a new university.* [< Medieval Latin *assessare* fix a tax < Latin *assidere* sit by, attend < *ad-* by + *sedere* sit] —**assess′a ble,** *adj.*

In which of the following sentences is a form of **assess** used correctly?
__a. A town assesses all property for the tax rolls.
__b. She was tried at the local assesses.
__c. In each town an official assesses business and private property.

31c

c

im per a tive (im per′ə tiv), *adj.* 1 not to be avoided; that must be done; urgent: *It is imperative that this very sick child should stay in bed.* 2 expressing a command or request: *an imperative statement.* 3 (in grammar) having to do with a verb form which expresses a command, request, or advice. "Go!" and "Stop, look, listen!" are in the imperative mood. —*n.* 1 something imperative; command: *The great imperative is "Love thy neighbor as thyself."* 2 a verb form in the imperative mood. 3 the imperative mood. [< Latin *imperativus* < *imperare* to command] —**im per′a tive ly,** *adv.* —**im per′a tive ness,** *n.*

Check the sentence(s) in which **imperative** is used correctly.
__a. She had an imperative manner.
__b. It is imperative that nurses follow instructions during surgery.
__c. He used the imperative in telling me to leave.
__d. I felt imperative about being so late.
__e. A sentry uses an imperative tone in halting a trespasser.

57a

a, b, c, e

in ver te brate (in vėr′ tə brit, in vėr′ tə brāt)

Most of the early life-forms on our planet were **invertebrates**. And at first glance, the creature seemed to belong to this group.

Write a definition or synonym:

82a

a, d, e

ger mi nate (jėr′ mə nāt)

Each spring, Mrs. Samuelson waited impatiently for her seeds to **germinate**.

Write a definition or synonym:

107b

Many members of the crew were related to the **bereaved** family. These men would not tolerate the Stanleys' outrageous comments. After a brief conversation, the crew members went into action. They grabbed all the food supplies and pulled over to the river bank and disembarked. Minutes later, the Stanleys were floating down the river in lonely majesty.

Bereaved means:
__a. mournful crowd
__b. remaining alive
__c. deprived by death
__d. no longer breathing

132b

Modern space vehicles have a vast number of **components** assembled so intricately that the repair of a single part is extremely difficult. But the space scientists located the problem, and soon the satellite was rocketed into orbit.

Another word for **component** is:
__a. item
__b. unit
__c. mechanism
__d. part

294c

c

rit u al (rich'u al), n. 1 form or system of rites. The rites of baptism, marriage, and burial are parts of the ritual of most churches. 2 a prescribed order of performing a ceremony or rite. Secret societies have a ritual for initiating new members. 3 book containing rites or ceremonies. 4 the carrying out of rites. —adj. of or having to do with rites or rituals; done as a rite: a ritual dance. ritual laws. —rit'u al ly, adv.

Check the sentence(s) in which **ritual** can be correctly substituted for the italicized word.

—**a.** He hurried off to work without *ceremony*.
—**b.** Part of the *ceremony* is the exchanging of rings.
—**c.** She made a *ceremonial* offering.

270a

1. b
2. a,c

be fall (bi fôl')

Naturalists all over the world are interested in what **befalls** the animals of Africa.

Write a definition or synonym:

245a

b, d

o ra to ry (ôr' ə tôr' ē, ôr' ə tōr' ē; or' ə tôr' ē, or' ə tōr' ē)

Of course, on the opening day there would be the usual **oratory**.

Write a definition or synonym:

220b

After the last hurricane, members of the volunteer fire department spent several days **hewing** the wood from fallen trees. The wood had to be reduced to pieces that were small enough for the sanitation department trucks to haul away.

Hew means:

—**a.** burn up
—**b.** cut or chop
—**c.** slice into pieces
—**d.** manufacture

195b

We try to obtain at least one professional soloist for our spring concert. Last year we were lucky to have a singer who was at the **apex** of his career and who was received with acclaim all over the world.

Another word for **apex** is:

—**a.** origin
—**b.** pinnacle
—**c.** bottom
—**d.** midpoint

170c

d

in duce ment (in düs'mant, in dyüs'mant), n. 1 something that influences or persuades; incentive. 2 act of influencing or persuading.

Match the **inducement** in the first column with the subject most likely to be **induced** by it.

— money   **a.** man
— candy   **b.** rabbit
— carrot   **c.** child
— catnip   **d.** kitten

7a

_a, c_

ap pro pri a tion (ə prō′ prē ā′ shən)

Jamison wanted Congress to vote an **appropriation** large enough to let his committee study the problem for another two years.

Write a definition or synonym:

32a

_b, c, e_

al lay (ə lā′)

As soon as he was admitted to the hospital, Legs started complaining and carrying on. The nurse gave him some aspirin to **allay** his fever and told him to stop acting like such a big baby.

Write a definition or synonym:

57b

Invertebrates, such as spiders or flies, may be easily damaged since they have no backbone to hold them rigid. That's why most **invertebrates** are quite small.

Invertebrate means:
__a. backless
__b. having no backbone
__c. one-celled
__d. microscopic

82b

It sometimes takes several weeks for a seed to **germinate**. But when the first tiny green leaves appeared above the earth, Mrs. Samuelson was always excited. It was almost like having children again.

A synonym for **germinate** is:
__a. ripen
__b. enlarge
__c. mature
__d. sprout

107c

_c_

be reave (bi rēv′), _v.t._, **-reaved** or **-reft,** **-reav ing.** 1 leave desolate and alone: _The family was bereaved by the death of the father._ 2 deprive ruthlessly; rob: _bereaved of hope._ [Old English _berēafian_ < _be-_ away + _rēafian_ rob]

Which of the following have been **bereaved**?
__a. pioneer
__b. orphan
__c. delinquent
__d. adolescent
__e. widower
__f. divorcée

132c

_d_

com po nent (kəm pō′nənt), _n._ one of the parts that make up a whole; necessary part: _Because alcohol is a solvent, it is a component of many liquid medicines._ See **element** for synonym study. —_adj._ that composes; constituent: _Blade and handle are the component parts of a knife._ [< Latin _componentem_ put together < _com-_ together + _ponere_ put]

ANALOGY component : whole ::
__a. faucet : water
__b. radio : station
__c. fuel : gas
__d. rocket : spaceship
__e. cylinder : engine

170b

Maharaji wouldn't listen to Jim's pleading. "No **inducement** is great enough to make me leave my people and my work here," he said. "You couldn't offer me anything that would mean more to me than serving my own people."

A synonym for **inducement** is:
__a. prize
__b. salary
__c. encouragement
__d. incentive

195a

a,b,c

a pex (ā′ peks)

The **apex** of our season comes with the spring concert.

Write a definition or synonym:

220a

b,d,e

hew (hyü)

Once the hurricane has run its course, the inhabitants will have to **hew** the fallen trees.

Write a definition or synonym:

244c

b

rev el (rev′əl), *v.,* **-eled, -el ing** or **-elled, -el ling,** *n.* —*v.i.* **1** take great pleasure *(in): The children revel in country life.* **2** make merry. —*n.* a noisy good time; merrymaking. [< Old French *reveler* be disorderly, make merry < Latin *rebellare.* Doublet of REBEL.] —**rev′el er, rev′el ler,** *n.*

Check the sentence(s) in which **revel** is used correctly.
__a. Many children revel against their parents.
__b. She reveled in her misery.
__c. The bugler sounded revel.
__d. The birthday party turned into a revel.
__e. He did not revel the answer.

269c

c

el o quence (el′ə kwəns), *n.* **1** flow of speech that has grace and force. **2** power to win by speaking; the art of using language so as to stir the feelings.
el o quent (el′ə kwənt), *adj.* **1** having eloquence. **2** very expressive: *eloquent eyes.* [< Latin *eloquentem* speaking out < *ex-* out + *loqui* speak] —**el′o quent ly,** *adv.*

1. An **eloquent** speaker can be correctly described as:
   __a. gossipy
   __b. silver-tongued
   __c. wordy
2. In which of the following phrases is **eloquent** used correctly?
   • __a. an eloquent performance
   __b. an eloquent dress
   __c. an eloquent glance

294b

The **ritual** most apparent to the outsider is that of facing Mecca to pray at certain times during the day.

Ritual means:
__a. an everyday occurrence
__b. a ceremony for tourists
__c. a carrying out of ceremonies
__d. a religion

7b

Sally believed Congress should act immediately. A two-year study would cost a great deal and cause an unnecessary delay. Sally's committee wrote letters protesting the **appropriation**.

Appropriation means:
_ **a.** assessment
_ **b.** allotment
_ **c.** collection
_ **d.** reinforcement

32b

"Aspirin will bring your fever down and relieve your headache," Dr. Cardiac told Legs. "I don't know what I can do to **allay** your fear of hospitals!"

"Send me home!" Legs said quickly. "I have no fear of hospitals when I'm on the outside looking in!"

Another word for **allay** is:
_ **a.** increase
_ **b.** activate
_ **c.** eliminate
_ **d.** relieve

57c

b

in ver te brate (in vėr′tə brit, in vėr′tə-brāt), *adj.* 1 without a backbone. 2 of or having to do with invertebrates. —*n.* animal without a backbone. Worms and insects are invertebrates.

ANALOGY **invertebrate : spider :: mammal :**
_ **a.** flower
_ **b.** tomato
_ **c.** animal
_ **d.** giraffe
_ **e.** biology

82c

d

ger mi nate (jėr′mə nāt), *v.,* **-nat ed, -nat ing.** —*v.i.* begin to grow or develop; sprout: *Seeds germinate in the spring.* —*v.t.* cause to grow or develop. [< Latin *germinatum* sprouted < *germen* sprout] —**ger′mi na′tor,** *n.*

Check the sentence(s) in which a form of **germinate** is used correctly.
_ **a.** An idea germinated in his brain.
_ **b.** The bacteria germinated in the test tube.
_ **c.** Many illnesses are spread by germinates.
_ **d.** She germinated the interview abruptly.
_ **e.** It is possible to get seeds to germinate indoors.

108a

b, e

preg nant (preg′ nənt)

The moment was **pregnant** with possibilities. Lord and Lady Stanley were too dumbfounded to speak.

Write a definition or synonym:

133a

e

dis in te grate (dis in′ tə grāt)

The communications team reported that the rocket would begin to fall back toward earth in twenty minutes. When it entered the earth's atmosphere, it would **disintegrate**.

294a
b,c,e

rit u al (rich' ü al)

The company my husband worked for sent us a book explaining the local customs. As we learned, most Arabs are Moslems. We found it interesting to compare Moslem **rituals** with those of our own religion.

Write a definition or synonym:

269b
d

For many years the public and the government seemed indifferent to the fact that the elephant was becoming extinct. **Eloquent** appeals from conservationists finally moved the African governments to become concerned with the problem and then to take action.

The meaning of **eloquent** is:
— **a.** humorous
— **b.** persistent
— **c.** expressive
— **d.** very angry

244b

Those who enjoy organizing, **revel** in all the planning. Those who just enjoy having a good time, **revel** in the party.

Revel means:
— **a.** revolt against
— **b.** take great pleasure in
— **c.** concentrate one's attention on
— **d.** relax in

219c
d

tur bu lent (ter′byə lənt), *adj.* 1 causing disorder; disorderly; unruly; violent: *a turbulent mob.* 2 stormy; tempestuous: *turbulent weather, turbulent water.* [< Latin *turbulentus < turba* turmoil] —**tur′bu lent ly,** *adv.*

Which of the following words mean about the same as **turbulent?**
— **a.** breezy
— **b.** agitated
— **c.** staunch
— **d.** raging
— **e.** wild

194c
a

en rap ture (en rap′chər), *v.t.,* **-tured, -tur ing.** move to rapture; fill with great delight.

Which of the following would be likely to **enrapture** most people?
— **a.** a superbly decorated community Christmas tree
— **b.** a stunning victory by your school football team
— **c.** an exciting theatrical performance
— **d.** an essay on manners
— **e.** a bowl of dessert

170a
a, b, d

in duce ment (in düs′ mənt, in dyüs′ mənt)

Jim wanted Maharaji to make a tour of North America. He tried to think of an **inducement** to offer the holy man.

Write a definition or synonym:

7c

b

ap pro pri ate (*adj.* ə prō′prē it; *v.* ə prō′prē āt), *adj.*, *v.*, **-at ed, -at ing.** —*adj.* especially right or proper for the occasion; suitable; fitting: *Plain, simple clothes are appropriate for school wear.* See **fit¹** for synonym study. —*v.t.* **1** set apart for a special purpose: *The legislature appropriated a billion dollars for foreign aid.* **2** take for oneself; use as one's own: *You should not ap-* *propriate other people's belongings without their permission.* [< Late Latin *appropriatum* made one's own < Latin *ad-* to + *proprius* one's own] —**ap pro′pri ate ly,** *adv.* —**ap pro′pri ate ness,** *n.* —**ap pro′pri a′tor,** *n.*

ap pro pri a tion (ə prō′prē ā′shən), *n.* **1** sum of money or other thing appropriated **2** act of appropriating. **3** a being appropriated.

Check the sentence(s) in which a form of **appropriation** is used correctly.
— **a.** The town's appropriation of his land upset him.
— **b.** They voted an appropriation for a new park.
— **c.** His appropriation showed good color sense.
— **d.** The ancient Greeks made appropriations to their gods.

32c

d

al lay (ə lā′), *v.t.*, **-layed, -lay ing. 1** put at rest; quiet: *My fears were allayed by the news that my family was safe.* **2** relieve (pain, trouble, thirst, etc.); alleviate. [Old English *ālecgan* < *ā-* away, off + *lecgan* to lay] —**al lay′er,** *n.*

ANALOGY allay : irritate :: comfort :
— **a.** distress
— **b.** discover
— **c.** soothe
— **d.** quiet
— **e.** pain

58a

d

nu cle us (nü′ klē əs, nyü′ klē əs)

Alice took some skin tissue from the creature and prepared a slide. Then she studied it under the microscope to discover the size and shape of one cell's **nucleus**.

Write a definition or synonym:

83a

a, b, e

de fi cient (di fish′ ənt)

Each year, Mrs. Samuelson called a man from the state government to test the soil in her garden. She wanted to make sure the soil was not **deficient**.

Write a definition or synonym:

108b

As the distance between the boat and the shore increased, the Stanleys stared at each other in shock. Then the **pregnant** silence was broken by Lady Stanley's scream.

Pregnant means:
— **a.** significant
— **b.** wealthy
— **c.** unborn
— **d.** unhappy

133b

When a rocket **disintegrates** in space, it comes apart bit by bit. In a week or so, the separate pieces are scattered far and wide in space. The satellite continued on course, as planned.

Disintegrate means:
— **a.** melt
— **b.** disappear
— **c.** break up
— **d.** fall

169c

horoscope (hôr′ə skōp, hor′ə skōp), *n.* 1. the relative position of the planets at a particular time, especially at the hour of a person's birth, regarded as influencing his life. 2 diagram of the twelve signs of the zodiac, showing the arrangement of the heavens at a particular time. A horoscope is used in telling fortunes by the planets and the stars. 3 a fortune told by this means. 4 **cast a horoscope,** discover the influence that the stars and planets are supposed to have upon a person's life. [< Greek *hōroskopos* < *hōra* hour + *skopos* watcher]

c

One can secure a **horoscope**:
— **a.** from a newspaper
— **b.** from an astrologer
— **c.** at an observatory
— **d.** from a book on astrology
— **e.** from a psychiatrist

194b

A first-rate performance **enraptures** the audience, and it gives the singers great delight as well.

To **enrapture** is:
— **a.** to entrance
— **b.** to entertain
— **c.** to enslave
— **d.** to ensnare

219b

The gale winds make the water **turbulent,** causing breakers and whitecaps.

Turbulent means:
— **a.** frothy
— **b.** cold
— **c.** noisy
— **d.** violent

244a

c

rev el (rev′ əl)

Most of the townspeople **revel** in these affairs.

Write a definition or synonym:

269a

a, c

el o quent (el′ ə kwənt)

Eloquent appeals have been made to save certain species of animals from extinction.

Write a definition or synonym:

293c

d

in fat u ate (in fach′ü āt), *v.t.*, **-at ed, -at ing.** 1 inspire with a foolish or extreme passion. 2 make foolish. [< Latin *infatuatum* made foolish < *in-* + *fatuus* foolish]

Someone who is **infatuated** is:
— **a.** "a plain Jane"
— **b.** "head over heels"
— **c.** "smitten"
— **d.** "teacher's pet"
— **e.** "swept off one's feet"

8a

a, b

e con o mize (i kon′ ə mīz)

However, when Jamison requested his appropriation, Congress was in a mood to **economize**.

Write a definition or synonym:

33a

a

ne ces si tate (nə ses′ ə tāt)

Legs asked whether his knee operation would **necessitate** total anesthesia.

Write a definition or synonym:

58b

"No matter what it is," Thornbill said, "it must have a **nucleus** in each cell. Without the **nucleus**, which directs all the cell's activities, the cell could not survive."

A synonym for **nucleus** is:
___**a.** center
___**b.** brain
___**c.** skeleton
___**d.** structure

83b

If soil is **deficient**, the necessary minerals and plant foods must be added. Mrs. Samuelson's "babies" could not grow strong and healthy unless they received the proper food.

Another word for **deficient** is:
___**a.** defective
___**b.** improper
___**c.** coarse
___**d.** weak

108c

a

preg nant (preg′nənt), *adj.* 1 having an embryo or embryos developing in the uterus; being with child or young. 2 filled; loaded. 3 fertile; rich; abounding: *a mind pregnant with ideas.* 4 filled with meaning; very significant: *a pregnant saying, pregnant years.* [< Latin *praegnantem* < *prae-* pre- + *gen-* to bear] **—preg′nant ly,** *adv.*

Check the phrase(s) in which **pregnant** is used correctly.
___**a.** pregnant woman
___**b.** pregnant moment
___**c.** pregnant gun
___**d.** pregnant void

133c

c

dis in te grate (dis in′tə grāt), *v.,* **-grat ed, -grat ing.** —*v.t.* break up; separate into small parts or bits. —*v.i.* 1 become disintegrated; break up. 2 (of atomic nuclei) undergo disintegration. **—dis in′te gra′- tor,** *n.*

Which of the following agents would most likely cause **disintegration**?
___**a.** termites
___**b.** glue
___**c.** magnet
___**d.** bomb
___**e.** fire

293b

I had been so **infatuated** with the romantic stories in the *Arabian Nights* that I really believed life in Arabia would contain all the beauty and excitement of those fairy tales.

Infatuate means:
—a. become convinced of something
—b. make aware of
—c. make a strong impression
—d. inspire with a foolish passion

268c

vis u al ize (vizh′ü ə līz), *v.,* -ized, -iz ing.
—*v.t.* 1 form a mental picture of: *visualize a friend's face when she is away.* 2 make visible. —*v.i.* form mental pictures.
—vis′u al i za′tion, *n.* —vis′u al iz′er, *n.*

b

Check the sentence(s) in which a form of **visualize** is used correctly.
—a. We visualized a scheme by which we would make a fortune.
—b. She visualized the eye chart as the doctor pointed to the letters.
—c. An artist usually visualizes a painting before touching the canvas.

243c

ga la (gā′lə, gal′ə), *adj.* of festivity: festive.
—*n.* a festive occasion; festival. [< Italian < Old French *gale* merriment < Germanic]

c

ANALOGY **gala** : festive :: **solemn** :
—a. joyful
—b. restful
—c. serious
—d. depressing
—e. appalling

219a

tur bu lent (tér′ byə lənt)

Down at the beach, the waters have been growing more and more **turbulent**.

c, f

Write a definition or synonym:

194a

en rap ture (en rap′ chər)

Our aim is to **enrapture** our audience.

a, c,
e, f

Write a definition or synonym:

1695

A person's **horoscope** is determined by the appearance of the heavens at the hour of his or her birth. Some people believe, as Jim did, that one's fortunes may be predicted by consulting it.

Horoscope is:
—a. a person supposedly able to predict the future
—b. the cultivation of plants
—c. a diagram of the heavens used in fortune-telling
—d. the direction a person's life may take

8b

Since Congress wanted to **economize**, there was a chance that no money would be appropriated. In fact, Jamison's budget would probably be reduced.

The meaning of **economize** is:
__a. spend money
__b. cut expenses
__c. revise laws
__d. stop spending

33b

"A knee operation does not **necessitate** total anesthesia," Dr. Cardiac said. "I'll give you a shot to put your leg to sleep. You can stay awake during the operation."

The meaning of **necessitate** is:
__a. rule out
__b. order
__c. require
__d. obligate

58c

a

nu cle us (nü′klē əs, nyü′klē əs), n., pl. **-cle i** or **-cle us es.** 1 a central part or thing around which other parts or things are collected. 2 a beginning to which additions are to be made. 3 the central part of an atom, consisting of a proton or protons, neutrons, and other particles. The nucleus carries a positive charge and forms a core containing most of the mass of an atom around which electrons orbit. 4 the fundamental, stable arrangement of atoms in a particular compound. 5 (in biology) a mass of specialized protoplasm found in most plant and animal cells without which the cell cannot grow and divide. See **cell** for diagram. 6 (in astronomy) the dense central part of a comet's head. 7 a specialized mass of gray matter in the brain or spinal cord. [< Latin, kernel < *nux, nucis* nut]

Write the letter of the appropriate **nucleus** in the blanks provided.
__ political convention   a. pianist
__ nut   b. proton
__ fortune   c. candidate
__ atom   d. dollar
__ party   e. kernel

83c

a

de fi cient (di fish′ənt), adj. 1 not complete: defective: *His knowledge of geography is deficient.* 2 not sufficient in quantity, force, etc.; lacking: *This milk is deficient in fat.* —*n.* person or thing that is deficient. [< Latin *deficientem* lacking, failing < *de-* down + *facere* do] —**de fi′cient ly,** *adv.*

Which of the following words mean the *opposite* of **deficient**?
__a. adequate
__b. complete
__c. faulty
__d. perfect
__e. miserable
__f. sufficient

109a

a, b

waif (wāf)

As the Stanleys' boat rounded another bend in the river, they spotted a small **waif** standing on the bank, waving to them.

Write a definition or synonym:

134a

a, d

ca nine (kā′ nīn)

The satellite that was just launched is carrying a single **canine** passenger.

Write a definition or synonym:

169a

b, d, e

ho ro scope (hôr′ ə skōp, hor′ ə skōp)

When Jim asked Maharaji if he would object to Jim's having his **horoscope** read, the old man simply smiled.

Write a definition or synonym:

193c

c

ar dor (är′dər), *n.* **1** warmth of emotion; passion. **2** great enthusiasm; eagerness; zeal: *patriotic ardor.* [< Latin < *ardere* to burn]

Which of the following words mean about the same as **ardor**?

__a. zeal
__b. indifference
__c. passion
__d. slothfulness
__e. enthusiasm
__f. fire

218c

c

ax i om (ak′sē əm), *n.* **1** statement taken to be true without proof; self-evident truth: *It is an axiom that if equals are added to equals the results will be equal.* **2** a well-established principle; rule or law. [< Latin *axioma* < Greek *axiōma* < *axios* worthy]

Which of the following are **axioms**?

__a. messages
__b. statements denied by most people
__c. statements accepted by most people
__d. statements questioned by most people
__e. fables
__f. "Everyone must die."

243b

The **gala** spirit of the celebration would be enhanced by dancing, as well as performances by all of the talented people of the area. Everyone looked forward to the evening's activities.

A synonym for **gala** is:

__a. amateur
__b. pleasant
__c. festive
__d. musical

268b

Many people, when they think of Africa, **visualize** first the animals of that great continent. Then, perhaps, other images come to mind: the jungle, mountains, waterfalls, and so on.

The meaning of **visualize** is:

__a. explore thoroughly
__b. picture mentally
__c. analyze in detail
__d. make a list of

293a

b, c

in fat u ate (in fach′ ü āt)

I had become **infatuated** with the holy city of Mecca when I was still a child.

Write a definition or synonym:

8c

b

e con o mize (i kon′ə mīz), v., **-mized,**
-miz ing. —v.t. manage so as to avoid waste;
use to the best advantage. —v.i. cut down
expenses. —**e con′o miz′er,** n.

Which of the following expressions mean about the
same as **economize**?

—**a.** "burn the candle at both ends"
—**b.** "provide for a rainy day"
—**c.** "wish on a star"
—**d.** "make ends meet"
—**e.** "watch pennies"

33c

c

ne ces si tate (nə ses′ə tāt), v.t., **-tat ed,**
-tat ing. 1 make necessary; require;
demand: *His broken leg necessitated an ope-*
ration. 2 compel, oblige, or force: *What*
necessitated you to take this action? —**ne-**
ces′si ta′tion, n.

Which of the following events might **necessitate**
immediate action?

—**a.** a forest fire
—**b.** a nightmare
—**c.** a plane crash
—**d.** a head cold
—**e.** an approaching storm

59a

c, e,
d, b,
a

em bry o (em′ brē ō)

"It's too bad we have no chance to study an **embryo** of
this life-form," Alice said.

Write a definition or synonym:

84a

a, b,
d, f

sol u ble (sol′ yə bəl)

Mrs. Samuelson learned that it was important to use a
plant food that was **soluble** in water.

Write a definition or synonym:

109b

The crew members decided to have a feast to
celebrate their freedom from the Stanleys. All of the
villagers joined in. Carlos made sure that even the
smallest **waif** had plenty to eat. It made him happy to
see every thin and neglected child eating well.

The meaning of **waif** is:

—**a.** delinquent
—**b.** badly behaved child
—**c.** homeless child
—**d.** thin child

134b

Canines are often used in medical experiments on
earth. In this satellite, one puppy is being put to sleep,
frozen, and kept in orbit. The animal will be revived
several months later. This experiment will help
determine whether or not humans can be frozen for
years at a time during longer trips to outer space.

Another word for **canine** is:

—**a.** mammal
—**b.** horse
—**c.** elephant
—**d.** dog

168c

ap pall ing (ə pô′ling), *adj.* causing consternation and horror; dismaying; terrifying.
—**ap pall′ing ly,** *adv.*

Which of the following might you find **appalling**?
__a. a hot day
__b. a brutal murder
__c. a glass of sour milk
__d. a bombing
__e. a mine disaster

193b

At every concert we give, our **ardor** is felt by the members of the audience and they, in turn, reward us with a warm reception.

Ardor means:
__a. hard work
__b. disease
__c. enthusiasm
__d. ability

218b

It is wise to observe this **axiom** as it has been tested and proved many times over.

An **axiom** is:
__a. a story with a moral
__b. a wise precaution
__c. an established principle
__d. a fictitious statement

243a

, b, e

ga la (gā′ lə, gal′ ə)

According to all the advance reports, the centennial would be a **gala** occasion.

Write a definition or synonym:

268a

d, e

vis u al ize (vizh′ ü ə līz)

It is hard to **visualize** Africa without its game animals.

Write a definition or synonym:

292c

d

pil grim age (pil′grə mij), *n.* 1 a pilgrim's journey; journey to some sacred place as an act of religious devotion. 2 a long journey.

Check the sentence(s) in which a form of **pilgrimage** is used correctly.
__a. I made a pilgrimage to the corner for the bus.
__b. Pilgrimages are often made to shrines.
__c. We all went on the long pilgrimage together.
__d. After the ceremonies, they went to the pilgrimage.

9a

b, d, e

cur tail (kėr′ tāl′)

Jamison learned that his study group would have to **curtail** its investigation.

Write a definition or synonym:

34a

a, c, e

ster ile (ster′ əl)

The head nurse helped Dr. Cardiac put on her **sterile** gloves, and the operation began.

Write a definition or synonym:

59b

From a careful study of the **embryo**, a biologist can learn much about an organism's development before birth or germination. At this stage, when the organs are too primitive to function independently, some clue to the creature's origin might be found.

An **embryo** is a plant or animal that is:
__a. full grown
__b. undeveloped
__c. mature
__d. small

84b

When a plant food is water **soluble**, it can be made into liquid by the rain and carried deep into the soil to feed the plant roots.

Something that is **soluble** is easily:
__a. hardened
__b. dissolved
__c. melted
__d. made solid

109c

c

waif (wāf), *n.* 1 person without home or friends, especially a homeless or neglected child. 2 anything without an owner; stray thing, animal, etc. [< Anglo-French; probably < Scandinavian]

Which of the following would be described as a **waif**?
__a. lost mitten
__b. abandoned baby
__c. refugee child
__d. traveling salesperson
__e. adopted child
__f. stray dog

134c

d

ca nine (kā′nin), *adj.* 1 of or like a dog: *canine faithfulness.* 2 like that of a dog: *The glutton had a canine appetite.* 3 of or belonging to the family of carnivorous mammals that includes dogs, foxes, jackals, and wolves. —*n.* 1 a dog. 2 any animal belonging to the canine family. 3 a canine tooth. [< Latin *caninus* < *canis* dog]

In which of the following places would you be most likely to find a **canine**?
__a. on a farm
__b. in the lion house
__c. in your mouth
__d. at the circus

292b

A **pilgrimage** to Mecca may be made by ship, train, or camel.

The meaning of **pilgrimage** is:
—**a.** short trip
—**b.** vacation
—**c.** round trip
—**d.** religious journey

267c

c **pas sé** (pä sā′, pas′ā), *adj.* out of date; outmoded. [< French, passed]

Which of the following words mean about the same as **passé?**
—**a.** modern
—**b.** novel
—**c.** unique
—**d.** obsolete
—**e.** antiquated

242c

a **pro vin cial** (prə vin′shəl), *adj.* 1 of a province: *provincial government.* 2 belonging or peculiar to some particular province or provinces rather than to the whole country; local: *provincial customs.* 3 having the manners, speech, dress, point of view, etc., of people living in a province. 4 lacking refinement or polish; narrow: *a provincial point of view.* —*n.* 1 person born or living in a province. 2 a provincial person. —**pro vin′cial ly,** *adv.*

Provincial can be correctly used to describe which of the following?
—**a.** a local newspaper
—**b.** a country bumpkin
—**c.** a national television network
—**d.** a world traveler
—**e.** a narrow-minded person

218a

b **ax i om** (ak′ sē əm)

"It is better to be safe than sorry" is an **axiom** that applies to hurricane preparations.

Write a definition or synonym:

193a

e **ar dor** (är′ dər)

The chorus always sings with **ardor** at a concert.

Write a definition or synonym:

168b

Much of Jim's behavior to date had been equally **appalling** to Maharaji and his followers. Jim's habit of shouting at the sacred cows struck them as dismaying, and even a bit terrifying.

Appalling means:
—**a.** horrifying
—**b.** strange
—**c.** rude
—**d.** inconsiderate

9b

With his own study **curtailed**, Jamison would not be able to collect much information about pollution of the sea. He decided to rely on the information that The Friends of the Sea had already collected.

A synonym for **curtail** is:
—**a.** confirm
—**b.** renew
—**c.** reduce
—**d.** exaggerate

34b

Everything in the operating room, including the doctors' gloves and masks, must be **sterile** to prevent germs from entering the patient's body.

Sterile means:
—**a.** germ-free
—**b.** boiled
—**c.** shining
—**d.** anesthetic

59c

b

em bry o (em′brē ō), *n.*, *pl.* **-bry os**, *adj.*
—*n.* **1** animal during the period of its growth from the fertilized egg until its organs have developed so that it can live independently. The embryo of a mammal is usually called a fetus in its later stages (in human beings, more than three months after conception). **2** an undeveloped plant within a seed. **3 in embryo,** in an undeveloped stage. —*adj.* undeveloped; embryonic. [< Medieval Latin < Greek *embryon* < *en-* in + *bryein* to swell]

Which of the following would be an **embryo**?
—**a.** an unborn child
—**b.** an adolescent
—**c.** an unhatched chicken
—**d.** a fertilized egg
—**e.** a tadpole

84c

b

sol u ble (sol′yə bəl), *adj.* **1** that can be dissolved or made into liquid: *Salt is soluble in water.* **2** that can be solved: *This problem is hard but soluble.* [< Latin *solubilis* < *solvere* dissolve] —**sol′u ble ness,** *n.* —**sol′u bly,** *adv.*

Which of the following are *not* **soluble** in water?
—**a.** sugar
—**b.** rock dust
—**c.** arithmetic problems
—**d.** sand
—**e.** jello
—**f.** crossword puzzle

110a

b, c, f

glut ton (glut′ n)

The crew members and villagers all made **gluttons** of themselves.

Write a definition or synonym:

135a

a, c, d

tol er a ble (tol′ ər ə bəl)

Flights to the stars could take as long as fifty years. The only way to make conditions **tolerable** is to freeze the travelers before the journey begins and wake them years later, a few months before they reach their destination.

Write a definition or synonym:

53

292a

pil grim age (pil' grə mij)

Our first stop was Mecca. This city is the goal of the **pilgrimage** which devout Moslems hope to make at least once in their lives.

b, c

Write a definition or synonym:

267b

At one time, a millionaire might go big-game hunting in Africa with dozens of servants and guides, and every luxury. This type of display is **passé** today because simplicity is considered stylish.

A synonym for **passé** is:

—**a.** extinct
—**b.** old
—**c.** out-of-date
—**d.** up-to-date

242b

The editor of the local newspaper took a strong position on this subject. Her editorial stated that Andersonville should be proud of its **provincial** ways. She wrote: "We should be proud of our small-town manners. People like to visit Andersonville because we are so different from the typical city."

Provincial means:

—**a.** belonging to a locality
—**b.** referring to a national custom
—**c.** in the process of changing
—**d.** profitable

217c

bland (bland), *adj.* 1 gentle or soothing; balmy; *a bland summer breeze.* 2 smoothly agreeable and polite: *a bland smile.* 3 soothing to the palate or digestive tract; not irritating: *a bland diet of baby food.* [< Latin *blandus* soft] —**bland/ly,** *adv.* —**bland/ness,** *n.*

a

ANALOGY **bland : spicy :: pale :**

—**a.** dull
—**b.** colorful
—**c.** pepper
—**d.** unexciting
—**e.** agreeable

192c

o ver ture (ō'vər chùr), *n.* 1 proposal or offer: *The enemy is making overtures for peace.* 2 a musical composition played by the orchestra as an introduction to an opera, oratorio, or other long musical composition. [< Old French < Latin *apertura* opening, Doublet of APERTURE.]

b

ANALOGY **overture : beginning ::**

—**a.** bill : pay
—**b.** house : cleaner
—**c.** bank : rob
—**d.** agreement : break
—**e.** conclusion : end

168a

ap pall ing (ə pô' ling)

c, d

At first, Jim found the caste system **appalling**.

Write a definition or synonym:

9c

c

cur tail (kẻr′tāl′), *v.t.* cut short; cut off part of; reduce; lessen. See **shorten** for synonym study. [< obsolete *curtal,* adjective, cut short (especially of tails) < Old French *curtald* < *court* short < Latin *curtus* cut short] —**cur′tail′er,** *n.* —**cur′tail′ment,** *n.*

ANALOGY curtail : activities ::
—**a.** hide : conceal
—**b.** busy : industrious
—**c.** lengthen : stretch
—**d.** shorten : sleeves
—**e.** money : bank

34c

a

ster ile (ster′əl), *adj.* 1 free from living germs or microorganisms: *keep surgical instruments sterile.* 2 not producing seed, offspring, crops, etc.: *sterile land, a sterile cow.* 3 not producing results: *sterile hopes.* 4 mentally or spiritually barren. [< Latin *sterilis*] —**ster′ile ly,** *adv.*

Which of the following words mean the *opposite of* **sterile?**
—**a.** fruitful
—**b.** beneficial
—**c.** abundant
—**d.** unproductive
—**e.** arid
—**f.** infected

60a

a, c, d

mu ta tion (myü tā′ shən)

The biologists found evidence that the slime creature was a **mutation.**

Write a definition or synonym:

85a

b, d

hy brid (hī′ brid)

To tell the truth, Mrs. Samuelson was not entirely satisfied with the way her plant "children" were turning out. Perhaps that's why she began experimenting with **hybrids.**

Write a definition or synonym:

110b

Not one gave a thought to the Stanleys. The two of them deserved whatever fate had in store for them. Every man, woman, and child ate like a **glutton** until every last morsel of the Stanleys' food was gone.

A **glutton** is:
—**a.** a hungry animal
—**b.** a starving insect
—**c.** a pest
—**d.** a greedy eater

135b

No human being could endure a fifty-year voyage, and the problems of sanitation and supply would be insurmountable. The deep-freeze technique holds the promise of making a long space voyage **tolerable** for humans.

Tolerable means:
—**a.** favorable
—**b.** endurable
—**c.** pleasant
—**d.** perfect

291c

b

be troth (bi trôth', bi trŏth'), v.t. engage (two persons, one to the other) with a view to marriage.

To become **betrothed**, one:
—**a.** "hops a fast freight"
—**b.** "pops the question"
—**c.** "asks for one's hand"
—**d.** "ties the knot"
—**e.** "gets hitched"

267a

b

pas sé (pa sā', pas' ā)

A glamorous, luxurious African big-game hunt, in which all the comforts of home are brought along, is now considered **passé**.

Write a definition or synonym:

242a

b

pro vin cial (pra vin' shal)

People living in a small town are often sensitive about being called **provincial**.

Write a definition or synonym:

217b

The violent winds of a hurricane are certainly different from the **bland** summer breezes that precede them.

A synonym for **bland** is:
—**a.** mild
—**b.** dull
—**c.** strong
—**d.** warm

192b

Most choral works are preceded by an **overture** which introduces the themes of the composition.

A synonym for **overture** is:
—**a.** speech
—**b.** introduction
—**c.** chorus
—**d.** symphony

167c

d

fu tile (fyü'tl, fyü'til), adj. 1 not successful; useless; ineffectual: *He fell down after making futile attempts to keep his balance.* See **vain** for synonym study. 2 not important; trifling. [< Latin *futilis* pouring easily, worthless < *fundere* pour] —**fu'tile ly,** adv.

Check the sentence(s) in which **futile** is used correctly.
—**a.** She was given to wearing futile jewelry.
—**b.** Don't ask futile questions.
—**c.** The heiress idled away her time in futile pursuits.
—**d.** It would be futile for you to try to escape.

10a

d

dig ni tar y (dig′ nə ter′ ē)

Rupert Jamison and Sally Kendall decided to work together. They each enlisted the support of many **dignitaries**.

Write a definition or synonym:

35a

a, c, f

trans fu sion (tran sfyü′ zhən)

Legs stayed calm until he saw the **transfusion** equipment standing next to the operating table.

Write a definition or synonym:

60b

Mutations, which can occur in both plants and animals, can be inherited. The Manx cat is an example of an animal which lost its tail through a **mutation**. The slime creature was obviously another **mutated** life-form. With luck, we'll never see another one of that type.

Another word for **mutation** is:
__a. movement
__b. removal
__c. disease
__d. change

85b

She planned to select the best features of two different bushes in order to make a **hybrid**. One rose bush had especially large blossoms; the other was unusually resistant to plant disease. Her **hybrid** rose would have the best qualities of each.

Hybrid means:
__a. beautiful plant
__b. pure form
__c. crossbreed
__d. mixture

110c

d

glut ton (glut′n), *n.* 1 a greedy eater; person who eats too much. 2 person who never seems to have enough of something: *a glutton for punishment.* 3 the European name for the wolverine. [< Old French *glouton* < Latin *gluttonem*]

ANALOGY **glutton : greedy** ::
__a. miser : stingy
__b. feast : dinner
__c. kitchen : eating
__d. coward : fearful
__e. soldier : war

135c

b

tol er a ble (tol′ər ə bəl), *adj.* 1 able to be borne or endured; bearable. 2 fairly good; passable: *She is in tolerable health.* —**tol′er a ble ness,** *n.* —**tol′er a bly,** *adv.*

A performance that is **tolerable** is:
__a. "nothing to brag about"
__b. "second-rate"
__c. "top-notch"
__d. "second to none"
__e. "first class"

291b

Although we had been **betrothed** for only a few months, we decided to advance our wedding date so that I could accompany him.

The meaning of **betroth** is:

—a. be acquainted
—b. engage
—c. be together
—d. be in love

266c

gro·tesque (grō tesk'), adj. 1 odd or unnatural in shape, appearance, manner, etc.; fantastic; queer: *pictures of dragons and other grotesque monsters.* 2 ridiculous; absurd: *The monkey's grotesque antics made the children laugh.* 3 (of painting or sculpture) in or resembling the grotesque. —n. painting, sculpture, etc., combining designs, ornaments, figures of persons or animals, etc., in a fantastic or unnatural way, much used in the Renaissance. [< French < Italian *grottesco,* literally, of caves, cavelike < *grotta.* See GROTTO.] —**gro·tesque'ly,** adv. —**gro·tesque'ness,** n.

ANALOGY **grotesque : ordinary** ::

—a. beast : monster
—b. flawed : perfect
—c. horrible : loathesome
—d. beautiful : actress
—e. movie : film

d

241c

cen·ten·ni·al (sen ten'ē əl, sen ten'yəl), adj. 1 of or having to do with 100 years or the 100th anniversary. 2 100 years old. —n. 1 a 100th anniversary: *The town is celebrating its centennial.* 2 celebration of the 100th anniversary. [< Latin *centum* hundred + English -nial] —**cen·ten'ni·al·ly,** adv.

Check the sentence(s) in which a form of **centennial** is used correctly.

—a. The man was a centennial.
—b. By its centennial year, the college's enrollment had increased tenfold.
—c. Married couples frequently celebrate their centennials.

d

217a

bland (bland)

A **bland** breeze and a light rainfall can be the forerunners of a violent hurricane.

Write a definition or synonym:

c, d

192a

o·ver·ture (ō'vər chùr, ō'vər chər)

The orchestra usually plays an **overture** before the choral singing begins.

Write a definition or synonym:

b, e

167b

Today there are "untouchables" in some of the highest positions in government. Although some members of this caste still perform most of the menial tasks, hope of advancement is no longer **futile**.

Futile means:

—a. imaginary
—b. worthwhile
—c. understandable
—d. useless

10b

With Jamison adding his strength, the public would pay more attention to The Friends of the Sea. The addition of **dignitaries** serving as honorary members would lend even more importance to the committee's work.

The meaning of **dignitary** is:
—**a.** government employee
—**b.** member of a royal family
—**c.** member of the armed forces
—**d.** person of high rank

35b

Fresh blood is always kept on hand in case a patient bleeds too much and needs a blood **transfusion.**
"Put me to sleep!" Legs demanded. "I can't stand the sight of blood!"

Another word for **transfusion** is:
—**a.** removal
—**b.** transaction
—**c.** clot
—**d.** transfer

60c

d

mu ta tion (myü tā′shən), *n.*　1 act or process of changing; change; alteration. 2 change within a gene or chromosome of animals or plants resulting in the appearance of a new, inheritable feature or character. 3 a new genetic character or new variety of plant or animal formed in this way; mutant. [< Latin *mutationem* < *mutare* to change]

Check the sentence(s) in which **mutation** is used correctly.
—**a.** His accident had caused him severe mutation.
—**b.** An odd mutation would be a purple dog.
—**c.** Many birds carry out an annual mutation.
—**d.** Grafting of fruits may produce a mutation.

85c

c

hy brid (hī′brid), *n.*　1 offspring of two animals or plants of different varieties, species, races, etc. The loganberry is a hybrid because it is a cross between a dewberry and the red raspberry. The mule is a hybrid of a female horse and a male donkey.　2 (in genetics) offspring of two individuals that differ in at least one gene. 3 anything of mixed origin. A word formed of parts from different languages is a hybrid. —*adj.* 1 bred from two different species, varieties, etc. A mule is a hybrid animal. 2 of mixed origin. [< Latin *hybrida*]

ANALOGY hybrid fruit : nectarine :: hybrid animal :
　—**a.** vegetable
　—**b.** apple
　—**c.** mule
　—**d.** garden
　—**e.** roses

a, d

LESSON 12

Competition in Women's Gymnastics

Kim Andrews and Paula Lazlo were two of the strongest contenders for the national championship in gymnastics. There were perhaps a dozen other women who could provide serious competition at the two-day meet sponsored by the U.S. Gymnastics Federation. But it was generally agreed that the top honors would go to either Kim or Paula.

136a

a, b

cos mic (koz′ mik)

According to the report of the USSR-USA Commission, the deep-freeze satellite is the first step in **cosmic** exploration.

Write a definition or synonym:

167a

fu tile (fyü′ tl, fyü′ tīl)

Until recently, it would have been **futile** for any of the "untouchables" to try to change their lot in life.

Write a definition or synonym:

191c

en sem ble (än säm′bəl), *n.* **1** all the parts of a thing considered together; general effect. **2** a united performance of the full number of singers, musicians, etc.: *After the solo all the singers joined in the ensemble.* **3** group of musicians or the musical instruments used in such a performance: *Two violins, a cello, and a harp made up the string ensemble.* **4** set of clothes of which each item is chosen to match or complement the others; a complete, harmonious costume. [< French < Latin *in-simul* at the same time < *in-* + *simul* at the same time]

Which of the following would be considered an **ensemble**?
_**a.** matching coat, shoes, and hat
_**b.** all the members of an opera company
_**c.** a number of paintings by one artist
_**d.** pianist
_**e.** a string quartet

216c

but tress (but′ris), *n.* **1** a support built against a wall or building to strengthen it. **2** a support like this; prop. —*v.t.* **1** strengthen with a buttress. **2** support and strengthen. [< Old French *bouterez* (plural) < *bouter* thrust against]

Check the sentence(s) in which a form of **buttress** is used correctly.
_**a.** I buttressed my head with a pillow.
_**b.** The soldiers were safe inside the buttress.
_**c.** A strong faith can be a buttress against fear.
_**d.** We buttressed the side of the house with bricks.

241b

A fiftieth anniversary is somewhat important, but a **centennial** is certainly something to celebrate with enthusiasm.

Centennial means:
_**a.** 25th anniversary
_**b.** birthday
_**c.** wedding anniversary
_**d.** 100th anniversary

266b

The **grotesquely** long neck of the giraffe and the equally **grotesque** prehistoric look of the rhinoceros are two examples of nature's strange ways.

Grotesque means:
_**a.** supernatural
_**b.** humorous
_**c.** carnivorous
_**d.** strange

291a

be troth (bi trōŦH′, bi trôth′)

At the time that my husband was told he was being assigned to Saudi Arabia, we were **betrothed**.

Write a definition or synonym:

10c

d

dig ni tar y (dig′nə ter′ē), *n.,* *pl.* **-tar ies.** person who has high rank or a position of honor. A bishop is a dignitary of the church.

Check the sentence(s) in which **dignitary** is used correctly.
- __a. He felt it was beneath his dignitary.
- __b. A dignitary of our church opened the meeting.
- __c. I was asked to be a dignitary of the will.
- __d. The prime minister is an important dignitary.

35c

d

trans fuse (tran sfyüz′), *v.t.,* **-fused, -fus ing.** 1 pour (a liquid) from one container into another. 2 transfer (blood) from the veins of one person or animal to another. 3 inject (a solution) into a blood vessel. 4 infuse; instill: *The speaker transfused his enthusiasm into the audience.*
trans fu sion (tran sfyü′zhən), *n.* 1 act or fact of transfusing. 2 transfer of blood from one person or animal to another.

Check the sentence(s) in which a form of **transfusion** is used correctly.
- __a. The sale of a house is a business transfusion.
- __b. A doctor gives transfusions to promote recovery.
- __c. The victim of an airplane crash may need a transfusion.
- __d. A chemist may perform transfusions with his test tubes.

LESSON 7

b, d

Can You Dig It?

Paul Andrades had been on leave from the university for a year and a half so that he could direct an archaeological project in Greece. In archaeology, which is the scientific study of ancient times, an investigation of ancient ruins is called a "dig." With the help of several hundred local laborers, Paul and his colleagues made an important discovery.

86a

c

pres tige (pre stēzh′, pre stēj′)

In a few years, Mrs. Samuelson's hybrid roses brought their owner a great deal of **prestige**.

Write a definition or synonym:

111a

su per la tive (sə pėr′ lə tiv, sù pėr′ lə tiv)

Both Kim and Paula were **superlative** athletes.

Write a definition or synonym:

136b

Here is part of the Commission's report: "We have already explored our solar system and our galaxy. **Cosmic** exploration is the next step. Having learned about our nearest neighbors, we are now ready to learn more about the universe as a whole."

The meaning of **cosmic** is:
- __a. worldwide
- __b. scientific
- __c. of the universe
- __d. of the earth

c

166c

seg re gate (v. seg′rə gāt; adj. seg′rə git, seg′rə gāt), v., **-gat ed, -gat ing,** adj. —v.t. 1 separate from others; set apart; isolate: *The doctor segregated the sick child.* 2 separate or keep apart (one race, people, etc.) from another or from the rest of society by maintaining separate schools, separate public facilities, etc. —v.i. 1 separate from the rest and collect in one place. 2 (in genetics) undergo segregation. —adj. segregated. [< Latin *segregatum* segregated < *se-* apart from + *gregem* herd]

Check the sentence(s) in which a form of **segregate** is used correctly.
_**a.** Boys and girls are segregated for certain school activities.
_**b.** She was segregated until she recovered.
_**c.** Every now and then I like to be segregated.

191b

The members of the **ensemble** who accompany us take their places first. Then, for about three minutes, they "tune-up."

Another word for **ensemble** is:
_**a.** stage crew
_**b.** soloists
_**c.** members of an audience
_**d.** group of musicians

216b

Sandbags are commonly used to **buttress** sea walls. The water is less likely to shift sandbags, for they are heavy and hard to move.

Another word for **buttress** is:
_**a.** backlog
_**b.** backstop
_**c.** support
_**d.** lining

241a

cen ten ni al (sen ten′ ē əl, sen ten′ yəl)

Last year, the village leaders found a perfect excuse for a celebration: the town's **centennial**.

Write a definition or synonym:

266a

a, c, e

gro tesque (grō tesk′)

Some of the animals in Africa are **grotesque**.

Write a definition or synonym:

a, c

LESSON 30

An Arabian Adventure

My husband and I were among the few couples who had the opportunity to take a honeymoon trip to Saudi Arabia. My husband is a geologist with one of the large oil companies. We spent our first year of married life on the Arabian desert.

b, d

LESSON

Leopard Lovers

Howard and Janice Austin had produced many films on African wildlife for the Museum of Natural History, but they had never realized how *wild* wildlife can actually be until they began to shoot their film on the African leopard. After arriving in Kenya, they headed west across the grasslands into the tropical rain forest.

36a

b, c

vig i lant (vij′ ə lənt)

As she worked, Dr. Cardiac explained why the fresh blood was nearby. All the doctors and nurses remained **vigilant**.

Write a definition or synonym:

61a

am phi the a ter (am′ fə thē′ ə tər)

Near Athens, the capital of Greece, Paul's team discovered an ancient **amphitheater**.

Write a definition or synonym:

86b

When the hybrid roses began winning blue ribbons at flower shows, the other gardeners began to regard Mrs. Samuelson with admiration and respect. She enjoyed her new **prestige** and was glad to pass helpful hints on to the other garden club members.

Another word for **prestige** is:
__**a.** fame
__**b.** reputation
__**c.** knowledge
__**d.** pride

111b

Nothing can equal the **superlative** performance of a champion at the top of her form.

Another word for **superlative** is:
__**a.** exaggerated
__**b.** dramatic
__**c.** powerful
__**d.** supreme

136c

c

cos mic (koz′mik), *adj.* 1 of or belonging to the cosmos; having to do with the whole universe: *Cosmic forces produce stars and meteors.* 2 vast: *a cosmic explosion.* —**cos′mi cal ly,** *adv.*

Something **cosmic** is *not*:
__**a.** large
__**b.** in disorder
__**c.** petty
__**d.** in space
__**e.** minute

290c

a

tem·per·ance (tem'pər əns), *n.* 1 a being moderate in action, speech, habits, etc.; self-control. 2 a being moderate in the use of alcoholic drinks. 3 the principle and practice of not using alcoholic drinks at all.

A person without **temperance** can be called **intemperate.** In which of the following activities would an **intemperate** person be most likely to engage?

__a. overeating
__b. lecturing on the evils of drink
__c. extravagant spending

265c

b

ma·ter·nal (mə ter'nl), *adj.* 1 of or like a mother; motherly. 2 related on the mother's side of the family; a *maternal* uncle, *maternal grandparents.* 3 received or inherited from one's mother: *His blue eyes were a maternal inheritance.* [< Middle French *maternel* < Latin *maternus* < *mater* mother] —**ma·ter·nal·ly**, *adv.*

Which of the following might be **maternal**?

__a. cow
__b. ram
__c. lioness
__d. colt
__e. sow
__f. grandfather

LESSON 25

b, c, d

The Biggest Little Town in the World

Andersonville is a small town that loves a celebration. Any excuse that people can find to celebrate is seized upon immediately. Before you know it, you are a member of one of the numerous committees formed to plan the festivities.

216a

c

but·tress (but'ris)

People who live near the water try to **buttress** their sea walls against the hurricane's force.

Write a definition or synonym:

191a

en·sem·ble (än säm' bəl)

Most of the choral works which we perform call for an orchestral **ensemble**.

Write a definition or synonym:

166b

At one time, the lowest class, the caste of the "untouchables," was so completely **segregated** that it was impossible for a member of this caste to converse with members of the higher castes.

A synonym for **segregate** is:

__a. remove
__b. unite
__c. separate
__d. exalt

11a

com pile (kəm pīl′)

Howard and Janice Austin had **compiled** a great deal of data on the African leopard.

Write a definition or synonym:

36b

Slowly, Legs began to relax. His mind wandered; he felt a little sleepy. But everyone else in the operating room remained **vigilant** in case of unexpected complications.

A synonym for **vigilant** is:
__a. erect
__b. tense
__c. alert
__d. anxious

61b

The **amphitheater** was large enough to hold several thousand people. The people sat in a series of circles, each one a little higher than the next, around a central stage.

A synonym for **amphitheater** is:
__a. showplace
__b. stadium
__c. theater
__d. movie house

86c

b

pres tige (pre stēzh′, pre stēj′), *n.* reputation, influence, or distinction based on what is known of one's abilities, achievements, opportunities, associations, etc. [< Middle French, illusion, magic spell < Latin *praestigiae* tricks]

Check the sentence(s) in which **prestige** is used correctly.
__a. The man was held in high prestige.
__b. She had to keep up a lot of prestige to fool the enemy.
__c. The prize carried a great deal of prestige with it.
__d. His fine game of tennis gave him prestige at the club.

111c

d

su per la tive (sə pėr′lə tiv, sù pėr′lə tiv), *adj.* 1 of the highest kind; above all others; supreme: *King Solomon had superlative wisdom.* 2 showing the highest degree of comparison of an adjective or adverb. *Fairest, best,* and *most slowly* are the superlative forms of *fair, good,* and *slowly.* —*n.* 1 person or thing above all others; supreme example. 2 the highest degree of comparison of an adjective or adverb. 3 form or combination of words that shows this degree. 4 **talk in superlatives,** exaggerate. [< Late Latin *superlativus,* ultimately < *super-* beyond + *latum* brought, carried] —**su per′la tive ly,** *adv.* —**su per′la tive ness,** *n.*

Check the sentence(s) in which a form of **superlative** is used correctly.
__a. He was a silly man who talked too much, always using superlatives.
__b. "Warmer" is the superlative for "warm."
__c. Mt. Whitney is a superlative mountain.
__d. Many people consider champagne the superlative of wines.
__e. Brushing one's teeth is a superlative experience.

137a

b, c, e

cull (kul)

From the information gathered in the first cosmic probe, certain facts will be **culled**.

Write a definition or synonym:

166a

c

seg re gate (*v.* seg′ rə gāt; *adj.* seg′ rə git, seg′ rə gāt)

One feature of the Hindu religion is the caste system that rigidly **segregates** the different classes of society.

Write a definition or synonym:

LESSON 20

b, d

All Together Now...

I am a member of our town's chorus, which specializes in performing the great choral works of the masters. Each year we present two or three concerts, for which we rehearse for several months. On the night of the concert, everyone is at a high pitch of excitement.

215c

b

vig il (vij′əl), *n.* 1 a staying awake for some purpose; a watching; watch: *All night the mother kept vigil over the sick child.* 2 a night spent in prayer. 3 **vigils,** *pl.* devotions, prayers, services, etc., on the night before a religious festival. 4 the day and night before a solemn religious festival. [< Latin *vigilia* < *vigil* watchful]

ANALOGY vigil : sleepy :: fast :
__a. kitchen
__b. candle
__c. hungry
__d. quick
__e. guard

240c

c

pic to ri al (pik tôr′ē əl, pik tōr′ē əl), *adj.* 1 having to do with pictures; expressed in pictures. 2 making a picture for the mind; vivid. 3 illustrated by pictures: *a pictorial history.* 4 having to do with painters or painting. [< Latin *pictorius* < *pictor* painter] —**pic to′ri al ly,** *adv.*

Which of the following are **pictorial**?
__a. tables of statistics
__b. comic books
__c. good descriptive writing
__d. collections in art museums
__e. bird calls

265b

Animal mothers are fiercely **maternal** in protecting their young from harm.

Maternal means:
__a. fatherly
__b. motherly
__c. feminine
__d. clever

290b

It is especially important for a swimmer to use **temperance** in preparing for an important meet. It is easy to overdo one's training and to practice to excess.

Temperance means:
__a. moderation
__b. a time schedule
__c. modesty
__d. eccentricity

11b

From first-hand accounts and official records, they had **compiled** a long list of places where leopards had attacked farm animals and human beings.

Compile means:
_a. identify
_b. analyze
_c. discover
_d. collect

36c

c

vig i lant (vij′ə lənt), *adj.* keeping steadily on the alert; watchful; wide-awake: *The dog kept vigilant guard.* See **watchful** for synonym study. —**vig′i lant ly,** *adv.*

Which of the following expressions mean about the same as **vigilant**?
_a. "heads up"
_b. "at ease"
_c. "on guard"
_d. "on the safe side"
_e. "on the lookout"

61c

b

am phi the a ter or **am phi the a tre** (am′fə thē′ə tər), *n.* 1 a circular or oval building with tiers of seats around a central open space. 2 place of public contest; arena. 3 something resembling an amphitheater in shape.

Which of the following events would most likely be held in an **amphitheater**?
_a. county fair
_b. track meet
_c. football game
_d. rifle-shooting competition
_e. dog show

87a

c, d

phe nom e nal (fə nom′ ə nəl)

By crossbreeding her rose bushes, Mrs. Samuelson often achieved results that were quite **phenomenal**.

Write a definition or synonym:

112a

a, d

pin na cle (pin′ ə kəl)

At seventeen, Paula was at the **pinnacle** of her career as a gymnast.

Write a definition or synonym:

137b

Not all the information will be needed, so the important facts must be **culled** from the rest. If the right facts are chosen, the building of the starships to carry settlers to the ends of the universe will be no problem.

Another word for **cull** is:
_a. include
_b. report
_c. select
_d. locate

165c

c

her it age (her′ə tij), *n.* what is handed down from one generation to the next; inheritance: *The heritage of freedom is precious to Americans.* [< Old French < *heriter* inherit < Late Latin *hereditare* < Latin *hereditatem* heredity]

ANALOGY **heritage : past :: prediction :**
- __a. witchcraft
- __b. tradition
- __c. future
- __d. church
- __e. prophecy

190c

d

es teem (e stēm′), *v.t.* **1** have a very favorable opinion of; think highly of: *We esteem courage.* See **value** for synonym study. **2** think; consider: *Men have often esteemed happiness the greatest good.* —*n.* a very favorable opinion; high regard: *Courage is held in esteem.* [< Old French *estimer* < Latin *aestimare* to value]

Check the sentence(s) in which **esteem** can be correctly substituted for the italicized word.
- __a. He does not *think* clearly.
- __b. We do not *consider* wealth as the measure of real success.
- __c. I will not even *consider* going out in this storm.
- __d. I *value* her friendship.

215b

The day and night **vigil** of the weather people is necessary to keep track of the hurricane, for it may change direction at any time.

Another word for **vigil** is:
- __a. worry
- __b. watch
- __c. fear
- __d. warning

240b

A **pictorial** style of writing, which uses words to suggest pictures to the mind, is a great asset in radio broadcasting because radio cannot use actual pictures to put its message across.

Pictorial means:
- __a. auditory
- __b. oral
- __c. illustrative
- __d. accurate

265a

c, f

ma ter nal (mə tėr′ nl)

The **maternal** instinct of most female animals is very strong.

Write a definition or synonym:

290a

b, c

tem per ance (tem′ pər əns)

Another quality which any champion athlete must have is **temperance**.

Write a definition or synonym:

11c

d

com pile (kəm pil′), *v.t.,* **-piled, -pil ing.**
1 collect and bring together in one list or
account. 2 make (a book, a report, etc.) out
of various materials. [< Latin *compilare* pile
up < *com-* together + *pilare* press] **—com-
pil′er,** *n.*

Which of these people would be most likely to **compile**
data?
___a. a dancer
___b. an insurance agent
___c. a card player
___d. a biologist

37a

a, c, e

con sult ant (kən sult′ nt)

Two of the doctors in the room were serving as
medical **consultants**.

Write a definition or synonym:

62a

b, c

de i ty (dē′ ə tē)

Paul believed that the amphitheater had been
dedicated to more than one **deity**.

Write a definition or synonym:

87b

On one plant, the size of the flowers was astonishing.
However, it was the color—a deep, soft purple—
which everyone found **phenomenal**.

The meaning of **phenomenal** is:
___a. abnormal
___b. brightly colored
___c. extraordinary
___d. extremely fragrant

112b

Kim was becoming a better competitor with each
meet, but she had not yet taken the national
championship. People agreed that she had not reached
the **pinnacle** of her gymnastic career.

Another word for **pinnacle** is:
___a. peak
___b. middle
___c. bottom
___d. perfection

137c

c

cull (kul), *v.t.* 1 pick out; select: *The lawyer
culled important facts from the mass of evidence.* 2 pick over; make selections from.
—n. something picked out as inferior or
worthless. Poor fruit, stale vegetables, and
animals not up to standard are called culls.
[< Old French *coillir* < Latin *colligere* col-
lect] **—cull′er,** *n.*

ANALOGY **cull : choose :: discard :**
___a. select
___b. piece
___c. reject
___d. demand
___e. arrange

289c

dis use (*n.* dis yüs′; *v.* dis yüz′), *n.*, *v.*, -used, -us ing. —*n.* lack of use; not being used: *Many words common in Shakespeare's time have fallen into disuse.* —*v.t.* discontinue the use or practice of.

c

Something in **disuse** is likely to be:
— **a.** exploited
— **b.** in poor condition
— **c.** covered with dust
— **d.** employed
— **e.** active

264c

in ev i ta ble (in ev′a ta bal), *adj.*, not to be avoided; sure to happen; certain to come: *Death is inevitable.* [< Latin *inevitabilis* < *in-* not + *evitare* avoid < *ex-* out + *vitare* shun] —in ev′i ta ble ness, *n.* —in ev′i ta bly, *adv.*

d

Check the word(s) that mean(s) the *opposite* of **inevitable.**
— **a.** fated
— **b.** likely
— **c.** uncertain
— **d.** probable
— **e.** positive
— **f.** avoidable

240a

pic to ri al (pik tôr′ ē al)

During the state fair last week, Sandra's station covered the same events as its competitor. The station manager said Sandra's **pictorial** style of reporting helped them capture the larger part of the listening audience.

b, d, e

Write a definition or synonym:

215a

vig il (vij′ al)

Weather people keep a **vigil** over every hurricane.

b, c, d

Write a definition or synonym:

190b

The **esteem** for the successful businessman is based not only on his skill and industry, but on his commitment to the company. The businessman regards his company as a second family. It is a source of personal pride and pleasure.

A synonym for **esteem** is:
— **a.** friendship
— **b.** love
— **c.** adoration
— **d.** respect

165b

Like many ancient lands, India has a rich and complex **heritage.** Side by side with age-old religious beliefs exists a modern legal system based on the British model. Indians today benefit from both traditions.

Another word for **heritage** is:
— **a.** characteristic
— **b.** right
— **c.** inheritance
— **d.** gift

12a

b, d

in ten si ty (in ten′ sə tē)

As the Austins moved into the rain forest toward the latest trouble spot, the **intensity** of the heat slowed their progress.

Write a definition or synonym:

37b

Dr. Cardiac spoke with the two **consultants** several times and asked for their comments and advice. With their many years of experience, they were a valuable source of information and assistance.

Another word for **consultant** is:
__**a.** specialist
__**b.** adviser
__**c.** official
__**d.** authority

62b

From the statues and the symbols carved in the stone walls, it seemed that the structure had originally been built to honor a major **deity**, the sun god Apollo.

Another word for **deity** is:
__**a.** symbol
__**b.** idol
__**c.** idea
__**d.** god

87c

c

phe nom e nal (fə nom′ə nəl), *adj.* 1 of or having to do with a phenomenon or phenomena. 2 having the nature of a phenomenon. 3 extraordinary; remarkable: *a phenomenal memory.* —**phe nom′e nal ly,** *adv.*

phe nom e non (fə nom′ə non), *n.*, *pl.* **-na** (or **-nons** for 4). 1 fact, event, or circumstance that can be observed: *Lightning is an electrical phenomenon.* 2 any sign, symptom, or manifestation: *Fever and inflammation are phenomena of disease.* 3 any exceptional fact or occurrence: *historical phenomena.* 4 an extraordinary or remarkable person or thing. A genius or prodigy is sometimes called a phenomenon. [< Greek *phainomenon* < *phainesthai* appear]

ANALOGY phenomenal : ordinary ::
__**a.** unusual : strange
__**b.** discover : find
__**c.** incredible : unbelievable
__**d.** event : happening
__**e.** riches : poverty

112c

a

pin na cle (pin′ə kəl), *n.* 1 a high peak or point of rock. 2 the highest point: *at the pinnacle of one's fame.* 3 a slender turret or spire. [< Old French *pinacle* < Latin *pinnaculum,* diminutive of *pinna* wing, point]

Which of the following would be most likely to have a **pinnacle** (or **pinnacles**)?
__**a.** mountain range
__**b.** cathedral
__**c.** plateau
__**d.** prestige
__**e.** skyline
__**f.** baseball player's career

138a

c

tab u late (*v.* tab′ yə lāt; *adj.* tab′ yə lit, tab′ yə lāt)

Before the first starship is launched, the results of all earlier space shots will be **tabulated**.

Write a definition or synonym:

165a

c, d

her it age (her′ ə tij)

In India, the cow is a sacred animal. Jim refrained from criticizing the beliefs of the Indian people. Their ancient religion is a part of their **heritage**.

Write a definition or synonym:

190a

a, d, e

es teem (e stēm′)

In Japanese society today, a successful businessman is held in high **esteem**.

Write a definition or synonym:

214c

c

can cel la tion (kan′sə lā′shən), *n.* **1** a canceling. **2** a being canceled. **3** marks made when something is canceled or crossed out. **4** something that is canceled.

Check the sentence(s) in which **cancellation** is used correctly.
___**a.** There was a cancellation of our meeting until next week.
___**b.** A cancellation on a stamp means it was used.
___**c.** Cancellation is often used in multiplying or dividing fractions.
___**d.** There will be a cancellation of the space shot if all parts do not check out properly.

239c

d

si mul ta ne ous (sī′məl tā′nē əs, sim′əl-tā′nē əs), *adj.* **1** existing, done, or happening at the same time: *The two simultaneous shots sounded like one.* **2** indicating two or more equations or inequalities, with two or more unknowns, for which a set of values of the unknowns is sought that is a solution of all the equations or inequalities. [< Medieval Latin *simultaneus* simulated < Latin *similis* like; confused in sense with Latin *simul* at the same time] —**si′mul ta′ne ous ly**, *adv.* —**si′mul ta′ne ous ness**, *n.*

Check the groups of people who are doing exactly the same thing **simultaneously**.
___**a.** people at a carnival
___**b.** soldiers marching in a parade
___**c.** musicians in an orchestra
___**d.** women in a chorus line
___**e.** congregation reciting a prayer in church

264b

Some African tribes live only by hunting. When they cannot get meat, it is **inevitable** that they will perish, unless they learn to farm and raise their food.

A synonym for **inevitable** is:
___**a.** essential
___**b.** important
___**c.** necessary
___**d.** unavoidable

289b

Muscles that are not exercised regularly grow soft and flabby from **disuse**.

Disuse means:
___**a.** rest
___**b.** worthlessness
___**c.** lack of use
___**d.** abuse

12b

The **intensity** of the fierce tropical heat can cause sunstroke or heat exhaustion to those who are not accustomed to it.

The meaning of **intensity** is:
- __**a.** extreme degree
- __**b.** heat
- __**c.** temperature
- __**d.** great quantity

37c

b

con sult ant (kən sult′nt), *n.* **1** person who gives professional or technical advice. **2** person who consults another.

ANALOGY consultant : advice ::
- __**a.** doctor : office
- __**b.** dentist : teeth
- __**c.** politician : votes
- __**d.** police officer : ticket
- __**e.** father : mother

62c

d

de i ty (dē′ə tē), *n., pl.* **-ties.** **1** one of the gods worshiped by a people or a tribe; god or goddess. **2** divine nature; being a god. **3 the Deity,** God. [< Old French *deite* < Latin *deitatem* < *deus* god]

ANALOGY deity : Apollo :: planet :
- __**a.** stars
- __**b.** Earth
- __**c.** space
- __**d.** orbit
- __**e.** galaxy

88a

e

sym me try (sim′ ə trē)

Mrs. Samuelson planned her own garden to achieve the greatest possible **symmetry**.

Write a definition or synonym:

113a

a, b,
d, e,
f

in vin ci ble (in vin′ sə bəl)

Anyone watching Paula do her double back flips might think of her as **invincible**.

Write a definition or synonym:

138b

Tabulating the important results organizes them and makes them easier to study and understand.

The meaning of **tabulate** is:
- __**a.** put in shorter form
- __**b.** arrange in tables
- __**c.** make a record of
- __**d.** type neatly

289a

a

dis use (*n.* dis ūs'; *v.* dis ūz')

Disuse of any muscles makes them weak.

Write a definition or synonym:

264a

a, b, d

in ev i ta ble (in ev' a ta bal)

Although it is **inevitable** that there will be some poaching, the game wardens keep this to a minimum on most game preserves.

Write a definition or synonym:

239b

If there is an event of national importance, such as an election, it will have **simultaneous** coverage by local radio stations and national networks. At these times it makes little difference which station we tune in.

The meaning of **simultaneous** is:

- —a. on the same day
- —b. spontaneous; unplanned
- —c. repeated
- —d. at the same time

214b

There has also been a **cancellation** of the Lions Club annual meeting. Rather than have a poorly attended meeting, the members decided not to meet at all.

Something that is **canceled** is:

- —a. postponed
- —b. reorganized
- —c. done away with
- —d. changed

189c

b

bane (bān), *n.* 1 cause of death, ruin, or harm. 2 destruction of any kind; ruin; harm. [Old English *bana* murderer.]

Which of the following words would best describe the word **bane?**

- —a. disastrous
- —b. delirious
- —c. advantageous
- —d. injurious
- —e. evil
- —f. beneficial

164c

b

ex as pe rate (eg zas'pə rāt'), *v.t.,* **-rat ed, -rat ing.** irritate very much; annoy extremely; make angry: *The little boy's constant noise exasperated his father.* [< Latin *exasperatum* irritated < *ex-* completely + *asper* rough] —**ex as'pe rat'ing ly,** *adv.*

Which of the following words might be used to describe an **exasperated** person?

- —a. subdued
- —b. bewildered
- —c. red-faced
- —d. agitated
- —e. unique
- —f. smiling

12c

a

in ten si ty (in ten′sə tē), *n., pl.* **-ties.**
1 quality of being intense; great strength: *the intensity of sunlight.* 2 extreme degree; great vigor; violence: *intensity of thought, intensity of feeling.* 3 amount or degree of strength of electricity, heat, light, sound, etc., per unit of area, volume, etc.

Which of the following might have **intensity**?
_a. a storm
_b. an emotion
_c. a tree
_d. a light breeze
_e. a color

38a

d

chron ic (kron′ ik)

The next thing Legs remembered was Dr. Cardiac smiling down at him and telling him the operation was a success.
"Don't worry," she said, "you do not have a **chronic** condition."

Write a definition or synonym:

63a

b

por tal (pôr′ tl, pōr′ tl)

As the digging progressed, the team uncovered massive blocks of stone which had once formed a great **portal**.

Write a definition or synonym:

88b

"The trouble with Mother Nature," she would often say, "is that she has no order or design. She lets her wild flowers grow every which way." Mother Samuelson loved **symmetry**. Her flowers were planted in a definite order with a carefully balanced design.

Symmetry means:
_a. form
_b. design
_c. purpose
_d. balance

113b

Sure enough, as she competed on the uneven bars and the balance beam, Paula easily outscored her opponents. Kim won almost as many points. However, at the end of the meet only one girl would be called **invincible**.

A synonym for **invincible** is:
_a. superlative
_b. unconquerable
_c. beaten
_d. standing

138c

b

tab u late (*v.* tab′yə lāt; *adj.* tab′yə lit, tab′yə lāt), *v.,* **-lat ed, -lat ing,** *adj.* —*v.t., v.i.* arrange (facts, figures, etc.) in tables or lists. —*adj.* shaped like a table or a tablet.

In which of the following would you most likely use **tabulating**?
_a. bricklaying
_b. physics
_c. mathematics
_d. painting

164b

What **exasperated** Jim most was driving through a crowded narrow street. He found his way completely blocked by cars and people. No one was allowed to disturb the two cows that were lying down in the middle of the street.

Another word for **exasperate** is:
- __a. tease
- __b. irritate
- __c. alarm
- __d. discourage

189b

Residents of Tokyo are so accustomed to earthquakes that a small one may pass almost unnoticed. They regard severe earthquakes as the **bane** of their lives and take many precautions to minimize damage to life and property.

Another word for **bane** is:
- __a. burn
- __b. ruin
- __c. noise
- __d. excitement

214a

b, d

can cel la tion (kan′ sə lā′ shən)

We assume there will be a **cancellation** of the bowling league party that was scheduled for tonight.

Write a definition or synonym:

239a

b, c

si mul ta ne ous (sī′ məl tā′ nē əs, sim′ əl tā′ nē əs)

Sometimes two stations will have **simultaneous** coverage of an event.

Write a definition or synonym:

263c

b

il le git i mate (il′i jit′ə mit), *adj.* 1 not according to the law or the rules. 2 born of parents who are not married to each other; bastard. 3 not logical; not according to good usage; improper. —**il′le git′i mate ly**, *adv.*

Check the phrase(s) in which **illegitimate** is used correctly.
- __a. an illegitimate usage of a word
- __b. an illegitimate play in a card game
- __c. making an illegitimate deduction from the facts
- __d. adopting an illegitimate child

288c

d

tor so (tôr′sō), *n., pl.* -sos. 1 the trunk of the human body. 2 the trunk or body of a statue without any head, arms, or legs. 3 something left mutilated or unfinished. [< Italian, originally, stalk < Latin *thyrsus* < Greek *thyrsos*]

Check the sentence(s) in which **torso** can be correctly substituted for the italicized word.
- __a. The archaeologists unearthed a broken statue, with only the legs and *body* remaining.
- __b. The child had measles, and his entire *body* was covered with red spots.

13a

a, b, e

list less (list′ lis)

When the temperature stayed at 50° Celsius for the fourth day in a row, both Howard and Janice were **listless**.

Write a definition or synonym:

38b

"If you take it easy for a while, your knee will be as good as new," the doctor said. "You shouldn't have any more trouble. This injury will not lead to a **chronic** condition."

A synonym for **chronic** is:
__a. constant
__b. short-lived
__c. nervous
__d. serious

63b

Thousands of years ago, people had entered the amphitheater through this huge **portal**. It was decorated with statues of flying horses and a symbol of the shining sun.

Another word for **portal** is:
__a. stage
__b. path
__c. window
__d. entrance

88c

d

sym me try (sim′ə trē), *n., pl.* **-tries.** 1 a regular, balanced arrangement on opposite sides of a line or plane, or around a center or axis. 2 pleasing proportions between the parts of a whole; well-balanced arrangement of parts; harmony. [< Greek *symmetria* < *syn-* together + *metron* measure]

Which of the following usually need **symmetry** to be acceptable?
__a. rice pudding
__b. a wedding cake
__c. an airplane
__d. a steak
__e. a show dog
__f. patchwork quilt

113c

b

in vin ci ble (in vin′sə bəl), *adj.* unable to be conquered; impossible to overcome; unconquerable: *invincible courage, an invincible fighter.* [< Latin *invincibilis* < *in-* not + *vincere* conquer] **—in vin′ci ble ness,** *n.* **—in vin′ci bly,** *adv.*

ANALOGY invincible : winner :: vulnerable :
__a. loser
__b. fighter
__c. singer
__d. player
__e. runner

139a

b, c

the o rem (thē′ ər əm, thir′ əm)

The computation of the starship's path will be based on several new mathematical **theorems**.

Write a definition or synonym:

164a

a, b

ex as pe rate (eg zas′ pə rāt′)

Jim found much to admire as he walked beside Maharaji. But he found much to **exasperate** him too.

Write a definition or synonym:

189a

e, d, f

bane (bān)

Earthquakes are still the **bane** of many Japanese cities.

Write a definition or synonym:

213c

a

pes si mis tic (pes′ə mis′tik), *adj.* 1 having a tendency to look at the dark side of things or to see all the difficulties and disadvantages. See **cynical** for synonym study. 2 expecting the worst: *He is pessimistic about the outcome of the trial.* 3 having to do with pessimism. —**pes′si mis′ti cal ly**, *adv.*

Which of the following expressions best describe a **pessimistic** person?
—**a.** "looking for the silver lining"
—**b.** "full of gloom and doom"
—**c.** "casting away care"
—**d.** "wet blanket"
—**e.** "life of the party"

238c

c

au to ma tion (ô′tə mā′shən), *n.* 1 the use of automatic controls in the operation of a machine or group of machines. In automation, electronic or mechanical devices do many of the tasks formerly performed by people. 2 method of making a manufacturing process, a production line, etc., operate more automatically by the use of built-in or supplementary controls in a machine or number of machines.

Automation can be correctly described as:
—**a.** out of date
—**b.** efficient
—**c.** modern
—**d.** clumsy
—**e.** handcrafted

263b

Poachers use **illegitimate** means to get into the preserves to hunt. If they are caught, they are fined heavily.

Another word for **illegitimate** is:
—**a.** forbidden
—**b.** illegal
—**c.** cruel
—**d.** licensed

288b

Lu Ann's arms and legs were as slim and muscular as her **torso**.

Torso means:
—**a.** physique
—**b.** neck
—**c.** head
—**d.** trunk

13b

The guides were not at all **listless**. While Howard and Janice remained quiet on their cots, the men made camp, checked the equipment, prepared a good meal, and discussed the expedition with interest.

A synonym for **listless** is:
__a. restless
__b. indifferent
__c. useless
__d. diseased

38c

a

chron ic (kron′ik), *adj.* 1 lasting a long time: *Rheumatism is often a chronic disease.* 2 suffering long from an illness: *a chronic invalid.* 3 never stopping; constant; habitual: *a chronic liar.* [< Greek *chronikos* of time < *chronos* time] —**chron′i cal ly,** *adv.*

Check the sentence(s) in which **chronic** is used correctly.
__a. A chronic smoker often regrets having started smoking.
__b. She had a chronic expression.
__c. A sore throat is not a chronic disease.
__d. The doctor told me to take a chronic.
__e. The man is a chronic complainer.

63c

d

por tal (pôr′tl, pōr′tl), *n.* door, gate, or entrance, usually an imposing one. —*adj.* of or having to do with the portal vein. [< Medieval Latin *portale* < Latin *porta* gate]

Which of the following would you most likely enter through a **portal** (or **portals**)?
__a. a castle
__b. an ocean liner
__c. a cottage
__d. a mansion
__e. a cave

89a

), c, e

en hance (en hans′)

"A beautiful rose garden will **enhance** the charm of your house," she would say, "and it will increase the market value."

Write a definition or synonym:

114a

a

ad ept (*n.* ad′ ept; *adj.* ə dept′)

Kim had been working hard since the last meet. She was particularly **adept** at the floor exercise.

Write a definition or synonym:

139b

Teams of Soviet and U.S. mathematicians will work with the latest in computer technology to develop new mathematical **theorems**. Not until the **theorems** are proved will the first human-bearing starship be launched.

A **theorem** is a statement:
__a. that can be proved to be true
__b. that expresses an opinion
__c. that is probably true
__d. that can be disputed

163c

a

pu trid (pyü′trid), *adj.* 1 decaying; rotten: *putrid meat.* 2 characteristic of putrefying matter; foul: *a putrid odor.* 3 thoroughly corrupt or depraved; extremely bad. [< Latin *putridus* < *puter* rotten] **—pu′trid ly,** *adv.* **—pu′trid ness,** *n.*

To which of the following might **putrid** be applied?
__a. corrupt politics
__b. an overripe peach
__c. freshly baked bread
__d. perfume
__e. a Girl Scout

188c

b

de mure (di myùr′), *adj.,* **-mur er, -mur est.** 1 artificially proper; assuming an air of modesty; coy: *the demure smile of a flirt.* 2 reserved or composed in demeanor; serious and sober. See **modest** for synonym study. [< *de-* + Old French *meür* discreet, mature < Latin *maturus*] **—de mure′ly,** *adv.* **—de mure′ness,** *n.*

Which of the following words mean the *opposite* of **demure**?
__a. prudish   __d. jovial
__b. temperate   __e. humble
__c. loud   __f. forward

213b

The weather people believe that it is better to keep reports **pessimistic** so that people will prepare for the worst.

Pessimistic means:
__a. taking a gloomy view
__b. optimistic
__c. oppressive
__d. full of danger

238b

It is true that **automation** has caused the loss of some jobs in the broadcasting industry. But most of the important work is still being done by men and women, and not by machine.

Automation means:
__a. making less paper work
__b. cutting down costs
__c. making something run more automatically
__d. using more men and machinery

263a

a

il le git i mate (il′ i jit′ ə mit)

Now that many game animals are protected, poachers use **illegitimate** methods to find prey.

Write a definition or synonym:

288a

e

tor so (tôr′ sō)

Years of exercise had not thickened Lu Ann's slender **torso**.

Write a definition or synonym:

13c

b

list less (list′lis), *adj.* seeming too tired to care about anything; not interested in things; not caring to be active; languid. [< *list*⁴] —**list′less ly,** *adv.* —**list′less ness,** *n.*

ANALOGY listless : bored :: fatal :
___**a.** impulsive
___**b.** tired
___**c.** incurable
___**d.** indifferent
___**e.** arrogant

39a

a, c, e

re cu pe rate (ri kyü′ pə rāt′, ri kü′ pə rāt′)

Legs wanted to know how long it would take him to **recuperate**.

Write a definition or synonym:

64a

a, d

crypt (kript)

The very next day, Paul's team unearthed the entrance to a large **crypt**.

Write a definition or synonym:

89b

"No matter how well you have decorated a room, a vase of roses will **enhance** its charm, making it even more pleasant and attractive."

Another word for **enhance** is:
___**a.** enlarge
___**b.** heighten
___**c.** scent
___**d.** detract from

114b

Kim's jumping and tumbling showed signs of long practice. She showed complete mastery when she moved into the handstands and back flips. She was equally **adept** in every phase of the floor exercise.

Another word for **adept** is:
___**a.** expert
___**b.** sensational
___**c.** strong
___**d.** unusual

139c

a

the or em (thē′ər əm, thir′əm), *n.* 1 statement or rule in mathematics that has been or is to be proved. 2 statement of mathematical relations that can be expressed by an equation or formula. 3 any statement or rule that can be proved to be true. [< Greek *theōrēma* < *theōrein* consider. See THEORY.]

Check the sentence(s) in which a form of **theorem** is used correctly.
___**a.** Everyone had a different theorem as to who committed the crime.
___**b.** The final examination contained many theorems.
___**c.** He expressed the theorem in a formula.

163b

There seemed to be no one source for the terrible smell. But if the holy man noticed anything **putrid**, he didn't let on. He seemed to be beyond worrying about such matters.

Another word for **putrid** is:
— **a.** foul
— **b.** sooty
— **c.** poor
— **d.** frightening

188b

For example, when a Japanese girl is embarrassed about something, she might giggle **demurely** behind her upraised hand. This air of proper modesty is typical of girls raised in the traditional manner.

Demure means:
— **a.** dainty
— **b.** coy
— **c.** petite
— **d.** silly

213a

b, d

pes si mis tic (pes′ ə mis′ tik)

We turn the radio up to catch the latest weather report. Like the others, this one is **pessimistic**.

Write a definition or synonym:

238a

, c, d

au to ma tion (ô′ tə mā′ shən)

Sandra was a little worried when she learned that her station would be using more and more **automation** in the years to come.

Write a definition or synonym:

262c

c

be lat ed (bi lā′tid), *adj.* 1 happening or coming late or too late; delayed: *The belated letter arrived at last.* 2 overtaken by darkness: *The belated travelers lost their way.* —**be lat′ed ly,** *adv.* —**be lat′ed ness,** *n.*

ANALOGY belated : timely :: greeting :
— **a.** farewell
— **b.** retirement
— **c.** promotion
— **d.** announcement
— **e.** address

287c

a

li a bil i ty (lī′ə bil′ə tē), *n., pl.* **-ties.** 1 state of being susceptible: *liability to disease.* 2 state of being under obligation: *liability for a debt.* 3 **liabilities,** *pl.* debts or other financial obligations of a business. 4 something that is to one's disadvantage: *Poor handwriting is a liability for a teacher.*

ANALOGY liability : asset :: minus :
— **a.** short
— **b.** riches
— **c.** debit
— **d.** value
— **e.** plus

82

14a

c

ex ot ic (eg zot′ ik)

The temperature dropped when the first rains came. Janice became interested in the **exotic** tropical plants and flowers.

Write a definition or synonym:

39b

"You might start walking in a week," Dr. Cardiac replied. "You can begin to run in a month or so, but it might take a little longer before you **recuperate** fully. Then your knee will be as good as it ever was."

Recuperate means:
__a. rest
__b. regain
__c. recover
__d. stand up

64b

The **crypt** lay directly under the center of the stage of the amphitheater. There were jewels, golden statues, and other valuable articles inside the **crypt**.

Another word for **crypt** is:
__a. vault
__b. box
__c. closet
__d. playroom

89c

b

en hance (en hans′), *v.t.*, **-hanced, -hanc ing.** make greater in quality, value, or importance; add to; heighten: *The gardens enhanced the beauty of the house.* [< Anglo-French *enhauncer*, variant of Old French *enhaucier* < *en-* on, up + *haucier* raise] —**en hance′ment**, *n.*

Which of the following would most likely **enhance** the quality of your schoolwork?
__a. a good throwing arm
__b. a fine voice
__c. ability to read effectively
__d. ability to listen well
__e. long hours of study

114c

a

a dept (*adj.* ə dept′; *n.* ad′ept), *adj.* thoroughly skilled; expert. —*n.* person thoroughly skilled in some art, science, occupation, etc. [< Medieval Latin *adeptum* skilled (in alchemy) < Latin < *ad-* to + *apisci* reach] —**a dept′ly**, *adv.* —**a dept′ness**, *n.*

Check the sentence(s) in which a form of **adept** is used correctly.
__a. The professor is an adept in her field.
__b. A baseball player who hits many home runs is adept in the sport.
__c. We are thinking of adepting a baby.
__d. Slipshod work is the sign of an adept person.

140a

b, c

spasm (spaz′ əm)

Five years have passed. The time has come for reentry of the dog's satellite. The dog is to be revived in time for the landing. All of the scientists eagerly watch the display panels which show the dog's vital signs. They wait for a **spasm** of activity.

Write a definition or synonym:

83

287b

Swimmers with muscular arms and shoulders tend to be fairly heavy. Their strength makes up for their weight. Lu Ann's slender arms were not that strong. The only way to turn this **liability** into an asset was to try harder.

Another word for **liability** is:
—a. disadvantage
—b. condition
—c. asset
—d. necessity

262b

It is hoped that these **belated** efforts to preserve some species will be successful. "Better late than never," say those who are concerned with the survival of the animals.

A synonym for **belated** is:
—a. premature
—b. disorganized
—c. delayed
—d. incorrect

237c

ex ploit (n. ek'sploit, ek sploit'; v. ek-sploit'), n. a bold, unusual act; daring deed. —v.t. 1 make use of; turn to practical account: *A mine is exploited for its minerals.* 2 make unfair or selfish use of: *Nations used to exploit their colonies, taking as much wealth out of them as they could.* [< Old French *esploit* < Popular Latin *explicitum* achievement < Latin, an unfolding < *ex-* out + *plicare* to fold] —ex ploit'a ble, *adj.* —ex ploit'er, *n.*

Check the sentence(s) in which a form of **exploit** is used correctly.
—a. Crossing the Atlantic by balloon is an exploit that was widely hailed.
—b. It takes courage to exploit the wilderness.
—c. She exploited her friends by sponging on them.
—d. He exploited his war experiences by turning them into popular fiction.

212c

sat u rate (sach'ə rāt'), *v.t.*, -rat ed, -rat ing. 1 soak thoroughly; fill full: *During the fog, the air was saturated with moisture.* 2 cause (a substance) to unite with the greatest possible amount of another substance. A saturated solution of sugar or salt is one that cannot dissolve any more sugar or salt. [< Latin *saturatum* filled < *satur* full] —sat'u rat'er, sat'u ra'tor, *n.*

Which of the following can be described as **saturated**?
—a. a street full of sunlight
—b. a scholar who has been studying a subject for years
—c. a cup filled to the brim with liquid
—d. a blanket that was left out in the rain

188a

de mure (di myŭr')

Tourists from America find many Japanese girls and women to be quite **demure**.

Write a definition or synonym:

163a

pu trid (pyü' trid)

Jim needed some fresh air, so he asked Maharaji to walk with him along the banks of the Ganges River. Even there, Jim could not help noticing a **putrid** odor.

Write a definition or synonym:

14b

After a few days, when she became used to them, the flowers no longer seemed **exotic**. They seemed as ordinary and familiar as the flowers back home.

Another word for **exotic** is:
- __a. foreign
- __b. brilliant
- __c. rare
- __d. beautiful

39c

c

re cu pe rate (ri kyü′pə rāt′, ri kü′pə rāt′), *v.*, **-rat ed, -rat ing.** —*v.i.* recover from sickness, exhaustion, loss, etc. —*v.t.* 1 restore to health, strength, etc. 2 get back; regain. [< Latin *recuperatum* recovered] —**re cu′pe ra′tion,** *n.*

From which of the following situations might you **recuperate**?
- __a. a long illness
- __b. the loss of a book
- __c. a restful vacation
- __d. an accident
- __e. a stock market crash

64c

a

crypt (kript), *n.* an underground room or vault. The crypt beneath the main floor of a church was formerly often used as a burial place. [< Latin *crypta* < Greek *kryptē* vault < *kryptos* hidden. Doublet of GROTTO.]

Check the sentence(s) in which a form of **crypt** is used correctly.
- __a. Crypts are likely to be cold and damp.
- __b. He crypt to the refrigerator.
- __c. Important people used to be buried in a church crypt.
- __d. Your message was so crypt, I could not understand it.
- __e. There was a crypt beneath our house that was formerly used for housing fugitives.

90a

c, d, e

im ma ture (im′ ə chür′, im′ ə tür′, im′ ə tūr′)

Mrs. Samuelson always advised her friends to pick **immature** blossoms when they gathered flowers to decorate their houses.

Write a definition or synonym:

115a

a, b

stance (stans)

Stance is an important part of the competition on the long beam.

Write a definition or synonym:

140b

After the first **spasm** of activity, the tracks on the display panels slow to a normal level. "It's a success!" cries one of the scientists. "The puppy is alive and well, and we're on our way to the stars!"

A **spasm** is a:
- __a. series of loud noises
- __b. brief spell of unusual activity
- __c. part of a satellite
- __d. noisy confusion

98

162c

ANALOGY hovel : manor ::
___a. lawn : field
___b. shed : hut
___c. shovel : spade
___d. gravel : dirt
___e. cabin : mansion

hov el (huv′əl, hov′əl), n. 1 house that is small, crude, and unpleasant to live in. 2 an open shed for sheltering cattle, tools, etc. [Middle English]

b

187c

ANALOGY girth : around ::
___a. depth : height
___b. leaves : flowers
___c. height : branches
___d. circle : measure
___e. width : across

girth (gėrth), n. 1 the measure around anything; *a man of large girth, the girth of a tree.* 2 strap or band that keeps a saddle, pack, etc., in place on a horse's back. See harness for picture. 3 girdle. — v.t. 1 fasten with a strap or band. 2 surround; girdle. — v.i. measure a certain amount in girth. [< Scandinavian (Old Icelandic) *gjǫrth* gir-dle. Related to GIRD.]

a

212b

We know that the ground will be saturated, too, once the hurricane has passed. Flooding will result when the soil has absorbed all the water it can hold.

A synonym for saturate is:
___a. wet
___b. touch
___c. soak
___d. cover

237b

In a city where there is competition among many stations, standards can be set higher, and it becomes more difficult to exploit the public.

A meaning for exploit is:
___a. enlighten
___b. take advantage of
___c. make the best of
___d. steal from

262a

be lat ed (bi lā′ tid)

This belated plan to preserve the animals has great merit.

Write a definition or synonym:

a, b

287a

li a bil i ty (lī′ ə bil′ ə tē)

A slight build like Lu Ann's can be a liability in competitive swimming.

Write a definition or synonym:

b, e

14c

ex ot ic (eg zot′ik), *adj.* 1 from a foreign country; not native: *We saw many exotic plants at the flower show.* 2 fascinating or interesting because strange or different: *an exotic tropical island.* —*n.* an exotic person or thing. [< Greek *exōtikos* < *exō* outside < *ex* out of] —**ex ot′i cal ly,** *adv.*

ANALOGY exotic : familiar :: grief :
- __a. sorrow
- __b. joy
- __c. emotion
- __d. excitement
- __e. funeral

40a

con va les cent (kon′ və les′ nt)

Legs said he didn't want to remain **convalescent** for more than three days.

Write a definition or synonym:

65a

ge ol o gy (jē ol′ ə jē)

A number of Greek archaeologists had joined the dig. One of them commented that **geology** was most helpful when working in ancient ruins.

Write a definition or synonym:

90b

"The older and larger blossoms will not last as long indoors as the **immature** ones. I like to see the little roses open up and spread their petals as they become more fully developed."

A synonym for **immature** is:
- __a. unripe
- __b. fresh
- __c. rare
- __d. embryonic

115b

The long wooden beam is four feet off the floor and only four inches wide. The position of the feet, when making each jump or turn, is all important. Paula's **stance** seemed a little awkward when she landed on the beam after a handstand.

Stance means:
- __a. attention
- __b. position of feet
- __c. position of hands
- __d. appearance

140c

spasm (spaz′əm), *n.* 1 a sudden, abnormal, involuntary contraction of a muscle or muscles. 2 any sudden, brief fit or spell of unusual energy or activity. [< Greek *spasmos* < *span* draw up, tear away]

A **spasm** is:
- __a. deliberate
- __b. sudden
- __c. planned
- __d. a cramp
- __e. restful

162b

The **hovel** had no running water or electricity. There were no windows, and the place looked dirty. But Maharaji seemed peaceful and quite content.

A synonym for **hovel** is:
__a. tent
__b. hut
__c. apartment
__d. pen

187b

The boys who start training for sumo are larger than average to begin with. They are fed the most fattening foods to increase their **girth**.

A synonym for **girth** is:
__a. circumference
__b. height
__c. neck size
__d. muscles

212a

a, c

sat u rate (sach′ ə rāt′)

Before a hurricane strikes, the air usually feels **saturated**.

Write a definition or synonym:

237a

, c, d

ex ploit (*n.* ek′ sploit, ek sploit′; *v.* ek sploit′)

Sandra said that in a one-station town, it would be easy for unethical station managers to **exploit** the public.

Write a definition or synonym:

261c

a

an ni hi late (ə nī′ə lāt), *v.t.,* **-lat ed, -lat ing.** destroy completely; wipe out of existence: *The flood annihilated over thirty towns and villages.* [< Late Latin *annihilatum* brought to nothing < Latin *ad-* to + *nihil* nothing] —**an ni′hi la′tor,** *n.*

Check the sentence(s) in which a form of **annihilate** is used correctly.
__a. The general annihilated the opposition and won a stunning victory.
__b. The village was annihilated by volcanic eruptions.
__c. He annihilated the sandwich and cookies.
__d. Although the bees' nest was annihilated, many of the insects were still alive.

286c

a

per se ver ance (pèr′sə vir′əns), *n.* a sticking to a purpose or an aim; a persevering; tenacity. See **persistence** for synonym study.

If you do something with **perseverance**, you are:
__a. dogged
__b. strong-willed
__c. irresolute
__d. wavering
__e. steadfast

15a

b

in ac ces si ble (in′ ək ses′ ə bəl)

The Austins were the first Americans to penetrate this deeply into the forest. The trees were so thick that the area had been considered **inaccessible** to all but the most experienced guides and hunters.

Write a definition or synonym:

40b

Dr. Cardiac said he would remain **convalescent** until he was fully recuperated. Legs offered her a free season pass to the home soccer games if she could speed up the time it took him to get better. Dr. Cardiac just laughed and said Legs could take her out to dinner as soon as he was able to stand without crutches.

Convalescent means:
___a. immune
___b. bored
___c. recovering
___d. inactive

65b

The study of **geology** helps identify the types of rocks and minerals used in the ruin. It also gives information about the ancient society which built them. For example, the stones in the main portal had been cut many miles from the amphitheater. Armies of slaves were needed to haul them to the building site.

Geology means:
___a. study of the world
___b. study of the earth's crust
___c. study of treasures
___d. study of science

90c

a

im ma ture (im′ə chür′, im′ə tür′, im′ə- tyür′), *adj.* not mature; undeveloped. —**im′ma ture′ly,** *adv.* —**im′ma ture′- ness,** *n.*

Which of the following are **immature**?
___a. colt
___b. steer
___c. adolescent
___d. rosebud
___e. grandfather

115c

b

stance (stans), *n.* 1 position of the feet of a player when swinging at the ball in golf, baseball, or other games. 2 manner of stand- ing; posture. 3 attitude; point of view. [< Old French *estance*, ultimately < Latin *stare* to stand]

Stance is important to:
___a. a boxer
___b. a singer
___c. a swimmer
___d. a lecturer
___e. a baseball player

b, d

LESSON 15

Mr. Grandstand

Last year, our college football team went into its final game undefeated. None of our players were really outstanding, but we were strong in all departments, and we had team spirit. That's what made winners. Or that's what we had been told. Unfortunately, no one told us what to do about an athlete like Rafe Barlow, our opponents' star fullback.

162a

hov el (huv′ əl, hov′ əl) — a

Write a definition or synonym:

After weeks of searching, Jim Rosen found Maharaji,
the holy man he had been seeking. Maharaji was living
with a few followers in a tiny **hovel**.

187a

girth (gĕrth) — d, e

Write a definition or synonym:

An exception to the usually slim Japanese is the sumo
wrestler, whose **girth** is tremendous.

211c

prel ude (prel′yūd, prē′lūd, prā′lūd), n., v.,
-ud ed, -ud ing. —n. 1 anything serving as
an introduction, preliminary performance,
action, event, condition, etc.: *The German
invasion of Poland was a prelude to World
War II.* 2 in music: a a composition, or part
of it, that introduces another composition or
part. b a short, independent instrumental
composition of an imaginative, improvised
nature. c a composition played at the beginning of a church service, especially an organ
solo. —v.t. 1 be a prelude or introduction to.
2 introduce with a prelude. 3 (in music) play
as a prelude. —v.i. give a prelude or in-
troductory performance. (Definition adapted) — d

Check the sentence(s) in which **prelude** is used
correctly.
—a. A song was a prelude to the ceremonies.
—b. The young man hesitated to speak to the girl
without a proper prelude.
—c. The pianist did not play the prelude, but started
with the main theme.

236c

re voke (rǐ vōk′), v., -voked, -vok ing, n.
—v.t. take back; repeal; cancel; withdraw:
revoke a driver's license. —v.i. fail to follow
suit in playing cards when one can and
should; renege. —n. (in cards) a failure to
follow suit when one can and should; renege.
[< Latin *revocare* < *re-* back + *vocare* to
call] — b

Which of the following *cannot* be **revoked**?
—a. an inevitable fate
—b. a law
—c. a spoken word
—d. an umpire's decision
—e. a driver's license
—f. a decision

261b

Fortunately, some of the African nations have set up
game preserves to prevent greedy and careless
hunters from **annihilating** entire species.

Annihilate means:
—a. wipe out
—b. remove
—c. shoot
—d. capture

286b

To do anything well, one must have great
perseverance and never lose sight of one's goal.

Another word for **perseverance** is:
—a. persistence
—b. aimlessness
—c. strength
—d. courage

15b

To reach leopard country, they left the river bank and moved inland to an almost **inaccessible** part of the rain forest.

Inaccessible means:
—**a.** hard to enter
—**b.** hard to understand
—**c.** uninteresting
—**d.** hard to leave

40c

c

con va les cent (kon/və les/nt), *adj.* recovering health and strength after illness. —*n.* person recovering after illness.

Check the sentence(s) in which **convalescent** is used correctly.
—**a.** An impatient person is a poor convalescent.
—**b.** While convalescent, he spent part of each day in a wheelchair.
—**c.** A convalescent no longer needs constant care.
—**d.** I had to be convalescent before my illness.

65c

b

ge ol o gy (jē ol/ə jē), *n., pl.* **-gies.** 1 science that deals with the earth's crust, the layers of which it is composed, and their history. 2 features of the earth's crust in a place or region; rocks, rock formation, etc., of a particular area: *the geology of North America.*

Which of the following would you study in a **geology** class?
—**a.** glaciers
—**b.** planets
—**c.** vertebrates
—**d.** granite
—**e.** volcanoes
—**f.** comets

LESSON 10 | Mysteries of the Mind

, c, d

Although medical science has wiped out many serious physical diseases, much remains unknown about mental illness. Considerable attention is being devoted to this problem today. Because most people know so little about mental health, a campaign is under way to educate the public.

116a

a, e

mo men tum (mō men' təm)

Suddenly, Paula's foot slipped. The **momentum** her body had acquired was enough to send her sliding off the beam to the floor.

Write a definition or synonym:

141a

pre ma ture (prē' mə chůr', prē' mə tůr', prē' mə tyůr')

With Rafe Barlow in the hospital, we felt confident of victory. We later learned our confidence had been **premature**.

Write a definition or synonym:

161c

c

pop u late (pop′yə lāt), *v.t.,* **-lat ed, -lat ing. 1** live in; inhabit: *This city is dense-ly populated.* **2** furnish with inhabitants; people: *Europeans populated much of America.*

Check the sentence(s) in which a form of **populate** is used correctly.

__**a.** Indians no longer populate the western prairies.
__**b.** That house is populated by an eccentric old man.
__**c.** The theater was populated on opening night.

186c

c

pe tite (pə tēt′), *adj.* of small stature or size; little, especially with reference to a woman or girl. [< Old French, feminine of *petit*]

Which of the following words mean the *opposite* of **petite**?

__**a.** miniature
__**b.** minute
__**c.** narrow
__**d.** enormous
__**e.** titanic

211b

A period of calm, when the air is very still, is often a **prelude** to a hurricane. Later, there is another calm period, which marks the middle of the storm, when the "eye" of the hurricane is passing through.

Another word for **prelude** is:

__**a.** companion
__**b.** component
__**c.** finale
__**d.** introduction

236b

Licenses are reviewed every few years. If a station has failed to do its proper job, its license may be **revoked**.

Revoke means:

__**a.** release
__**b.** cancel
__**c.** deny
__**d.** permit

261a

an ni hi late (ə nī′ ə lāt)

Hunters and poachers have nearly **annihilated** some species of African animals.

Write a definition or synonym:

286a

a,d

per se ver ance (pėr′ sə vir′ əns)

Becoming a championship swimmer requires **perseverance**.

Write a definition or synonym:

15c

in ac ces si ble (in′ək ses′ə bəl), *adj.*
1 hard to get at; hard to reach or enter: *The house on top of the steep hill is inaccessible.*
2 not accessible; that cannot be reached or entered at all. —**in′ac ces′si bly,** *adv.*

In which of the following sentences is **inaccessible** used correctly?
__a. Poison should be stored where it is inaccessible to children.
__b. It is inaccessible to make such a mistake.
__c. The top of a mountain is often inaccessible.

LESSON 5

The Slime Creature, Part 1

"What has ten legs, two heads, sharp teeth, and is covered with horrible green slime?" Tom Millard asked his wife Peggy.

"I don't know, dear," Peggy answered as she stepped out of the bus to begin their weekend in the country.

"I don't know either," Tom laughed, "but it's crawling up the side of your neck!" Tom didn't know then just how prophetic his joke would prove to be.

66a

stra ta (strā′ tə, strat′ ə)

Beneath the earth, there were several **strata** of sandstone between the harder rocks.

Write a definition or synonym:

91a

psy chol o gy (sī kol′ ə jē)

Many people today are interested in **psychology**.

Write a definition or synonym:

116b

Paula's feet were completely still as she reached the top of her handstand. As she brought her legs down toward the narrow beam, they picked up more **momentum**. If her legs had been shorter, or she had weighed less, her feet would not have built up so much force when they hit the beam.

The meaning of **momentum** is:
__a. force of weight and speed
__b. rapid movement
__c. sense of importance
__d. increasing speed

141b

Just before the kickoff we heard that Rafe had been released. He was going to play after all! That's when we realized our victory plans had been **premature**.

Premature means:
__a. eager
__b. foresighted
__c. too soon
__d. over confident

161b

In the major cities, like Calcutta or New Delhi, there are so many people living close together that there is hardly enough room to turn around. Even the countryside is heavily **populated**.

Populate means:
- _**a.** ventilate
- _**b.** evacuate
- _**c.** inhabit
- _**d.** fill up

186b

A tall American girl looks even bigger next to her **petite** Japanese counterpart.

Petite means:
- _**a.** poor
- _**b.** skinny
- _**c.** tiny
- _**d.** fat

211a

prel ude (prel′ yüd, prē′ lüd, prä′ lüd)

A falling barometer can be a **prelude** to a hurricane.

Write a definition or synonym:

236a

b, d

re voke (ri vōk′)

The license that is issued to a radio station may be **revoked** at any time.

Write a definition or synonym:

---

c, d

LESSON 27

Born Free?

Big game hunting in Africa has declined in popularity. For one thing, it is a sport that is far too expensive for most people. A more important reason is that most game animals now live on reservations established by the governments to preserve the various species. Now the survival of many species is threatened by poachers who kill animals for their fur or sell them to zoos.

---

d

285c

hu mil i ty (hyü mil′ə tē), *n., pl.* **-ties.** humbleness of mind; meekness.

Which of the following expressions are descriptive of **humility**?
- _**a.** "hiding one's light under a bushel"
- _**b.** "nose in the air"
- _**c.** "fishing for compliments"
- _**d.** "taking a back seat"

16a

a, c

fur tive (fėr′ tiv)

When the Austins reached the area where the leopards had struck last, they built an observation post high in a tree. Late at night, Howard thought he saw **furtive** movements in the brush below.

Write a definition or synonym:

41a

ur ban (ėr′ bən)

Neither Tom nor Peggy Millard knew much about the countryside out in the lakes region. They had both spent most of their lives in **urban** surroundings. It was a treat for them to go to the country for a picnic.

Write a definition or synonym:

66b

When the workers uncovered the two layers of limestone beneath the floor of the crypt, there was great excitement. Since the limestone did not occur naturally, it meant that there was another ancient city buried under the amphitheater. To uncover it, they would have to dig through many **strata** of earth, rock, and ashes.

Strata means:
— **a.** levels
— **b.** intelligence
— **c.** culture
— **d.** civilization

91b

The student of **psychology** learns why people think and act and feel as they do.

Psychology is the science of:
— **a.** living bodies
— **b.** the mind
— **c.** earth
— **d.** man

116c

a

mo men tum (mō men′təm), *n., pl.* **-tums, -ta** (-tə). 1 quantity of motion of a moving body, equal to the product of its mass and velocity; force with which a body moves: *A falling object gains momentum as it falls.* 2 impetus resulting from movement: *The runner's momentum carried him far beyond the finish line.* [< Latin, movement < *movere* to move]

Check the sentence(s) in which **momentum** is used correctly.
— **a.** The huge boulder had so much momentum, he could not move it.
— **b.** The thrust of the rocket engine imparted great momentum to the launched missile.
— **c.** After the rocket engine ceased firing, the momentum of the missile carried it far into outer space.

141c

c

pre ma ture (prē′mə chůr′, prē′mə tůr′, prē′mə tyůr′), *adj.* before the proper time; too soon. A premature baby is one born more than two weeks early or weighing less than 5½ pounds. —**pre′ma ture′ly,** *adv.* —**pre′ma ture′ness,** *n.*

ANALOGY premature : baby ::
— **a.** tired : busy
— **b.** delayed : timely
— **c.** green : apple
— **d.** mother : hospital
— **e.** kickoff : football

161a

pop u late (pop′ yə lāt)

Like many Asian countries, India is heavily **populated**.

Write a definition or synonym:

186a

a, c,
e, f

pe tite (pə tēt′)

By Western standards, many Japanese women are quite **petite**.

Write a definition or synonym:

---

b, c, e

LESSON 22 | Hurricane Watch

At our Civil Defense headquarters, volunteers are studying the barometer. If the barometer falls much more, and if the wind continues to rise, our area will move from a hurricane *watch* to a hurricane *alert*. Everyone will begin taking all possible precautions against the damage that is typically caused by these fierce storms.

235c

a

en light en (en lit′n), *v.t.* give truth and knowledge to; free from prejudice, ignorance, etc.; inform; instruct. —**en light′en er**, *n.*

Check the word(s) that mean(s) about the same as **enlighten**.
__a. educate
__b. illuminate
__c. animate
__d. explain
__e. shine

260c

d

ul ti mate (ul′tə mit), *adj.* **1** coming at the end; last possible; final: *He never stopped to consider the ultimate result of his actions.* See **last¹** for synonym study. **2** that is an extremity; beyond which there is nothing at all; extreme: *the ultimate limits of the universe.* **3** fundamental; basic: *The brain is the ultimate source of ideas. The ultimate source of life has not been discovered.* **4** greatest possible: *He gave his life and thereby paid the ultimate price.* —*n.* an ultimate point, result, fact, etc. [< Medieval Latin *ultimatum* < Latin *ultimus* last, superlative of root of *ultra* beyond] —**ul′ti mate ly**, *adv.* —**ul′ti mate ness**, *n.*

Check the sentence(s) in which **ultimate** is used correctly.
__a. The politician's ultimate goal was the presidency.
__b. At last they came to the ultimate of the road.
__c. He refined his style until it was the ultimate in simplicity.
__d. The ultimate letter of the alphabet is *z*.

285b

Her **humility** was refreshing. It made a sharp contrast with some of the young girls, who were quite conceited.

Humility means:
__a. pride
__b. timidity
__c. chagrin
__d. modesty

16b

Howard watched carefully, knowing that the leopard would behave in a secretive and cautious manner. He knew that a leopard must be extremely **furtive** so its prey would not see it or hear it.

Another word for **furtive** is:
- __a. careful
- __b. silent
- __c. slow
- __d. stealthy

41b

For **urban** dwellers, the sight of the open country was refreshing. Even the rather dreary land near Gray Lake was a pleasant change from tall buildings and crowded streets.

Urban means:
- __a. living in the suburbs
- __b. having to do with a neighborhood
- __c. having to do with cities
- __d. living close to a city

66c

a

stra ta (strā′tə, strat′ə), *n.* a pl. of **stratum.**
stra tum (strā′təm, strat′əm), *n., pl.* **-ta** or **-tums.** 1 layer of material, especially one of several parallel layers placed one upon another: *lay several strata of gravel on a road.* 2 (in geology) bed or formation of sedimentary rock consisting throughout of approximately the same kind of material. 3 social level; group having about the same education, culture, development, etc.: *rise from a low to a high stratum of society.* 4 (in biology) a layer of tissue. [< Latin, something spread out < *sternere* to spread]

Check the sentence(s) in which a form of **strata** is used correctly.
- __a. The dessert was made of strata of cake and pudding.
- __b. Some societies have social strata that differ little from each other.
- __c. I used clever strata to defeat my enemy.
- __d. There are many different strata in the earth's crust.
- __e. Her family was of the highest social stratum.

91c

b

psy chol o gy (sī kol′ə jē), *n., pl.* **-gies.** 1 science or study of the mind; branch of science dealing with the actions, feelings, thoughts, and other mental or behavioral processes of people and animals. 2 the mental states and processes of a person or persons; mental nature and behavior.

Check the sentence(s) in which **psychology** is used correctly.
- __a. Her use of psychology made her a valuable employee.
- __b. I lost my psychology book on the bus.
- __c. That man has no psychology.
- __d. I am studying psychology to see how the heart functions.

117a

b, c

bol ster (bōl′ stər)

Paula climbed right back on the beam and continued her performance. But Paula had lost points. Paula's loss did a lot to **bolster** Kim's morale.

Write a definition or synonym:

142a

c

col le giate (kə lē′ jit, kə lē′ jē it)

Most people think **collegiate** football is the most exciting kind.

Write a definition or synonym:

LESSON 17

The Meaning of Life Is…

When he was younger, Jim Rosen had been quite impressed with the teachings of Eastern religion. He had admired the wisdom of the holy men from Tibet and India who came to North America to educate Western youth. Now that he was an adult, Jim decided to travel to India in search of a holy man who could help him discover the meaning of life.

a, b, e

185c

deft (deft), *adj.* quick and skillful in action; nimble: *the deft fingers of a surgeon.* See synonym study below. [variant of *daft*] —**deft′ly,** *adv.* —**deft′ness,** *n.*

Syn. Deft, dexterous, adroit mean skillful. Deft, usually confined to physical skill, suggests neatness and exceptional lightness and swiftness, particularly of the hands: *A surgeon must be deft in tying knots.* Dex-terous usually suggests easy, quick, smooth movements and lightness and sureness of touch coming from practice (*She is a dexter-ous pianist*), although it occasionally suggests having quick intelligence. Adroit is used less often of physical skill than of mental quick-ness, resourcefulness, and cleverness in han-dling situations: *The adroit stewardess kept the passengers on the plane cheerful during the storm.*

Check those jobs that require special **deftness.**
- —**a.** watchmaker
- —**b.** bricklayer
- —**c.** brain surgeon
- —**d.** teacher
- —**e.** pianist
- —**f.** dressmaker

d

210c

car·at (kar′ət), *n.* 1 unit of weight for pre-cious stones, equal to ⅕ gram. 2 karat. [< Middle French < Italian *carato* < Arabic *qīrāt* < Greek *keration,* diminutive of *keras* horn]

Check the sentence(s) in which a form of **carat** is used correctly.
- —**a.** Rabbits like carats.
- —**b.** I have a 14-carat gold ring.
- —**c.** Rubies and emeralds are measured in carats.
- —**d.** Iron nails are measured in carats.
- —**e.** The engagement ring is set with a two-carat diamond.

d

235b

Federal regulations require every radio station to spend a certain amount of time on news and public affairs. Thus, the stations cannot avoid the responsibility of **enlightening** their listeners.

The meaning of **enlighten** is:
- —**a.** inform
- —**b.** light up
- —**c.** amuse
- —**d.** enrich

260b

However, Maria is the first to admit that one's **ultimate** goal is rarely reached. Indeed, the last goal which some agents attain is a sudden and violent death.

Another word for **ultimate** is:
- —**a.** important
- —**b.** impending
- —**c.** certain
- —**d.** final

285a

hu·mil·i·ty (hyü mil′ə tē)

Lu Ann showed **humility** when she accepted her gold medal.

Write a definition or synonym:

a, c, e

16c

d

fur tive (fèr′tiv), *adj.* 1 done quickly and with stealth to avoid being noticed; secret: *a furtive glance into the forbidden room.* 2 sly; stealthy: *She had a furtive manner.* [< Latin *furtivus* < *furtum* theft < *fur* thief] **—fur′-tive ly,** *adv.* **—fur′tive ness,** *n.*

Which of the following people might act in a **furtive** manner?

__a. a salesperson
__b. a pickpocket
__c. an investigator
__d. a musician

41c

c

ur ban (èr′bən), *adj.* 1 of or having to do with cities or towns: *an urban district, urban planning.* 2 living in a city or cities: *the urban population, urban dwellers.* 3 characteristic of cities. 4 accustomed to cities. [< Latin *urbanus* < *urbs* city]

Which of the following would most likely be considered **urban**?

__a. an apartment house
__b. a field of corn
__c. a subway
__d. a large department store
__e. a volunteer fire department

67a

b, d,e

pul ve rize (pul′ vər īz)

When the team of archaeologists had dug twelve feet beneath the amphitheater, they found pottery which had been **pulverized**.

Write a definition or synonym:

92a

a, b

jar gon (jär′ gən, jär′ gon)

Books on psychology often contain a great deal of **jargon**.

Write a definition or synonym:

117b

Kim went through the balance beam performance with an almost perfect score. Her victory in this event continued to **bolster** her self-confidence. Now her spirits were up in the air, and her score began to show it.

Bolster means:
__a. soften
__b. enhance
__c. change
__d. support

142b

The players may not be quite as good as the pros, but their games mean more. Most spectators at a **collegiate** game are either students or alumni of the colleges involved. As a result, spirit runs very high.

Collegiate means having to do with:
__a. education
__b. athletics
__c. sports
__d. colleges

160c

c

ec cen tric (ek sen′trik), *adj.* 1 out of the ordinary; not usual; odd; peculiar. 2 not having the same center: *These circles ⊙ are eccentric.* 3 not perfectly circular: *The planets are in eccentric orbits around the sun.* 4 off center; having its axis set off center: *an eccentric wheel.* —*n.* 1 person who behaves in an unusual manner. 2 disk or wheel set off center so that it can change circular motion into back-and-forth motion. [< Medieval Latin *eccentricus* < Greek *ekkentros* off center < *ex-* out + *kentron* center] —**ec cen′tri cal ly,** *adv.*

Which of the following are most likely to be **eccentric**?
—**a.** a hermit
—**b.** path of a satellite
—**c.** the wheel of an automobile
—**d.** lawyers
—**e.** flighty persons

185b

One who is **deft** in this art can transform an ordinary piece of paper into an exquisite artificial flower in a matter of seconds.

Deft means:
—**a.** strong
—**b.** industrious
—**c.** small
—**d.** skillful

210b

A six-**carat** diamond is an extremely large stone—too heavy to be comfortable. The two men, who must have been diamond merchants, handled the stone without apparent concern for its value.

A **carat** is a:
—**a.** degree of hardness
—**b.** description of color
—**c.** measure of sparkle
—**d.** unit of weight

235a

a, b

en light en (en līt′ n)

One of the important functions of a radio station is to **enlighten** its listeners.

Write a definition or synonym:

260a

1. c
2. no

ul ti mate (ul′ tə mit)

Maria's **ultimate** goal is to retire and live anonymously to a ripe old age.

Write a definition or synonym:

284c

a

bois ter ous (boi′stər əs), *adj.* 1 noisily cheerful; exuberant: *a boisterous game.* 2 rough and stormy; turbulent: *a boisterous wind.* 3 rough and noisy; clamorous: *a boisterous child.* [Middle English *boistrous*] —**bois′ter ous ly,** *adv.* —**bois′ter ous ness,** *n.*

Which of the following would most likely be **boisterous**?
—**a.** a game of chess
—**b.** pep rally
—**c.** a touch-football game
—**d.** a waterfall
—**e.** hurricane winds

17a

b, c

di late (dī lāt′, də lāt′)

Janice knew that the pupils in a leopard's eyes **dilate** when it hunts at night.

Write a definition or synonym:

42a

a, c, d

se clud ed (si klü′ did)

Tom was ready to stop as soon as they had climbed the first hill. Peggy wanted to find an even more **secluded** spot.

Write a definition or synonym:

67b

Bits and pieces of ancient clay pots were all they could find. The rest of the pots had been **pulverized** into a fine powder by the weight of the stones above them.

Another word for **pulverize** is:
__a. crash; shatter
__b. crack
__c. wear out
__d. become dust

92b

A book that is written in the **jargon** of psychologists can be very difficult for an untrained person to understand. A good many words and expressions would mean little to the lay person.

Jargon means:
__a. falsehood
__b. baby talk
__c. foreign words
__d. special language

117c

d

bol ster (bōl′stər), *n.* **1** a long, firmly stuffed pillow, placed under the softer pillows on a bed or used as a back on a couch. **2** cushion or pad, often ornamental. —*v.t.* **1** support with a bolster. **2** keep from falling; support; prop. [Old English]

Check the sentence(s) in which a form of **bolster** is used correctly.
__a. He is a great bolster about his accomplishments.
__b. I have a pair of plaid bolsters on my bed.
__c. The sagging porch was bolstered by cement blocks.
__d. Her victory was bolstered by many votes.

142c

d

col le giate (kə lē′jit, kə lē′jē it), *adj.* **1** of or like a college. **2** of or like college students.

Check the sentence(s) in which **collegiate** is used correctly.
__a. Though over thirty, he still has a collegiate air.
__b. The collegiate environment stimulates the intellect.
__c. Most corporate presidents are collegiate.

160b

Pablo behaved in a conventional manner. He dressed and talked the way most people did. However his **eccentric** patrons dressed carelessly, talked in a strange manner, and drove a car which was painted purple. Pablo said he wasn't prejudiced against wealthy patrons who drove purple cars.

Eccentric means:
- __a. poor
- __b. mediocre
- __c. odd
- __d. unpleasant

185a

e

deft (deft)

Many Japanese are **deft** in origami, the art of folding paper.

Write a definition or synonym:

210a

b, c, e

car at (kar′ ət)

When I visit New York City, I like to go to the diamond center on Forty-Seventh Street. Last time I was there, I saw two men inspecting what looked like a six-**carat** diamond.

Write a definition or synonym:

234c

d

en vi ron ment (en vi′rən mənt), *n.*   1 all the surrounding things, conditions, and influences affecting the development of living things. A person's character is influenced by the social environment around him. Differences in environment often account for differences in the same kind of plant found in different places. 2 surroundings: *an environment of poverty.* 3 condition of the air, water, soil, etc.; natural surroundings: *a pollution-free environment.*

Check the sentence(s) in which **environment** is used correctly.
- __a. Tropical fish seem to enjoy the environment of water, greenery, and glass.
- __b. Psychologists disagree as to whether heredity or environment is the greater influence on character.
- __c. The artist painted an environment in oils.

259c

b

in crim i nate (in krim′ə nāt), *v.t.,* **-nat ed, -nat ing.**   accuse of a crime; show to be guilty: *In his confession the thief incriminated two others.* [< Late Latin *incriminatum* charged with a crime < Latin *in-* against + *crimen* a charge] **—in crim/i na/tion,** *n.*

1. In a trial, **incriminating** evidence:
   - __a. would be meaningless
   - __b. would not influence the jury
   - __c. would show a criminal's guilt
   - __d. would prove a person's innocence
2. Can you **incriminate** a crime?
   Yes _____   No _____

284b

The two **boisterous** kids jumped and twisted as they cheered. As a result, the people sitting next to them moved a few seats away.

Boisterous means:
- __a. loud and noisy
- __b. unpleasantly rude
- __c. genteel
- __d. childishly noisy

17b

The leopard's pupils **dilate** in the dark to allow more light to enter its eyes. As the pupils widen, more light enters, and the big cat's night vision improves. Janice hoped the leopard would see the zebra on the ground and not the two moviemakers up in the tree.

Dilate means:

___**a.** darken
___**b.** close
___**c.** expand
___**d.** contract

42b

Tom and Peggy had come out to the country with a busload of city people. There were so many people playing ball and picnicking all around them that they had trouble finding a **secluded** spot where they could be by themselves.

Another word for **secluded** is:

___**a.** undisturbed
___**b.** distant
___**c.** inhospitable
___**d.** desolate

67c

d

pul ve rize (pul′və riz′), v., **-rized, -riz ing.**
—v.t. 1 grind to powder or dust. 2 break to pieces; demolish. —v.i. become dust. [< Late Latin *pulverizare* < Latin *pulvis* dust] —**pul′ver i za′tion,** n. —**pul′ve‑riz′er,** n.

Which of the following could be **pulverized**?

___**a.** a china cup
___**b.** a crystal glass
___**c.** a rock
___**d.** ink
___**e.** a pudding

92c

d

jar gon (jär′gən, jär′gon), n. 1 confused, meaningless talk or writing. 2 language that is not understood. 3 language or dialect composed of a mixture of two or more languages, such as pidgin English. 4 language of a special group, profession, etc. Doctors, actors, and sailors have jargons. —v.i. talk jargon. [< Old French]

Which of the following would be most likely to use **jargon**?

___**a.** newspaper editorial writer
___**b.** doctors at a medical convention
___**c.** U.S. President giving a speech
___**d.** a delirious person
___**e.** group of sailors in a foreign port

118a

b, c

vi tal i ty (vī tal′ ə tē)

By the last event, Paula's **vitality** seemed to be diminishing.

Write a definition or synonym:

143a

a, b

en thrall (en thrôl′)

From the first quarter on, the spectators were **enthralled** by the play.

Write a definition or synonym:

284a

b

bois ter ous (boiʹ star as)

When Lu Ann's victory was announced, her younger brother and sister became a little too **boisterous**.

Write a definition or synonym:

255b

Because the people she worked with were always unaware of her identity, they could not **incriminate** her if they were caught by the police.

A synonym for **incriminate** is:

—a. confuse with another
—b. accuse of a crime
—c. offer testimony
—d. meet face-to-face

234b

If the **environment** is rural, the station will reflect this in its programming. If, however, the **environment** is urban, the programs will be directed to the interests of city people.

Another word for **environment** is:

—a. neighbors
—b. countryside
—c. heredity
—d. surroundings

209c

d

déb u tante or **dé bu tante** (debʹyə tänt, debʹyä tänt'), n. 1 a young woman during her first season in society. 2 woman making a debut. [< French débu-tante]

Which of the following phrases would describe a **débutante**?

—a. poverty-stricken
—b. youthful
—c. social
—d. expensive
—e. much-publicized

184c

b

con vey ance (kən vāʹəns), n. 1 a carrying; transmission; transportation. 2 thing that carries people and goods; vehicle. 3 communication. 4 transfer of ownership. 5 document showing such a transfer; deed.

ANALOGY **conveyance : vehicle ::**

—a. trailer : truck
—b. highway : bridge
—c. radio : television
—d. tractor : auto
—e. house : residence

160a

e

ec cen tric (ek senʹ trik)

Sonia knew that the couple who might become Pablo's patrons were quite **eccentric**.

Write a definition or synonym:

17c

c

di late (dī lāt′, də lāt′), *v.,* **-lat ed, -lat ing.**
—*v.t.* make larger or wider: *When you take a deep breath, you dilate your nostrils.* See **expand** for synonym study. —*v.i.*
1 become larger or wider: *The pupil of the eye dilates when the light gets dim.* See **expand** for synonym study. 2 speak or write in a very complete or detailed manner. [< Latin *dilatare* < *dis-* apart + *latus* wide] —**di-lat′a ble,** *adj.*

Which of the following would be likely to **dilate**?
__a. a puppy's stomach
__b. eyeglasses
__c. a scholar
__d. a growing child
__e. a debt

42c

a

se clud ed (si klü′did), *adj.* shut off from others; undisturbed: *a secluded cabin in the woods.* —**se clud′ed ly,** *adv.* —**se clud′-ed ness,** *n.*

ANALOGY secluded : crowded :: mountain :
__a. hill
__b. valley
__c. lake
__d. fortune
__e. rock

68a

a, b, c

ob liv i on (ə bliv′ ē ən)

Now the archaeologists were sure they had found a truly ancient city. They would rescue the city from **oblivion**.

Write a definition or synonym:

93a

b, d, e

psy chi a trist (sī kī′ ə trist, si kī′ ə trist)

Like psychologists, **psychiatrists** are concerned with the way the human mind works.

Write a definition or synonym:

118b

It was evident that Paula's **vitality** was diminishing. She walked more slowly; her step was not as quick and light.

Another word for **vitality** is:
__a. breath
__b. capacity
__c. strength
__d. health

143b

Fans on both sides of the field watched, **enthralled**, as a series of spectacular passes brought the ball to our five-yard line. Every person in the stands directed total attention to the action on the field.

Another word for **enthralled** is:
__a. captured
__b. captivated
__c. horror-struck
__d. delighted

159c

a

pa tron (pā′trən), *n.* 1 person who buys regularly at a given store or goes regularly to a given restaurant, hotel, etc. 2 person who gives his approval and support to some person, art, cause, or undertaking: *a patron of artists.* 3 a guardian saint or god. —*adj.* guarding; protecting. [< Latin *patronus* protector, patron < *pater* father. Doublet of PADRONE, PATROON.]

ANALOGY patron : artist ::
  —**a.** godparent : child
  —**b.** president : company
  —**c.** worker : boss
  —**d.** brother : sister
  —**e.** sponsor : TV show

184b

Today, the rickshaw is seldom used as a **conveyance**. Its place has been taken by the small taxi. Japan is also noted for its efficient, high-speed railroad transportation.

Another word for **conveyance** is:
—**a.** convenience
—**b.** vehicle
—**c.** automobile
—**d.** bicycle

209b

Many of today's wealthy young women have more serious concerns than "coming out" into society. For that reason, they do not wish to be **debutantes**.

A **debutante** is:
—**a.** an actress who plays juvenile roles
—**b.** a girl renowned for her beauty
—**c.** a very wealthy woman
—**d.** a girl during her first season in society

234a

b

en vi ron ment (en vī′ rən mənt)

A radio station is very much the product of its **environment**.

Write a definition or synonym:

259a

a, d, f

in crim i nate (in krim′ ə nāt)

Maria has always been careful not to **incriminate** any of the people she has worked with.

Write a definition or synonym:

283c

d

dog ged (dô′gid, dog′id), *adj.* not giving up; stubborn; persistent: *dogged determination.* [< *dog*] —**dog′ged ly,** *adv.* —**dog′ged ness,** *n.*

ANALOGY dogged : stubborn ::
  —**a.** feature : film
  —**b.** persist : continue
  —**c.** failure : success
  —**d.** producer : director
  —**e.** cowboy : rancher

18a

a, c

car niv or ous (kär niv′ ər əs)

A **carnivorous** animal, such as the leopard, must constantly be on the lookout for prey.

Write a definition or synonym:

43a

b

in vig o rat ing (in vig′ ə rāt ing)

At first, Tom and Peggy found the country air **invigorating**.

Write a definition or synonym:

68b

The Greek amphitheater and the sun god, Apollo, were well known. But the older city and its peoples had fallen into **oblivion**. Perhaps they had been unknown to the ancient Greeks themselves.

Something in **oblivion** is:
__a. well known
__b. forgotten
__c. prehistoric
__d. unknown

93b

It takes years of study to become a **psychiatrist**, because one must study medicine as well as psychology.

A **psychiatrist** is a:
__a. doctor of mental diseases
__b. eye and ear specialist
__c. nerve specialist
__d. brain surgeon

118c

c

vi tal i ty (vī tal′ə tē), *n., pl.* **-ties.** 1 vital force; power to live: *Her vitality was lessened by illness.* 2 power to endure and be active. 3 strength or vigor of mind or body; energy.

ANALOGY vitality : sloth ::
__a. interest : indifference
__b. active : energetic
__c. strength : exercise
__d. vigor : caution
__e. fame : fortune

143c

b

en thrall or **en thral** (en thrôl′), *v.t.,* **-thralled, -thrall ing.** 1 hold captive by beauty or interest; fascinate; charm. 2 make a slave of; enslave. —**en thrall′ment,** *n.*

ANALOGY enthrall : bore :: please :
__a. ignore
__b. disgust
__c. magic
__d. endure
__e. delight

159b

Artists with **patrons** (people who will buy regularly or possibly provide financial aid) are much more secure than those who have to rely on what they sell.

Another word for **patron** is:
- __a. sponsor
- __b. relative
- __c. donor
- __d. acquaintance

184a

a, e

con vey ance (kən vā′ əns)

Another symbol of change may be found in methods of **conveyance** in the cities.

Write a definition or synonym:

209a

c, d

deb u tante or **dé bu tante** (deb′ yə tänt,
                           deb′ yə tant,
                           deb′ yə tänt′)

In years past, **debutantes** were a center of interest for New York society.

Write a definition or synonym:

233c

c

au di to ry (ô′də tôr′ē, ô′də tōr′ē), *adj.* of or having to do with hearing, the sense of hearing, or the organs of hearing: *The auditory nerve transmits impulses from the ear to the brain.*

ANALOGY auditory : listen :: visual :
- __a. smell
- __b. see
- __c. touch
- __d. odor
- __e. hear

258c

d

ink ling (ingk′ling), *n.* a vague notion; slight suspicion; hint. [Middle English < *inclen* to whisper, hint < Old English *inca* doubt]

Which of the following words mean about the same as **inkling**?
- __a. suspicion
- __b. certainty
- __c. omen
- __d. clue
- __e. prediction
- __f. hunch

283b

Lu Ann's style was not the greatest, and she had had a bad start. But Lu Ann swam with **dogged** determination until she had overtaken the leaders and captured first place.

The meaning of **dogged** is:
- __a. slothful
- __b. resembling a dog
- __c. dog-paddling
- __d. persistent

18b

If a **carnivorous** animal is starving, it may attack a human but it prefers to feed on the flesh of other animals. Soon the leopard approached the zebra that the guides had killed that afternoon and left at the foot of the tree.

Carnivorous means:
___**a.** uncivilized
___**b.** flesh-eating
___**c.** vegetarian
___**d.** cannibalistic

43b

The coolness and the clean smell of the air were **invigorating**. Both Tom and Peggy felt refreshed and full of energy.

A synonym for **invigorating** is:
___**a.** exciting
___**b.** vital
___**c.** lusty
___**d.** stimulating

68c

b

o bliv i on (ə bliv′ē ən), *n.* 1 condition of being entirely forgotten: *Many ancient cities have long since passed into oblivion.* 2 fact of forgetting; forgetfulness. [< Latin *oblivionem* < *oblivisci* forget]

Check the sentence(s) in which **oblivion** is used correctly.
___**a.** Some of what one learns in school passes into oblivion.
___**b.** To say that black and white are opposite is to state the oblivion.
___**c.** He was oblivion to the truth about himself.
___**d.** A famous person may pass into oblivion after death.

93c

a

psy chi a trist (sī kī′ə trist, si kī′ə trist), *n.* doctor who treats mental and emotional disorders; expert in psychiatry.

Which of the following factors about a patient would interest a **psychiatrist**?
___**a.** attitude of parents
___**b.** family history
___**c.** dreams
___**d.** behavior
___**e.** eye color

119a

a

pro fi cient (prə fish′ ənt)

In the last event, however, Paula proved to be more **proficient**.

Write a definition or synonym:

144a

b

scrim mage (skrim′ ij)

Every **scrimmage** was greeted with a tremendous roar from both sides of the field. But at fourth down, it was still goal-to-go.

Write a definition or synonym:

159a

b, c

pa tron (pā′ trən)

By the end of the show, Pablo felt that it had been somewhat successful. Sonia knew better. She had been talking to a man and woman who wanted to become Pablo's **patrons**.

Write a definition or synonym:

183c

d

im per i al (im pir′ē əl), *adj.* 1 of or having to do with an empire, emperor, or empress. 2 of or having to do with the rule or authority of one country over other countries and colonies. 3 having the rank of an emperor. 4 supreme; majestic; magnificent. 5 of larger size or better quality. 6 according to the British standard of weights and measures. —*n.* 1 a small, pointed beard growing beneath the lower lip. 2 size of paper, 23 by 31 inches (in England 22 by 30 inches). [< Latin *imperialis* < *imperium* empire] —**im per′i al ly,** *adv.*

Which of the following were or are **imperial**?
— **a.** Queen Victoria's council
— **b.** an elected president
— **c.** a small fish
— **d.** a flowing beard
— **e.** The Roman Empire
— **f.** the Mississippi River

208c

a

re vue (ri vyü′), *n.* a theatrical entertainment with singing, dancing, parodies of recent movies and plays, humorous treatments of verse composition < *rhaptein* to stitch + *ōidē* song, ode]

Which of the following would you be likely to find in a **revue**?
— **a.** a recitation of the Gettysburg Address
— **b.** an essay on manners
— **c.** a soft-shoe routine
— **d.** jokes about current events
— **e.** an operatic aria

233b

As Sandra pointed out, television appeals to both eye and ear. Radio, however, is strictly an **auditory** means of communication.

Auditory means:
— **a.** having limitations
— **b.** having to do with the voice
— **c.** having to do with hearing
— **d.** old-fashioned; out-of-date

258b

If just one of any of half a dozen governments were to get the slightest **inkling** of Maria's true identity, her career, and probably her life, would be immediately ended.

Another word for **inkling** is:
— **a.** guess
— **b.** knowledge
— **c.** fact
— **d.** hint

283a

b, c

dog ged (dô′ gid, dog′ id)

Lu Ann's father explained that she was a very **dogged** person. He said that was the main reason she won the 400-meter freestyle race.

Write a definition or synonym:

b

18c

car niv or ous (kär niv′ər əs), *adj.* 1 of or having to do with an order of mammals that feed chiefly on flesh. 2 using other animals as food; flesh-eating: *the strong carnivorous eagle.* 3 (of plants) having leaves specially adapted to trap insects for food. [< Latin *carnivorus* < *carnem* flesh + *vorare* devour] —car niv′or ous ly, *adv.* —car niv′or- ous ness, *n.*

In which of the following sentences is **carnivorous** used correctly?
__a. A cow, chewing her cud, looks carnivorous.
__b. Elephants are not feared by other animals, because they are not carnivorous.
__c. Being without water makes one carnivorous.

d

43c

in vig o rate (in vig′ə rāt′), *v.t.,* -rat ed, -rat ing. give vigor to; fill with life and energy. —in vig′o rat′ing ly, *adv.* —in- vig′o ra′tion, *n.*

ANALOGY invigorating : refreshing ::
__a. confusing : clear
__b. tiring : exhausting
__c. business : order
__d. shower : bath
__e. running : exercise

a, d

69a

dil i gent (dil′ ə jənt)

To succeed as an archaeologist, according to Paul Andrades, one must be willing to work hard, and one must be **diligent**.

Write a definition or synonym:

a, b, c, d

94a

de spond ent (di spon′ dənt)

A **despondent** person may be urged to consult a psychiatrist.

Write a definition or synonym:

119b

In gymnastics, as in anything requiring strength and skill, the athlete with the most experience is often the most **proficient**.

Proficient means:
__a. talented
__b. satisfactory
__c. adept
__d. desirable

144b

After the last **scrimmage**, Rafe remained lying on the ground. The fight was no rougher this time than before. He must have slipped and fallen.

A **scrimmage** is a:
__a. pass
__b. touchdown
__c. episode
__d. football play

158c

b

e val u ate (i val′yü āt), *v.t.*, **-at ed, -at ing.**
find out the value or the amount of; estimate
the worth or importance of; appraise.

Check the sentence(s) in which a form of **evaluate** is
used correctly.
— **a.** She evaluated her friend highly.
— **b.** They had the property evaluated by an expert.
— **c.** The auctioneer came to evaluate the pieces.

183b

Until World War II, the Japanese **imperial** family
actually ruled the nation. Now the emperor is a
figurehead who rules in name only.

Imperial means:
— **a.** dating far back in history
— **b.** supernatural
— **c.** superhuman; godlike
— **d.** of an empire or its ruler

208b

This **revue** had been running on Broadway for several
months. Since I had not been to New York for several
years, I didn't understand the point of some of the
skits, but I enjoyed thoroughly the singing and
dancing.

A **revue** is a:
— **a.** variety show about current happenings
— **b.** interview show on television
— **c.** motion picture and variety show
— **d.** drama about historical events

233a

b, c

au di to ry (ô′ də tôr′ ē, ô′ də tōr′ ē)

Sandra felt that the most important characteristic of
radio broadcasting is that it is directed only to our
auditory senses.

Write a definition or synonym:

258a

b

ink ling (ingk′ ling)

Even today, no one has an **inkling** of Maria's true
identity.

Write a definition or synonym:

282c

c

com par a tive (kəm par′ə tiv), *adj.* 1 that
compares; of or having to do with comparison: *the comparative method of studying.*
2 measured by comparison with something
else; relative: *Screens give us comparative
freedom from flies.* 3 showing the second
degree of comparison of an adjective or
adverb. *Better* is the comparative form of
good. —*n.* 1 the second degree of comparison of an adjective or adverb. 2 form or
combination of words that shows this degree.
Fairer and *more slowly* are the comparatives
of *fair* and *slowly.* —**com par′a tive ly,**
adv. —**com par′a tive ness,** *n.*

Check the sentence(s) in which **comparative** is used
correctly.
— **a.** The speaker's one-sided view is comparative.
— **b.** After such a hot September, the cool October
days brought comparative relief.
— **c.** She did a comparative analysis of the three
books.

19a

b

maul (môl)

Although he knew the zebra was already dead, Howard caught his breath in alarm as the jungle cat began to **maul** its prey.

Write a definition or synonym:

44a

b

mire (mīr)

As they drew apart from the others and approached the edge of a quiet pond, Tom accidently stepped in the **mire**.

Write a definition or synonym:

69b

Each piece of broken pottery and each fragment of metal and wood in the buried city must be labeled, cleaned, examined, and stored with great care. After years of this **diligent** labor, it might be possible to identify the objects and their makers with certainty.

Diligent means:
_a. serious
_b. industrious
_c. sober
_d. swift

94b

Case studies made by psychiatrists show examples of people who become **despondent**. In some instances, the individuals become so discouraged, they lose the will to live.

Despondent means:
_a. rejected
_b. overlooked
_c. neglected
_d. dejected

119c

c

pro fi cient (prə fish′ənt), *adj.* advanced in any art, science, or subject; skilled; expert: *She was very proficient in music.* See **expert** for synonym study. [< Latin *proficientem* making progress < *pro-* forward + *facere* to make] —**pro fi′cient ly,** *adv.*

Which of the following expressions best describe a **proficient** person?
_a. "past master"
_b. "top-notch"
_c. "good Joe"
_d. "great gal"
_e. "a shark"
_f. "jack of all trades, master of none"

144c

d

scrim mage (skrim′ij), *n., v.,* **-maged, -mag ing.** —*n.* 1 a rough fight or struggle. 2 the play in football that takes place when the two teams are lined up and the ball is snapped back. 3 football playing for practice. —*v.i.* 1 take part in a rough fight or struggle. 2 (in football) take part in a scrimmage. —*v.t.* oppose in football practice. Also, BRITISH **scrummage.** [ultimately variant of *skirmish*] —**scrim′mag er,** *n.*

Check the synonym(s) for **scrimmage**.
_a. free-for-all
_b. roughhouse
_c. congregation
_d. assemblage
_e. skirmish

113

155b

Amateurs often wonder why a particular painting is priced so high. They do not always understand the standards art critics use when they **evaluate** a painting and judge its worth.

Evaluate means:

__a. make perfect
__b. fix the value of
__c. improve in value
__d. hold in high esteem

183a

a, c, d, e

im per i al (im pir´ ē al)

The **imperial** family reflects the many changes in Japanese life.

Write a definition or synonym:

208a

b, c, e

re vue (ri vyü´)

I told the police officer I was hurrying to the theater to see the new **revue**. He smiled and warned me not to risk any more injuries by jaywalking.

Write a definition or synonym:

232c

a

re im burse (rē´im bėrs´), v.t., -bursed, -burs·ing. pay back; repay (a person or a sum expended). [< re- + obsolete imburse < Medieval Latin imbursare < Latin in- into + Late Latin bursa purse] —re´im·burs´a-ble, adj. —re´im·burse´/ment, n.

Check the sentence(s) in which a form of **reimburse** is used correctly.

__a. When I finished shopping, I reimbursed the clerk for the groceries.
__b. Pay for my ticket; I will reimburse you.
__c. He was reimbursed for his loss.
__d. I wanted to reimburse her for the consideration she had shown.

257c

c

foi ble (foi´bəl), a weak point; weakness: Talking too much is one of her foibles. [< French, older form of faible feeble]

Check the sentence(s) in which **foible(s)** can be substituted for the italicized word(s).

__a. His illness left him with a great weakness.
__b. Although she had many small weaknesses, she had no great faults.
__c. They had to repair the weak point in the seawall before the storm came.

282b

A good contest shows the **comparative** quality of the competitors. In each event, the contestants are measured by the same standards.

Another word for comparative is:

__a. competitive
__b. obvious
__c. relative
__d. superficial

19b

Howard grimaced as he saw the leopard pull the animal about and **maul** it with its savage teeth and claws, dragging it this way and that. But Howard kept shooting, using his special film, as the leopard started to feed.

Maul means:
__a. defeat quickly
__b. discourage completely
__c. handle roughly
__d. cut and bruise

44b

The ground looked solid enough, but under Tom's weight it gave way. He sank into the slushy **mire** until he was up to his knees. Luckily, Peggy was able to pull him out before he sank any deeper.

Mire is:
__a. a deep puddle
__b. a small pond
__c. a dense thicket
__d. deep mud

69c

b

dil i gent (dil′ə jənt), *adj.* 1 hard-working; industrious. See **busy** for synonym study. 2 careful and steady: *a diligent search.* [< Latin *diligentem* < *dis-* apart + *legere* choose] —**dil′i gent ly,** *adv.*

Check those sentences in which a form of **diligent** is used *incorrectly*.
__a. The woman stared out the window diligently.
__b. She was diligent even in death.
__c. He pursued his studies diligently.
__d. Good housekeeping calls for diligent effort.
__e. The clock ticked diligently.

94c

d

de spond ent (di spon′dənt), *adj.* having lost heart, courage, or hope; discouraged; dejected. —**de spond′ent ly,** *adv.*

Check the word(s) that mean(s) the *opposite* of **despondent**.
__a. joyful
__b. melancholy
__c. elated
__d. dispirited
__e. anxious

120a

, b, e

ex u ber ant (eg zü′ bər ənt)

At the end of the meet, Paula was awarded the silver medal and Kim, the gold. Kim was the new champion, and she was **exuberant**.

Write a definition or synonym:

145a

, b, e

di a phragm (dī′ ə fram)

It was soon announced that Rafe had been hit in the **diaphragm**.

Write a definition or synonym:

282a

b, c

com par a tive (kəm par' ə tiv)

Lu Ann's parents discussed the **comparative** merits of the swimmers with the people sitting next to them.

Write a definition or synonym:

257b

By playing on a person's **foibles**, Maria has been able to get information which she might not have been able to obtain in any other way. Knowledge of an adversary's weak spots gives a spy a tremendous advantage.

Foible means:
—**a.** falsehood
—**b.** habit
—**c.** weakness
—**d.** illness

232b

Sandra's mother and father had loaned her several thousand dollars to attend college. Now she had to **reimburse** them at the rate of one hundred dollars a month.

Reimburse means:
—**a.** pay back
—**b.** replace
—**c.** renew
—**d.** play back

207c

b

pre cinct (prē'singkt), *n.* 1 district within certain boundaries, for government, administrative, or other purposes: *an election precinct, a police precinct.* 2 Often, **precincts,** *pl.* **a** space within a boundary: *Do not leave the school precincts during school hours.* **b** the region immediately surrounding a place; environs: *a factory and its precincts.* 3 boundary; limit. [< Medieval Latin *praecinctum* < Latin *praecingere* enclose < *prae- pre- + cingere* gird]

Which of the following is a **precinct?**
—**a.** eternity
—**b.** one's home and grounds
—**c.** school and schoolyard
—**d.** land
—**e.** parish
—**f.** sky

182c

c

pan o ram a (pan/ə ram/ə), *n.* 1 a wide, unbroken view of a surrounding region. 2 a complete survey of some subject: *a panorama of history.* 3 picture of a landscape or other scene, often shown as if seen from a central point; picture unrolled a part at a time and made to pass continuously before the spectators. 4 a continuously passing or changing scene: *the panorama of city life.* [< *pan- +* Greek *horama* view < *horan* to see]

Which of the following would be a **panorama?**
—**a.** photograph of the earth from space
—**b.** an underground cave
—**c.** a world history
—**d.** sights from the Empire State Building
—**e.** events during the lifetime of a generation

158a

a, b,
d, e

e val u ate (i val' yü āt)

It is difficult for an amateur to **evaluate** a painting.

Write a definition or synonym:

19c

c

maul (môl), *n.* a very heavy hammer or mallet for driving stakes, piles, or wedges. —*v.t.* beat and pull about; handle roughly: *The lion mauled its keeper badly.* [variant of *mall*] —**maul′er**, *n.*

Which of the following words mean the *opposite* of **maul**?
__a. batter
__b. caress
__c. hammer
__d. stroke
__e. pat
__f. mangle

44c

d

mire (mir), *n., v.,* **mired, mir ing.** —*n.* 1 soft, deep mud; slush. 2 wet, swampy ground; bog. —*v.t.* 1 cause to be stuck in mire. 2 soil with mud or mire. 3 involve in difficulties; entangle. —*v.i.* stick in mire; be bogged. [< Scandinavian (Old Icelandic) *mȳrr*]

Check the sentence(s) in which a form of **mire** is used correctly.
__a. Splashes of muddy water mired her clothes.
__b. The mire was cold and hard.
__c. She became mired in the tall grass.
__d. After the business failed, Mrs. Jones was mired in debt.

70a

a, b, e

delve (delv)

As the digging continued, Paul took several archaeologists back to Athens to **delve** into all the museums and libraries.

Write a definition or synonym:

95a

a,c

hys ter i a (hi stir′ ē ə, hi ster′ ē ə)

A psychiatrist is often called upon to treat **hysteria**.

Write a definition or synonym:

120b

Kim expressed her **exuberant** feelings by throwing herself into the air for a series of three back flips, throwing her arms around Paula, and giggling madly while she kissed the older girl on the cheek.

A synonym for **exuberant** is:
__a. moderate
__b. overflowing
__c. exciting
__d. hysterical

145b

Being hit in the **diaphragm**, right between the waist and the lungs, is no picnic. But getting the wind knocked out of you this way does happen fairly often in a football game.

Another word for **diaphragm** is:
__a. waist
__b. lungs
__c. head
__d. midriff

157c

a

cli en tele (klī/ən tel/), *n.* 1 clients as a group. 2 customers. 3 dependents; following. 4 number of clients.

Which of the following would *not* have a **clientele**?
__**a.** doctor
__**b.** poor student
__**c.** department store
__**d.** lecturer
__**e.** research chemist

182b

Viewing Japan from the summit of the mountain, one sees a **panorama** of green rice paddies, terraces of tea, crowded cities, and smoking factories.

The meaning of **panorama** is:
__**a.** cultural pattern
__**b.** natural history
__**c.** wide view
__**d.** geography

207b

Although the New York police force is centrally controlled, it is divided into **precincts** for administrative reasons. Times Square and the theater district are in the nineteenth **precinct**.

A synonym for **precinct** is:
__**a.** portion
__**b.** district
__**c.** parcel
__**d.** office

232a

b

re im burse (rē/ im bėrs/)

In addition to paying for her part of the family expenses, Sandra had to **reimburse** her parents for the money they had spent on her education.

Write a definition or synonym:

257a

b, c

foi ble (foi/ bəl)

An ability to spot the **foibles** of others is an invaluable asset to a spy.

Write a definition or synonym:

281c

c

an i ma tion (an/ə mā/shən), *n.* 1 liveliness of manner; spirit; vivacity: *She talks with great animation.* 2 an animating. 3 a being animated: *a case of suspended animation.* 4 the production of an animated cartoon.

Which of the following words mean the *opposite* of **animation**?
__**a.** lightheartedness
__**b.** dullness
__**c.** lifelessness
__**d.** gaiety

20a

b, d, e

scav en ger (skav′ ən jər)

Howard and Janice had shot hundreds of feet of film before the leopard moved away. In a few hours, they knew, the **scavengers** would appear.

Write a definition or synonym:

45a

a, d

sol i tude (sol′ ə tüd, sol′ ə tyüd)

Usually Tom and Peggy looked forward to periods of **solitude**.

Write a definition or synonym:

70b

The information about the buried city was probably stored right in Athens. But to find it, they would have to **delve** through room after room of ancient books and tablets which had been untouched for hundreds of years.

A synonym for **delve** is:
—**a.** study
—**b.** uncover
—**c.** search
—**d.** inquire

95b

People suffering from **hysteria** often become greatly excited for no reason. They may have so little control over their emotions that they are not responsible for some of their actions.

Hysteria is:
—**a.** severe pain
—**b.** misconduct
—**c.** a nervous disorder
—**d.** a contagious disease

120c

b

ex u ber ant (eg zü′bər ənt), *adj.* 1 very abundant; overflowing; lavish: *exuberant joy, an exuberant welcome.* 2 profuse in growth; luxuriant: *the exuberant vegetation of the jungle.* 3 abounding in health and spirits; overflowing with good cheer: *an exuberant young man.* [< Latin *exuberantem* growing luxuriantly < *ex-* thoroughly + *uber* fertile] —**ex u′ber ant ly,** *adv.*

Check the phrase(s) in which **exuberant** is used correctly.
—**a.** exuberant foliage
—**b.** exuberant embrace
—**c.** exuberant boredom
—**d.** exuberant celebration
—**e.** exuberant glance

145c

d

di a phragm (dī′ə fram), *n.* 1 a partition of muscles and tendons in mammals which separates the cavity of the chest from the cavity of the abdomen and is important in respiration; midriff. 2 a thin dividing partition, as in a galvanic cell, or in some shellfish. 3 a thin disk that vibrates rapidly when receiving or producing sounds, used in telephones, loudspeakers, microphones, and other instruments. 4 disk with a hole in the center for controlling the amount of light entering a camera, microscope, etc. —*v.t.* furnish with a diaphragm. [< Greek *diaphragma* < *dia-* across + *phragma* fence]

Check the sentence(s) in which **diaphragm** is used correctly.
—**a.** He was in a cast with a broken diaphragm.
—**b.** A diaphragm regulates the amount of light entering a camera.
—**c.** A trained singer breathes from the diaphragm.

119

157b

An artist's **clientele** is made up of art dealers and individual buyers who have money to spend on paintings they feel are worthwhile.

A synonym for **clientele** is:
—a. customers
—b. visitors
—c. friends
—d. critics

182a

pan o ram a (pan' ə ram' ə)

From Mount Fuji, a visitor sees a **panorama** of the Japanese countryside.

Write a definition or synonym:

a, d

207a

pre cinct (prē' singkt)

When I crossed an intersection in Times Square against the light, a police officer asked if I wanted to take a walk with him to his **precinct** headquarters.

Write a definition or synonym:

c

231c

main stay (mān'stā'), *n.* 1 rope or wire securing the head of the mainmast. See **mainmast** for picture. 2 main support: *Loyal friends are a person's mainstay in time of trouble.*

ANALOGY **mainstay** : support ::
—a. boss : worker
—b. amity : friendship
—c. trunk : leaves
—d. auto : trunk
—e. desk : chair

c

256c

in tu i tion (in'tü ish'ən, in'tyü ish'ən), *n.* 1 immediate perception or understanding of truths, facts, etc., without reasoning: *By experience with many kinds of people the doctor had developed great powers of intuition.* 2 truth, fact, etc., so perceived or understood. [< Late Latin *intuitionem* a gazing at < Latin *intueri* consider, look upon < *in-* + *tueri* to look]

Check the sentence(s) in which **intuition** is used correctly.
—a. She used her intuition to work out the algebra problem.
—b. Women are frequently accused of relying more on intuition than thought.
—c. My intuition tells me that you are trustworthy.
—d. The lovely painting was full of intuition.

c

281b

One group of children displayed an unusual amount of **animation** throughout the meet. When Lu Ann won an event, their excitement was impossible to miss.

Another word for **animation** is:
—a. indifference
—b. hostility
—c. liveliness
—d. amusement

20b

Scavengers, such as vultures and hyenas, usually do not make their own kills. They feed on what the carnivorous animals leave behind. The Austins climbed carefully down and signaled their guides. They had no room for hyenas in their movie.

A **scavenger**:
— **a.** eats decaying matter
— **b.** hunts smaller animals
— **c.** kills its own kind
— **d.** is a vegetarian

45b

A few hours of **solitude** should have been a welcome change from the crowded city life. Now, Tom and Peggy were glad they were together. If Tom had been completely by himself, he would have felt rather uneasy.

The meaning of **solitude** is:
— **a.** being alone
— **b.** being quiet
— **c.** loneliness
— **d.** meditation

70c

c

delve (delv), *v.i.,* **delved, delv ing.** 1 search carefully for information: *delve in books for facts to support a theory.* 2 ARCHAIC. dig. [Old English *delfan*] —**delv′er**, *n.*

ANALOGY delve : search :: ancient :
— **a.** cities
— **b.** ruin
— **c.** timely
— **d.** forgotten
— **e.** antique

95c

c

hys ter i a (hi stir′ē ə,   hi ster′ē ə),   *n.* 1 unrestrained excitement or emotion. 2 a mental disorder, or neurosis, characterized by a physical disability such as paralysis, blindness, digestive upsets, etc., resulting from anxiety. [< New Latin < Greek *hystera* uterus; because originally women were thought to be the only ones affected]

ANALOGY hysteria : uncontrollable laughter ::
— **a.** Spanish : romance language
— **b.** mental illness : paranoia
— **c.** sickness : German measles
— **d.** depression : suicidal thoughts
— **e.** excitement : crowds and noise

b, d

LESSON

Freedom Fighters

During World War II, Lou worked for the Office of Strategic Services. He was proficient in the languages of the Balkan states because his parents had been born there. For this reason, he was sent to Albania to work with a band of patriots behind enemy lines. One dark night, he parachuted into a prearranged spot high in the mountains to begin fighting for his parents' homeland.

146a

b,c

spon ta ne ous (spon tā′ nē əs)

When Rafe climbed back to his feet and waved aside the two men with the stretcher, a **spontaneous** cheer arose from both sides of the stands.

Write a definition or synonym:

121

157a

a, c

cli en tele (klī′ ən tel′)

Many people who attended the show would become part of the artist's **clientele**.

Write a definition or synonym:

181c

b

su per im pose (sü′pər im pōz′), *v.t.*, -posed, -pos ing. put on top of something else.

Check the sentence(s) in which a form of **superimpose** is used correctly.
— **a.** I superimposed the tissue on the picture.
— **b.** His lengthy visit was superimposing.
— **c.** The mayor has a superimposing manner.
— **d.** Elaborate carvings had been superimposed on the face of the building.

206c

b

or di nance (ôrd′n əns), *n.* 1 rule or law made by authority, especially one adopted and enforced by a municipal or other local authority; decree: *a traffic ordinance.* 2 an established religious ceremony. [< Old French *ordenance* < Latin *ordinare* arrange, regulate < *ordinem* order]

Which of the following can enact an **ordinance**?
— **a.** a state supreme court
— **b.** a police department
— **c.** a town council
— **d.** a labor union
— **e.** parents

231b

If she had been the **mainstay** of her family, the salary she earned as a beginner at the radio station would not have been enough.

Mainstay means:
— **a.** guardian
— **b.** loyal friend
— **c.** main support
— **d.** central point

256b

Government field agents like Maria come to value their **intuition**. There are many situations which simply cannot be handled by clear, rational fact-finding.

Intuition means:
— **a.** understanding truth by reasoning
— **b.** gaining knowledge through experience
— **c.** perceiving a truth without reasoning
— **d.** use of the senses to reach a conclusion

281a

an i ma tion (an′ ə mā′ shən)

All the faces at the Swimming Club showed great **animation** when Lu Ann's first event was announced.

Write a definition or synonym:

20c

a

scav en ger (skav′ən jər), *n.* 1 animal that feeds on decaying matter. Vultures are scavengers. 2 person who scavenges. [alteration of *scavager,* literally, inspector, ultimately < Old French *escauwer* inspect < Flemish *scauwen*]

In which of the following sentences is a form of **scavenger** used correctly?
— **a.** Scavengers search the trash baskets for scraps of food.
— **b.** The scavenger prepared to spring at its prey.
— **c.** A ragpicker is a scavenger.

45c

a

sol i tude (sol′ə tüd, sol′ə tyüd), *n.* 1 a being alone: *I like company and hate solitude.* 2 a lonely place. 3 loneliness.

Check the word(s) that mean(s) the *opposite* of **solitude.**
— **a.** privacy
— **b.** association
— **c.** companionship
— **d.** isolation
— **e.** togetherness

LESSON 8

e

The Most Wonderful Witch

Fairy tales have been part of our culture for centuries. Although most people no longer believe in the supernatural, parents still put their children to bed with tales of giants and fairies and goblins. The words "Once upon a time" still start a trip to the world of imagination. However, not everything you may hear in a fairy tale is imaginary.

96a

d

nar cot ic (när kot′ ik)

In the treatment of mental illness, use is sometimes made of hypnosis, shock treatments, or **narcotics.**

Write a definition or synonym:

121a

guer ril la (gə ril′ ə)

The **guerrilla** bands had established camps high in the mountains.

Write a definition or synonym:

146b

We were all rather surprised when we found ourselves cheering for the one man who could deprive us of victory. But there was no explaining it. The **spontaneous** cheering just happened.

A synonym for **spontaneous** is:
— **a.** unplanned
— **b.** aggressive
— **c.** skillful
— **d.** clever

156c

a

cru cial (krü′shəl), *adj.* 1 very important or decisive; critical. 2 very trying; severe. [< New Latin *crucialis* < Latin *crucem* cross; with reference to the fork of a road] —**cru′cial ly,** *adv.*

Check the sentence(s) in which a form of **crucial** is used correctly.
_**a.** He passed the crucial point of his illness.
_**b.** She tried crucially to pass the test.
_**c.** He completed the crucial experiment of the series.
_**d.** Our son is stationed in the crucial zone.

181b

The Oriental foundation of the Japanese culture remains. Now, however, Western ideas and methods have been **superimposed** upon it. The result is a strange mixture of Oriental and Western customs.

Another word for **superimpose** is:
_**a.** weight down
_**b.** add on to
_**c.** stamp over
_**d.** force into

206b

For example, there is a city **ordinance** against throwing litter in the streets. Litter baskets are provided at frequent intervals, and failure to use them may result in a fine.

Ordinance means:
_**a.** peculiarity
_**b.** regulation
_**c.** discrimination
_**d.** code

231a

main stay (mān′ stā′)

Fortunately, Sandra did not have to be the **mainstay** of her family.

Write a definition or synonym:

256a

b

in tu i tion (in′ tü ish′ ən, in′ tyü ish′ ən)

On more than one occasion, Maria's **intuition** has warned her that death was very near.

Write a definition or synonym:

c, d

LESSON 29 | Water Wings

I read a short story last week about a young girl named Lu Ann Simms. She broke the state records for the 200- and 400-meter freestyles without the benefit of extensive training or natural ability. What gave Lu Ann her victories was a fierce, driving will to win.

LESSON ③ She Killed Him with Kindness

Connie and Coward Craven separated last week after a year of marriage. Connie, who must have been the sweetest and the dumbest person in town, wrote Coward a note, asking him to dinner. Coward Craven, who was bad-tempered and ugly, did sit down to dinner with Connie. But he never lived to eat his dessert. That's why Connie called Berry Amazing, the famous criminal lawyer.

46a

stag nant (stag′ nənt)

"Did you notice the air?" Peggy asked as she stretched out on the only completely dry land around. "It's not invigorating anymore. It seems kind of **stagnant**."

Write a definition or synonym:

71a

nar rate (na rāt′, nar′ āt)

The tale I am going to **narrate** may be partly true. But it happened so long ago, it has been called a fairy tale. Today it is probably too late to separate fact from fiction.

Write a definition or synonym:

96b

Controlled use of a **narcotic** may relax patients suffering from hysteria enough to aid in their recovery. Narcotics would not be given to a patient who was already despondent, however.

A **narcotic** is:
__a. a stimulant
__b. a vitamin
__c. a nourishing drink
__d. a dulling drug

121b

The **guerrilla** bands were made up of volunteer fighters who plagued the enemy with sudden raids, usually at night.

A **guerrilla** is:
__a. a mountain animal
__b. a criminal
__c. an army officer
__d. an independent fighter

146c

spon ta ne ous (spon tā′nē əs), *adj.* 1 caused by natural impulse or desire; not forced or compelled; not planned beforehand: *Both sides burst into spontaneous cheers at the skillful play.* See **voluntary** for synonym study. 2 taking place without external cause or help; caused entirely by inner forces: *The eruption of a volcano is spontaneous.* 3 growing or produced naturally; not planted, cultivated, etc. [< Late Latin *spontaneus* < Latin *sponte* of one's own accord] —**spon ta′ne ous ly,** *adv.* —**spon ta′ne ous ness,** *n.*

Check the sentence(s) in which a form of **spontaneous** is used correctly.
__a. Spontaneous combustion can occur in oily rags.
__b. My carefully tended bushes grew spontaneously.
__c. Her laughter was easy and spontaneous.

125

156b

An artist's first one-man or one-woman show can be so important it becomes **crucial** to the artist's career. If the show is not fairly successful, the artist will not attract further notice. If the show is a smash success, the artist can become famous almost overnight.

Another word for **crucial** is:
_a. critical
_b. exciting
_c. middle
_d. turning

181a

su per im pose (sü′ pər im pōz′)

Over the years, the Japanese have **superimposed** other cultures upon their own.

Write a definition or synonym:

206a

b

or di nance (ôrd′ n əns)

New York has many **ordinances** of which the tourist is unaware.

Write a definition or synonym:

b, c

LESSON 24

In the Air, Everywhere!

As soon as Sandra D'Amato graduated from school she took a job at the local radio station. She had always wanted to work in broadcasting, and she decided the best way to gain experience would be to start working for a small station. In a year or so, she would be ready to move on.

255c

c

o bit u ar y (ō bich′ü er′ē), *n., pl.* **-ar ies,** *adj.* —*n.* a notice of death, often with a brief account of the person's life. —*adj.* of a death; recording a death or deaths. [< Medieval Latin *obituarius* < Latin *obitus* death < *obire (mortem)* meet (death) < *ob-* away + *ire* go]

ANALOGY obituary : funeral :: advertisement :
_a. birth
_b. sale
_c. wedding
_d. store
_e. party

280c

b

in tol er a ble (in tol′ər ə bəl), *adj.* too much to be endured; unbearable: *intolerable pain.* —**in tol′er a ble ness,** *n.* —**in tol′er a bly,** *adv.*

Something **intolerable** would be:
_a. "like rolling off a log"
_b. "changeable as the weather"
_c. "enough to provoke a saint"
_d. "enough to try the patience of Job"
_e. "six of one, half a dozen of the other"

21a

cryp tic (krip′ tik)

Berry Amazing was out of the office when Connie called to ask for his help. Connie left her name and phone number along with a **cryptic** message.

Write a definition or synonym:

46b

Tom commented on the **stagnant** waters of the nearby pond. No breezes stirred the surface. The waters had no ripples or any sign of motion.

Another word for **stagnant** is:
_a. shallow
_b. muddy
_c. rippling
_d. still

71b

Like many old stories, this one had been **narrated** for hundreds of years before it was first written down. People enjoyed telling stories and hearing them long before most people knew how to read or write.

Narrate means:
_a. read
_b. relate
_c. unfold
_d. relive

96c

d

nar cot ic (när kot′ik), *n.* 1 any drug that produces drowsiness, sleep, dullness, or an insensible condition, and lessens pain by dulling the nerves. Taken in excess narcotics, such as opium, cause systemic poisoning, delirium, paralysis, or even death. 2 anything that numbs, soothes, or dulls. —*adj.* 1 having the properties and effects of a narcotic. 2 of or having to do with narcotics or their use. [< Greek *narkōtikos* benumbing < *narkoun* benumb < *narkē* numbness] —**nar cot′i cal ly,** *adv.*

If you were under the influence of a **narcotic**, you would probably be:
_a. excited
_b. lonesome
_c. sleepy
_d. unconscious
_e. afraid
_f. numb

121c

d

guer ril la (gə ril′ə), *n.* member of a band of fighters who harass the enemy by sudden raids, ambushes, the plundering of supply trains, etc. Guerrillas are not part of a regular army. —*adj.* of or by guerrillas: *a guerrilla attack.* Also, **guerilla.** [< Spanish, diminutive of *guerra* war; of Germanic origin]

ANALOGY guerrilla : gorilla ::
_a. enemy : medicine
_b. soldier : tiger
_c. general : monkey
_d. knight : night
_e. attack : jungle

147a

a, c

il lus tri ous (i lus′ tri əs)

Rafe was an all-American choice and a famous sports figure as a collegiate player. But the team he played on was far from **illustrious**.

Write a definition or synonym:

127

156a

b, c, e

cru·cial (krü′shal)

Sonia knew the results of this one-man show would be crucial to Pablo's career. Why didn't he move around the room and meet people, instead of standing in the corner worrying?

Write a definition or synonym:

---

c, d

LESSON 19 The Land of the Rising Sun

In many ways, life in Japan is quite different from life in other Asian countries. For one thing, Japan has a temperate climate, a feature it shares only with parts of China. Japan is also the most industrialized country in Asia. Its standard of living is far higher than that of any other Asian nation.

205c

c

na·ive or na·ïve (nä ēv′), adj. simple in nature; like a child; not sophisticated; artless. Also, naïf. [< French naïve, feminine of naïf < Latin nativus. Doublet of NATIVE.] —na-ive′ly, na ïve′ly, adv. —na ive′ness, na-ïve′ness, n.

ANALOGY naïve : worldly :: innocent :

__a. tired
__b. guilty
__c. silent
__d. sincere
__e. unfortunate

230c

b

com·pul·sion (kəm pul′shən), n. 1 a compelling or a being compelled; use of force; coercion. A contract signed under compulsion is not legal. 2 impulse that is hard to resist: A compulsion to steal is not normal. [< Late Latin compulsionem < Latin compellere. See COMPEL.]

Check the sentence(s) in which compulsion is used correctly.

__a. The big plane moved through the air by compulsion.
__b. The woman had a compulsion to take things belonging to others.
__c. He studied only under compulsion.

255b

Maria has read her own obituary. It was printed in the newspaper when a fictitious character whose identity she had assumed was reported dead.

A synonym for obituary is:

__a. writing on a tombstone
__b. feature article
__c. death notice
__d. autobiography

280b

b, c, e

Rhoda's aunt was as restless as Rhoda herself. She found it intolerable to stay in bed when she could be out exploring another mysterious and romantic foreign city.

A synonym for intolerable is:

__a. uncomfortable
__b. unbearable
__c. necessary
__d. prejudiced

21b

After hearing about Connie's troubles, Berry knew she was innocent. All Berry Amazing's clients were innocent! But her phone message did seem to have a secret, hidden meaning. It was one of the most **cryptic** messages he had ever received.

Another word for **cryptic** is:
__a. mysterious
__b. ugly
__c. deadly
__d. criminal

46c

d

stag nant (stag′nənt), *adj.* 1 not running or flowing: *stagnant air, stagnant water.* 2 foul from standing still: *a stagnant pool of water.* 3 not active; sluggish; dull: *During the summer, business is often stagnant.* [< Latin *stagnantem*] —**stag′nant ly,** *adv.*

Which of the following would most likely become **stagnant**?
__a. the air on top of a mountain
__b. a pond with no outlet
__c. the outlook of a long-term convalescent
__d. the air in a cave
__e. water in a swimming pool
__f. a waterfall

71c

b

nar rate (nar′āt, na rāt′), *v.,* **-rat ed, -rat ing.** —*v.t.* give an account of; tell (a story, etc.) of; relate; recount: *narrate an incident.* —*v.i.* tell stories, etc. [< Latin *narratum* made known, told] —**nar′ra tor,** *n.*

Which of the following people are **narrating**?
__a. comedian telling what happened on the way to the theater
__b. teacher giving a homework assignment
__c. announcer giving the weather forecast
__d. old sailor spinning yarns to the children

97a

c, d, f

in duce (in düs′, in dyüs′)

A psychiatrist may sometimes use hypnosis to **induce** relaxation.

Write a definition or synonym:

122a

d

hav oc (hav′ ək)

The band Lou fought with was led by a tall, heavy man with a thick black mustache. His name was Costas. Each night they played **havoc** with the enemy's supplies.

Write a definition or synonym:

147b

The line was not outstanding; the receivers were only fair. But they had one outstanding and famous player: the **illustrious** Rafe Barlow.

The meaning of **illustrious** is:
__a. well educated
__b. outstanding
__c. dramatic
__d. talented

280a

a, c

in tol er a ble (in tol' ar a bal)

After a month of travel on the ocean liner, it would be **intolerable** not to be able to go ashore when the chance came.

Write a definition or synonym:

255a

c

o bit u ar y (ō bich' ū ar' ē)

Most people do not see their own **obituaries**.

Write a definition or synonym:

230b

John's **compulsion** had two causes. First, his contract required him to finish the bridge within a specified period. Second, he was scheduled to begin a long-needed vacation.

Another word for **compulsion** is:

—a. contest
—b. forcing
—c. request
—d. competition

205b

The **naïve** tourist is apt to spend more money than is necessary. Since tourists usually have money to spend, unethical merchants will try to take advantage of them.

Naïve means:

—a. uneducated
—b. stubborn
—c. artless
—d. unintelligent

180c

a

pre oc cu py (prē ok'ya pī), v.t., -pied, -py ing. 1 take up all the attention of: ab-sorb: *The question of getting to New York preoccupied her mind.* 2 occupy beforehand; take possession of before others: *Our favor-ite seats had been preoccupied.*

Check the sentence(s) in which a form of **preoccupy** is used correctly.

—a. A thing that interests me may preoccupy half my mind.
—b. Have you preoccupied this house long?
—c. We could not dine at our usual place as it had been preoccupied.
—d. I became preoccupied with my troubles.

155c

d

per ceive (par sēv'), v.t., -ceived, -ceiv ing. 1 be aware of through the senses; see, hear, taste, smell, or feel. See *see* for synonym study. 2 take in with the mind; observe; understand. (Definition adapted)

per cep tion (par sep/shan), n. 1 act of perceiving: *His perception of the change came in a flash.* 2 power of perceiving; a keen perception. 3 understanding that is the result of perceiving: *I now have a clear perception of what went wrong.* (Definition adapted)

Which of the following are examples of **perception**?

—a. receiving a paycheck
—b. understanding someone's mood
—c. sensing that something is wrong
—d. greeting someone at the door
—e. being aware of an odor

21c

cryp tic (krip′tik), *adj.* having a hidden meaning; secret; mysterious: *a cryptic message.* [< Late Latin *crypticus* < Greek *kryptikos* < *kryptos* hidden] —**cryp′ti cal ly,** *adv.*

ANALOGY cryptic : confusing :: clear :
— **a.** secret
— **b.** hidden
— **c.** message
— **d.** understandable
— **e.** forgiven

47a

o paque (ō pāk′)

"That's curious," Peggy said. "Now why would the air and the water be so still?" Peggy walked carefully down to the edge of the pond and looked into the **opaque** water.

Write a definition or synonym:

72a

man or (man′ ər)

Once upon a time, in the forests of Eastern Europe, there was a woman named Wanda who was the lady of a great **manor.**

Write a definition or synonym:

97b

Some patients, while fully awake, are unable to remember painful events. The psychiatrist may have trouble **inducing** them to talk freely without using hypnosis.

Another word for **induce** is:
— **a.** persuade
— **b.** prevent
— **c.** help
— **d.** force

122b

The enemy had more men and supplies than the guerrillas. On the night that Costas picked up Lou, the enemy army created **havoc** throughout the mountain area. Hardly a village was left standing, The guerrillas made plans for a swift, equally destructive revenge.

Havoc means:
— **a.** great destruction
— **b.** goodwill
— **c.** impatience
— **d.** shortage of materials

147c

il lus tri ous (i lus′trē əs), *adj.* **1** very famous; great; outstanding. **2** bringing or conferring glory; glorious. [< Latin *illustris* lighted up, bright < *in-* in + *lustrum* lighting] —**il lus′tri ous ly,** *adv.* —**il lus′tri ous ness,** *n.*

Check the word(s) that mean(s) the *opposite* of **illustrious.**
— **a.** unusual
— **b.** unknown
— **c.** customary
— **d.** popular

155b

Pablo's **perception** of the crowd's mood was completely different. He was sure he saw people frowning and heard them making critical comments. Sonia told him he was much too sensitive.

Perception means:
— **a.** sight
— **b.** ability
— **c.** taste
— **d.** insight

180b

I can shut myself up with my collection and become so **preoccupied** that I forget to eat. My happiest hours are spent absorbed in my stamp collection.

Preoccupy means:
— **a.** take up all the attention of
— **b.** put into a daze or trance
— **c.** become a business
— **d.** become boring

205a

a, c, d

na ïve or **na ive** (nä ēv′)

New York is no place for a **naïve** person.

Write a definition or synonym:

230a

a, b, e

com pul sion (kəm pul′ shən)

John explained that he was under **compulsion** to finish the bridge by a certain date.

Write a definition or synonym:

254c

d

spin ster (spin′stər), *n.*   **1** an unmarried woman.   **2** an elderly woman who has not married; old maid.   **3** woman who spins flax, wool, etc., into thread.

ANALOGY spinster : bachelor :: mare :
— **a.** colt
— **b.** marriage
— **c.** stallion
— **d.** maid
— **e.** widow

279c

d

in dis posed (in′dis pōzd′), *adj.*   **1** slightly ill.   **2** unwilling.

Check the sentence(s) in which **indisposed** is used correctly.
— **a.** He was indisposed to hard work of any type.
— **b.** I felt indisposed and ready to conquer the world.
— **c.** It is better to stay in bed if you feel indisposed.
— **d.** She was indisposed as to what to eat.

22a

d

de ment ed (di men′ tid)

When he had listened to Connie's story for the third time, Berry began to think his client was probably **demented**.

Write a definition or synonym:

47b

The sun was still shining, but the waters were not clear or sparkling. They were **opaque**. Peggy thought of going in for a swim. Then she changed her mind. For some reason, she began to imagine all sorts of unseen dangers lurking beneath the dark waters.

The meaning of **opaque** is:
___a. full of light
___b. not transparent
___c. not moving
___d. black and brown

72b

Brentwood **Manor** covered several hundred acres at the edge of a thick forest. The lord and lady, their children, and their servants lived in the manor house. Nearby lived over a hundred peasants. They farmed small portions of the **manor** land.

Another word for **manor** is:
___a. ranch
___b. farm
___c. development
___d. estate

97c

a

in duce (in düs′, in dyüs′), *v.t.,* **-duced, -duc ing. 1** lead on; influence; persuade: *Advertisements induce people to buy.* **2** bring about; cause: *Some drugs induce sleep.* **3** produce (an electric current, electric charge, or magnetic change) by induction. **4** infer by reasoning from particular facts to general truths or principles. [< Latin *inducere* < *in-* in + *ducere* to lead] —**in duc′er,** *n.*

Check the sentence(s) in which a form of **induce** is used correctly.
___a. To induce, one arrives at a general rule or principle through studying particular facts.
___b. He induced me to change my mind.
___c. The lectures induced new ideas for me.
___d. I couldn't help inducing my ideas into the discussion.

122c

a

hav oc (hav′ək), *n.* **1** very great destruction or injury; devastation; ruin: *Tornadoes, severe earthquakes, and plagues create widespread havoc.* **2 play havoc with,** injure severely; ruin; destroy. [< Anglo-French *havok,* variant of Old French *havot* plundering, devastation]

Check the sentence(s) in which **havoc** is used correctly.
___a. The rain played havoc with the harvest.
___b. The fire spread havoc throughout the city.
___c. The election of an honest sheriff played havoc among the law-abiding citizens.
___d. She was in a state of havoc.

148a

b

me di o cre (mē′ dē ō′ kər, mē′ dē ō′ kər)

Rafe's team may have been **mediocre**, but they scored twice in the third quarter and won the game with no trouble.

Write a definition or synonym:

155a

per cep tion (par sep' shan)

It was Sonia's **perception** that everyone at the show was favorably impressed.

Write a definition or synonym:

b, c

180a

pre oc cu py (prē ok' ya pī)

Stamp collecting completely **preoccupies** many people like myself. Not all of us are in the game to make money.

Write a definition or synonym:

a, b

204c

pa ro chi al (pa rō'kē al), adj. 1 of or in a parish: a parochial church. 2 narrow; limited: a parochial viewpoint. [< Late Latin parochialis < parochia parish. See PARISH.]

a

Check the sentence(s) in which **parochial** is used correctly.

—a. Many churches operate parochial schools.
—b. An internationalist has a parochial viewpoint.
—c. A small-town newspaper will concentrate largely on matters of parochial interest.
—d. The minister's parochial affairs kept him busy.

229c

em boss (em bôs', em bos'), v.t. 1 decorate with a design, pattern, etc., that stands out from the surface: Our coins are embossed with letters and figures. 2 cause to stand out from the surface: The letters on the book's cover had been embossed. —em boss'er, n. —em boss'ment, n.

Embossing might be found on:

—a. stationery
—b. chinaware
—c. a flower petal
—d. a newspaper
—e. a Braille book

254b

A married man or woman is seldom a useful spy. A bachelor or a **spinster** is more reliable, as long as he or she has no emotional attachments.

A **spinster** is:

—a. an unmarried person
—b. a career woman
—c. a homemaker
—d. an unmarried woman

279b

Rhoda hoped her aunt would not remain **indisposed** during the entire stopover in Calcutta. Perhaps she was only suffering from a mild case of seasickness.

Another word for **indisposed** is:

—a. delayed
—b. unhappy
—c. uninterested
—d. sick

22b

Berry thought that only a **demented** person would want to stay married to a man like Coward Craven. Connie would have to be crazy to have wanted to be with such a bad-tempered, ugly, unpleasant man. And no sane person would have served poison for dinner!

The meaning of **demented** is:
- __a. unusual
- __b. abnormal
- __c. uneducated
- __d. insane

47c

b

o paque (ō pāk′), *adj.* 1 not letting light through; not transparent or translucent. 2 not conducting heat, sound, electricity, etc. 3 not shining; dark; dull. 4 hard to understand; obscure. 5 stupid. —*n.* something opaque. [< Latin *opacus* dark, shady] —**o paque′ly,** *adv.* —**o paque′ness,** *n.*

Check the sentence(s) in which a form of **opaque** is used correctly.
- __a. I couldn't read anything through the opaque envelope.
- __b. When freshly polished, silver gleams opaquely.
- __c. His mind seemed opaque in its refusal to admit the rays of knowledge.
- __d. The opaque windows allowed the sunlight to pour into the room.

72c

d

man or (man′ər), *n.* 1 (in the Middle Ages) a feudal estate, part of which was set aside for the lord and the rest divided among his peasants, who paid the owner rent in goods, services, or money. If the lord sold his manor, the peasants or serfs were sold with it. 2 a large estate. 3 the main house or mansion of an estate. [< Old French *manoir* a dwelling < *maneir* dwell < Latin *manere* to stay]

ANALOGY manor : peasants ::
- __a. field : forest
- __b. house : yard
- __c. factory : workers
- __d. windows : roof
- __e. castle : stone

98a

a, b

e rad i cate (i rad′ ə kāt)

It is doubtful that mental illness can ever be completely **eradicated**.

Write a definition or synonym:

123a

a, b

en camp ment (en kamp′ ment)

Costas' guerrilla **encampment** lay close to an icy mountain stream.

Write a definition or synonym:

148b

A **mediocre** performance in football is never quite enough if you want to get to the top. Your performance, like Rafe Barlow's, must always be excellent.

Mediocre means:
- __a. below average
- __b. average
- __c. above average
- __d. failing

154c

a

pig ment (pig'mənt), *n.* 1 a coloring matter, especially a powder or some easily pulverized dry substance that constitutes a paint or dye when mixed with oil, water, or some other liquid. 2 the natural substance occurring in and coloring the tissues of an animal or plant. —*v.t.* color with or as if with pigment. [< Latin *pigmentum* < *pingere* to paint. Doublet of PIMENTO.]

Check the sentence(s) in which a form of **pigment** is used correctly.
—**a.** The evening sky was a beautiful pigment.
—**b.** Early artists ground their own pigments.
—**c.** His hair was white because it had no pigment.
—**d.** She wore a lovely dress of blue pigment.

179c

c

a non y mous (ə non'ə məs), *adj.* 1 by or from a person whose name is not known or given: *an anonymous letter.* 2 having no name; whose name is not known; nameless: *This book was written by an anonymous author.* [< Greek *anōnymos* < *an-* without + *onyma* name] —**a non'y mous ly**, *adv.* —**a non'y mous ness**, *n.*

Which of the following can be described as **anonymous**?
—**a.** a new, unnamed hybrid rose
—**b.** an unsigned telegram
—**c.** a person who cannot read or write
—**d.** a crowd at a political rally

204b

Although they like to accuse people from the rest of the country of being unsophisticated and poorly informed, some New Yorkers are so **parochial** that they think the United States ends at the Hudson River, which forms the western boundary of the city.

Another word for **parochial** is:
—**a.** limited
—**b.** poor
—**c.** feeble
—**d.** worldly

229b

A painted sign was rejected in favor of an **embossed** plate. It was felt that the raised bronze letters would be more in keeping with the design of the bridge.

An **embossed** design is one that is:
—**a.** carved
—**b.** painted
—**c.** raised
—**d.** lighted

254a

b, c

spin ster (spin' stər)

Maria fully expects to continue being a spy, and she expects to remain a **spinster**.

Write a definition or synonym:

279a

a, c, e

in dis posed (in' dis pōzd')

Rhoda's aunt was **indisposed** when they arrived at the port of Calcutta.

Write a definition or synonym:

22c

d

de ment ed (di men′tid), *adj.* mentally ill; insane; crazy. [< Latin *dementem* < *de-* out + *mentem* mind] —**de ment′ed ly,** *adv.* —**de ment′ed ness,** *n.*

In which of the following sentences is **demented** used correctly?
__a. A demented person should be given treatment.
__b. She was demented to corporal.
__c. Criminals are sometimes demented.

48a

a, c

rev er ie (rev′ ər ē)

Feeling strangely listless, the couple sat down by the edge of the pond and drifted into a **reverie**.

Write a definition or synonym:

73a

c

mal a dy (mal′ ə dē)

One year, more than half the peasants were stricken with a strange **malady**.

Write a definition or synonym:

98b

In individual cases, however, it is often possible to **eradicate** the illness by finding and removing its cause.

A synonym for **eradicate** is:
__a. heal
__b. relieve
__c. control
__d. eliminate

123b

The stream provided the **encampment** with an ample supply of water. The food was cooked over a crude fireplace made of rocks. The men slept each night beneath the trees.

An **encampment** is a:
__a. dormitory
__b. village
__c. settlement
__d. camp

148c

b

me di o cre (mē′dē ō′kər, mē′dē ō′kər), *adj.* neither good nor bad; of average quality; ordinary. [< Latin *mediocris,* originally, halfway up < *medius* middle + *ocris* jagged mountain]

Which of the following can **mediocre** describe?
__a. a mountain peak
__b. a performance
__c. a half-filled glass
__d. a tennis player
__e. a report card

278c

com mu ni ca ble (kə myū'nə kə bəl), *adj.* that can be communicated: *Ideas are communicable by words. Scarlet fever is a communicable disease.* —com mu'ni ca ble-ness, *n.* —com mu'ni ca bly, *adv.*

b

Which of the following are communicable?
__a. a cold
__b. a broken leg
__c. thoughts
__d. television set
__e. feelings

253c

fraught (frôt), *adj.* loaded or filled (with): *The attempt to climb Mount Everest was fraught with danger.* [originally past participle of obsolete *fraught* to load < *fraught* a load, freight < Middle Dutch or Middle Low German *vracht* freight]

b

Check the sentence(s) in which **fraught** is used correctly.
__a. The cup is fraught with coffee.
__b. We enjoy movies that are fraught with excitement.
__c. Her words are fraught with emotion.
__d. The coops were fraught with chickens.

229a

em boss (em bôs', em bos')

John said there had been some discussion about whether to have an **embossed** dedication plate on the bridge.

b, c, d

Write a definition or synonym:

204a

pa ro chi al (pə rō' kē əl)

Many New Yorkers are quite **parochial** in their viewpoints.

d

Write a definition or synonym:

179b

By remaining **anonymous**, collectors help ensure the safety of their stamp collections. This practice also protects them from dealers and other collectors who might track them down if their names were known.

The meaning of **anonymous** is:
__a. well-protected
__b. wearing a disguise
__c. without a name
__d. formless

154b

Pablo explained how he selected the proper colors for his paintings. Very often he mixed his own paint, carefully blending **pigment** and oils to achieve the desired effect.

Pigment means:
__a. coloring matter
__b. a kind of paint
__c. brushes for painting
__d. color sense

23a

a, c

cor o ner (kôr′ ə nər, kor′ ə nər)

The police sent for the **coroner** as soon as they reached the scene of the crime.

Write a definition or synonym:

48b

All too soon their pleasant, dreamy mood was shattered. Rising slowly from the center of the pond was a creature that changed their **reverie** into a nightmare!

Another word for **reverie** is:
__a. adoration
__b. thoughtfulness
__c. sleep
__d. daydream

73b

There seemed to be no cure for the mysterious **malady**. The people who fell sick died slowly and in great pain.

A synonym for **malady** is:
__a. thunderbolt
__b. problem
__c. rash
__d. disease

98c

d

e rad i cate (i rad′ə kāt), *v.t.*, -cat ed, -cat ing. 1 get rid of entirely; destroy completely; eliminate: *Yellow fever has been eradicated in the United States.* 2 pull out by the roots: *eradicate weeds.* [< Latin *eradicatum* rooted out < *ex-* out + *radicem* root] —e rad′i ca′tor, *n.*

ANALOGY eradicate : smallpox :: publish :
__a. fever
__b. write
__c. newspaper
__d. erase
__e. pencil

123c

d

en camp (en kamp′), *v.i.* 1 make a camp. 2 live in a camp for a time. —*v.t.* put in a camp: *They were encamped in tents.* —en-camp′ment, *n.*

ANALOGY encampment : tents :: village :
__a. houses
__b. people
__c. streets
__d. roof
__e. construction

149a

b, d, e

bed lam (bed′ ləm)

Bedlam reigned after the game as the crowd surged onto the field.

Write a definition or synonym:

278b

Officials are careful not to allow a person suffering from a **communicable** disease to land, as they do not wish the disease to spread.

Communicable means:
— **a.** childhood
— **b.** catching
— **c.** virus
— **d.** fatal

253b

Although there are many dull moments, a spy's life is often **fraught** with excitement. The danger of being discovered is ever present.

Fraught means:
— **a.** confused
— **b.** filled
— **c.** mixed
— **d.** lived

228c

a

lat er al (lat′ər əl), *adj.* of the side; at the side; from the side; toward the side. A lateral branch of a family is a branch not in the direct line of descent. —*n.* 1 a lateral part or outgrowth. 2 lateral pass. [< Latin *lateralis* < *latus* side] —**lat′er al ly**, *adv.*

Check the sentence(s) in which **lateral** is used correctly.
— **a.** She crossed to the other lateral of the room.
— **b.** The fish had two lateral fins.
— **c.** The man excluded his lateral relatives from his will.
— **d.** The miners dug a lateral tunnel.

203c

b

di a lect (dī′ə lekt), *n.* 1 form of speech characteristic of a class or region and differing from the standard language in pronunciation, vocabulary, and grammatical form. See **language** for synonym study. 2 one of a group of closely related languages: *Some of the dialects descended from the Latin language are French, Italian, Spanish, and Portuguese.* 3 words and pronunciations used by certain professions, classes of people, etc. —*adj.* dialectal. [< Latin *dialectus* < Greek *dialektos* discourse, conversation, ultimately < *dia-* between + *legein* speak]

ANALOGY **dialect : language ::**
— **a.** bridge : river
— **b.** tunnel : train
— **c.** earth : dig
— **d.** grape : fruit
— **e.** change : progress

179a

b, c, d

a non y mous (ə non′ ə məs)

Some large collectors choose to remain **anonymous**.

Write a definition or synonym:

154a

b, d

pig ment (pig′ mənt)

After scrutinizing the paintings, the art dealer asked Pablo what kind of **pigment** he used.

Write a definition or synonym:

23b

The **coroner** began an investigation into the cause of death. That was his job. Had the deceased, Mr. Coward Craven, died of natural causes, or had he been murdered?

A **coroner** is:
__a. an official who investigates deaths
__b. a physician who specializes in violent accidents
__c. a policeman who investigates murders
__d. a person who pries into the affairs of others

48c

d

rev er ie (rev′ər ē), *n.* **1** dreamy thoughts; dreamy thinking of pleasant things. **2** condition of being lost in dreamy thoughts. Also, **revery.** [< French *rêverie* < *rêver* to dream]

Match the people at the left with the **reveries** at the right.
a. housewife
b. 10-year-old boy
c. newlyweds
d. a math student
e. a sailor at sea
f. a nomad

__ an oasis
__ a new house
__ a port city
__ an electric dishwasher
__ sports
__ a computer

73c

d

mal a dy (mal′ə dē), *n., pl.* **-dies.** **1** any bodily disorder or disease, especially one that is chronic or deep-seated. **2** any unwholesome or disordered condition. [< Old French *maladie* < *malade* ill < Latin *male habitus* doing badly]

Check the sentence(s) in which **malady** is used correctly.
__a. His face was very pale, and he looked as though he suffered from a serious malady.
__b. She received a malady when she fell off her bicycle.
__c. Please play a malady on your banjo.
__d. When one has a malady, one is usually bedridden.

99a

c

re ha bil i tate (rē′ hə bil′ ə tāt)

Today many sufferers from mental illness can be **rehabilitated**.

Write a definition or synonym:

124a

a

skir mish (skėr′ mish)

Lou was wounded in the first **skirmish**.

Write a definition or synonym:

149b

In the **bedlam**, Rafe was lifted to the shoulders of his teammates and carried off the field. The goal posts were torn down. Even the police were unable to stop the wild celebration.

Another word for **bedlam** is:
__a. joy
__b. mirth
__c. fury
__d. uproar

278a

com·mu·ni·ca·ble (ka myu' na ka bal)

Officials in each port check the ship's passengers for **communicable** diseases.

Write a definition or synonym:

b, c, e

253a

fraught (frôt)

Maria is the first to agree that a spy's life is **fraught** with peril.

Write a definition or synonym:

b, d

228b

If one looks at the bridge only from the shore, the construction appears to progress slowly. But when one approaches from a **lateral** direction, one can see how much has been accomplished in a short time.

Another word for **lateral** is:

- —**a.** of the side
- —**b.** from the end
- —**c.** general
- —**d.** from above

203b

These differences in speech are due partly to the differences in national origins of the inhabitants. The **dialects**, however, differ in various parts of the city as well. After a while, some people can recognize the difference between a Bronx and a Brooklyn accent.

The meaning of **dialect** is:

- —**a.** custom; tradition
- —**b.** characteristic speech
- —**c.** national origin
- —**d.** peculiarity

178c

liq·ui·date (lik/wa dāt), v., -dat·ed, -dat·ing. —v.t. 1 clear off or pay (a debt or obligation): liquidate a mortgage. 2 settle the accounts of (a business, etc.) by distributing the assets; clear up the affairs of (a bankrupt). 3 get rid of (an undesirable person or thing). 4 kill ruthlessly; exterminate. —v.i. 5 liquidate debts, etc. [< Medieval Latin liquidatum made clear < Latin liquidus. See LIQUID.] —liq'ui·da'tion, n. —liq'ui·da'tor, n.

c

Check the sentence(s) in which a form of **liquidate** is used correctly.

- —**a.** The children liquidated the snow into water.
- —**b.** The dictator liquidated the revolutionaries.
- —**c.** The gardener liquidated the hornets' nest.
- —**d.** He liquidated all his debts on the first of the month.

153c

scru·ti·nize (skrüt/n iz), v.t., -nized, -niz·ing. examine closely; inspect carefully: The jeweler scrutinized the diamond for flaws. —scru'ti·niz'er, n. —scru'ti·niz'ing·ly, adv.

c

Which of the following would you be most likely to **scrutinize**?

- —**a.** a television show
- —**b.** a used car
- —**c.** a baseball game
- —**d.** a $100 bill

23c

co ro ner (kôr′ə nər, kor′ə nər), *n.* official of a local government whose principal function is to inquire in the presence of a jury into the cause of any death not clearly due to natural causes. [< Anglo-French *corouner* officer of the crown < *coroune*. See CROWN.]

In which of the following sentences is **coroner** used correctly?

__a. A coroner usually wears a crown.
__b. A coroner is a public servant.
__c. A coroner is always the foreman of a jury.
__d. A coroner is a member of the federal government.

49a

rav en ous (rav′ə nəs)

The slimy creature was unlike anything they had ever seen. Unable to move, they stared in horror at its loathesome face and **ravenous** mouth.

Write a definition or synonym:

74a

dis pel (dis pel′)

In the days before modern medicine, people believed in supernatural forces. Many peasants were convinced that Wanda, the lady of the manor, was a witch who could **dispel** their troubles.

Write a definition or synonym:

99b

Trained people help **rehabilitate** the mentally ill by encouraging them to use their talents or by teaching them new skills. More important to mental health, perhaps, is the rebirth of self-respect and self-confidence.

The meaning of **rehabilitate** is:

__a. restore to good condition
__b. return to place of origin
__c. change one's place of residence
__d. remodel

124b

The evening after Lou arrived the guerrillas were involved in a **skirmish** with a small band of enemy soldiers. Lou and the guerrillas were ambushed as they returned from a scouting trip.

The meaning of **skirmish** is:

__a. delaying action
__b. small conflict
__c. ambush
__d. massacre

149c

bed lam (bed′ləm), *n.* **1** noisy confusion; uproar. **2** ARCHAIC. insane asylum; madhouse. [< *Bedlam*, old name for the Hospital of St. Mary of *Bethlehem*, an insane asylum in London]

Check the synonym(s) for **bedlam**:

__a. haste
__b. turmoil
__c. mental hospital
__d. disturbance
__e. bewilderment

153b

A prospective buyer will **scrutinize** a painting closely before making a decision. He will spend considerable time looking at it both from a distance and at close range.

The meaning of **scrutinize** is:
_a. glance at
_b. touch gingerly
_c. inspect carefully
_d. react to

178b

Sometimes the heirs to a stamp collection have no interest in keeping it. They sell the stamps and other property at public auction when they **liquidate** the estate.

The meaning of **liquidate** is:
_a. divide
_b. melt down
_c. dispose of
_d. examine

203a

d, e

di a lect (dī′ ə lekt)

Many **dialects** are used in New York.

Write a definition or synonym:

228a

e

lat er al (lat′ ər əl)

Each day, John takes out his boat to get a **lateral** view of the construction.

Write a definition or synonym:

252c

c

dis cre tion (dis kresh′ən), *n.* **1** quality of being discreet; great carefulness in speech or action; good judgment; wise caution: *Use your own discretion.* **2** freedom to decide or choose: *It is within the principal's discretion to punish a pupil.*

Check each item that is an example of the use of **discretion**.
_a. being told to study one's lesson
_b. making a wise choice
_c. not knowing the answer to a question
_d. not saying something you know would anger someone

277c

a

ex press ly (ek spres′lē), *adv.* **1** in an express manner; plainly; definitely; clearly: *The package is not for you; you are expressly forbidden to touch it.* **2** for the express purpose; on purpose; specially: *You ought to talk to her, since she came expressly to see you.*

Which of the following mean the *opposite* of **expressly**?
_a. intentionally
_b. by chance
_c. uncertainly
_d. exactly
_e. involuntarily

24a

b

di lem ma (də lem′ ə)

The coroner couldn't be sure if the death was natural or not. So Berry Amazing's client was brought to trial for murder. Berry found himself faced with a **dilemma**.

Write a definition or synonym:

49b

The creature dropped below the surface. Tom and Peggy climbed as high as they could into the branches of the only tree nearby. The creature returned to the surface with a full-grown cow in its huge mouth. In an instant the cow disappeared, a victim of the creature's **ravenous** hunger.

Ravenous means:
__**a.** overly anxious
__**b.** very hungry
__**c.** very desirable
__**d.** ferocious

74b

A witch, they thought, might cast an evil spell by using her magical powers. But she might also **dispel** the evil, if she chose to, as easily as the wind scatters the dust from the road.

Dispel means:
__**a.** remove
__**b.** enlarge
__**c.** drive away
__**d.** exaggerate

99c

a

re ha bil i tate (rē′hə bil′ə tāt), *v.t.*, **-tat ed, -tat ing.** 1 restore to a good condition; make over in a new form: *The old neighborhood is to be rehabilitated.* 2 restore to former standing, rank, rights, privileges, reputation, etc.: *The former criminal completely rehabilitated himself and again became a trusted and respected citizen.* 3 restore to a condition of good health, or to a level of useful activity, by means of medical treatment and therapy. [< Medieval Latin *rehabilitatum* made fit again < Latin *re-* + *habilis* fit] —**re′ha bil′i ta′tion,** *n.*

Which of the following are examples of **rehabilitation?**
__**a.** rebuilding a bombed factory
__**b.** converting a barn
__**c.** painting a picture
__**d.** reorganizing a business firm
__**e.** learning to walk
__**f.** learning to walk after a broken leg

124c

b

skir mish (skėr′mish), *n.* 1 a brief fight between small groups of soldiers. 2 a slight conflict, argument, contest, etc. —*v.i.* take part in a skirmish. [< Old French *eskirmiss-,* a form of *eskirmir,* originally, ward off; of Germanic origin] —**skir′mish er,** *n.*

In which of the following places would a **skirmish** be most likely to occur?
__**a.** tea party
__**b.** hospital
__**c.** athletic field
__**d.** great battlefield
__**e.** classroom
__**f.** picket line

150a

, c, d

con clu sive (kən klü′ siv)

After the game, our coach told us that we had given him **conclusive** proof that the best team is not always the winning team.

Write a definition or synonym:

145

153a

d

scru ti nize (skrüt′ n īz)

At last it was opening day for Pablo's one-man show. The first person to arrive was an important art dealer. Pablo stood and watched as the dealer began to **scrutinize** each painting.

Write a definition or synonym:

178a

e, d, e

liq ui date (lik′ wə dāt)

I have acquired some of my most prized stamps from estates that are being **liquidated**.

Write a definition or synonym:

202c

d

di verse (də vèrs′, dī vèrs′), *adj.* 1 not alike; different: *diverse opinions.* 2 varied; diversified: *A person of diverse interests can talk on many subjects.* [variant of *divers*] —**diverse′ly**, *adv.* —**di verse′ness**, *n.*

Which of the following words mean about the same as **diverse**?
—**a.** many
—**b.** unusual
—**c.** uniform
—**d.** varied
—**e.** dissimilar

227c

b

e lon gate (i lông′gāt, i long′gāt), *v.,* **-gat ed, -gat ing,** *adj.* —*v.t., v.i.* make or become longer; lengthen; extend; stretch: *A rubber band elongates easily.* —*adj.* 1 long and thin: *the elongate leaf of a willow.* 2 lengthened. [< Latin *elongatum* lengthened < *ex-* out + *longus* long]

ANALOGY elongate : pull :: compress :
—**a.** stretch
—**b.** sag
—**c.** push
—**d.** lengthen
—**e.** squeeze

252b

A single lapse in **discretion** might blow Maria's cover and cost her her life.

Another word for **discretion** is:
—**a.** rashness
—**b.** direction
—**c.** caution
—**d.** ethics

277b

It is possible to find "authentic" souvenirs of one country that have been manufactured in another. These have been made **expressly** for the tourists who cannot tell the difference.

Expressly means:
—**a.** specially
—**b.** cheaply
—**c.** speedily
—**d.** by hand

24b

Should he allow his client, Connie Craven, to take the stand at her murder trial? She was so dumb, she would probably say the wrong thing. But it would look worse if she didn't testify in her own defense. It was a real **dilemma**.

Dilemma means:
__**a.** serious circumstances
__**b.** prejudiced jury
__**c.** difficult choice
__**d.** impossible decision

49c

b

rav en ous (rav′ə nəs), *adj.* **1** very hungry.
2 greedy. **3** rapacious. —**rav′en ous ly,**
adv. —**rav′en ous ness,** *n.*

Check any of the following that might be considered **ravenous.**
__**a.** people listening to an after-dinner speaker
__**b.** a fox watching a chicken yard
__**c.** a turtle sunning on a rock
__**d.** a construction worker opening a lunch box

74c

c

dis pel (dis pel′), *v.t.,* **-pelled, -pel ling.**
drive away and scatter; disperse. See **scatter**
for synonym study. [< Latin *dispellere* < *dis-*
away + *pellere* to drive]

Check the word(s) that mean(s) about the *opposite* of **dispel.**
__**a.** dismiss
__**b.** repel
__**c.** compel
__**d.** gather
__**e.** erase
__**f.** collect

100a

a, b,
d, f

stig ma (stig′ mə)

There is less **stigma** attached to mental illness today than in past years.

Write a definition or synonym:

125a

c, f

cha grin (shə grin′)

Much to Lou's **chagrin,** he was wounded in the leg.

Write a definition or synonym:

150b

Usually, an undefeated season is **conclusive** proof of a team's excellence. But in this case a mediocre team with one superlative player had walked off with the victory.

Conclusive means:
__**a.** defensive
__**b.** defeating
__**c.** decisive
__**d.** rewarding

152c

b

fru gal (frü′gəl), *adj.* **1** avoiding waste; tending to avoid unnecessary spending; saving; thrifty: *a frugal housekeeper.* See **economical** for synonym study. **2** costing little; barely sufficient: *He ate a frugal supper of bread and milk.* [< Latin *frugalis* < *frugi* temperate, useful, ultimately < *fructus* fruit, produce. See FRUIT.] —**fru′gal ly,** *adv.*

ANALOGY **frugal : lavish :: generous :**
__**a.** empty
__**b.** bare
__**c.** welcome
__**d.** stingy
__**e.** healthy

177c

d

cre den tial (kri den′shəl), *n.* **1** something that gives or recommends credit or confidence. **2 credentials,** *pl.* letters of introduction; references.

In which of the following situations would you need **credentials**?
__**a.** trying out for a school play
__**b.** going to church
__**c.** applying for a job
__**d.** registering for college
__**e.** getting access to secret government data

202b

It is sometimes called "the great melting pot" because the population is made up of so many **diverse** nationalities.

A synonym for **diverse** is:
__**a.** exotic
__**b.** divided
__**c.** foreign
__**d.** different

227b

As segments are added to each side of the bridge, the sides appear to **elongate**. Finally, they will meet in the middle.

A synonym for **elongate** is:
__**a.** build
__**b.** lengthen
__**c.** grow
__**d.** enlarge

252a

a, b, d, e

dis cre tion (dis kresh′ ən)

Many qualities are necessary to be a successful spy, but by far the most important is **discretion**.

Write a definition or synonym:

277a

a, d

ex press ly (ek spres′ lē)

Some manufacturers specialize in souvenirs made **expressly** for tourists.

Write a definition or synonym:

24c

c

di lem ma (də lem′ə), *n.* situation requiring a choice between two alternatives, which are or appear equally unfavorable; difficult choice. See **predicament** for synonym study. [< Greek *dilēmma* < *di-* two + *lēmma* premise]

Which of the following expressions might be used to express a **dilemma**?
—**a.** "duck soup"
—**b.** "in a fix"
—**c.** "nowhere to turn"
—**d.** "embarrassment of riches"

50a

b, d

strewn (strün)

As they ran from the creature, Tom and Peggy found themselves on a large field which was **strewn** with scraps of clothing. Peggy stumbled over a pile of bones.

Write a definition or synonym:

75a

d, f

in voke (in vōk′)

The peasants were sure they must **invoke** Wanda's help if their lives and the lives of their families were to be saved.

Write a definition or synonym:

100b

Unfortunately, the **stigma** of having once suffered from mental illness can haunt a person for life. People concerned with mental health look forward to the day when this stain on a person's reputation can be eradicated completely.

Stigma means:
—**a.** a bad smell
—**b.** confusion
—**c.** a feeling of horror
—**d.** a mark of disgrace

125b

His **chagrin** was caused not only by his shame at being wounded on his first expedition, but also by the knowledge that he would have to leave his newfound guerrilla friends.

Another word for **chagrin** is:
—**a.** rage
—**b.** embarrassment
—**c.** fear
—**d.** tantrum

150c

c

con clu sive (kən klü′siv), *adj.* decisive; convincing; final. —**con clu′sive ly,** *adv.* —**con clu′sive ness,** *n.*

Check the sentence(s) in which **conclusive** can be correctly substituted for the italicized word.
—**a.** The murderer's identity was revealed on the *final* page of the book.
—**b.** The witness's testimony was *decisive*, and the defendant was eventually convicted.

152b

Their shortage of funds made it necessary for Sonia to be **frugal**. Nevertheless, her talent for decoration allowed her to transform Pablo's quarters into an art gallery without much expense.

Another word for **frugal** is:
- __a. lean
- __b. saving
- __c. wasteful
- __d. careful

177b

If they provide me with **credentials** which show them to be ethical people, the stamps they are selling are likely to be genuine. Of course, not all letters of introduction or recommendation are genuine, either. But I hate to take unnecessary chances.

The meaning of **credentials** is:
- __a. statements
- __b. background
- __c. credit cards
- __d. references

202a

b, c

di verse (də vėrs′, dī vėrs′)

New York is made up of many **diverse** peoples and neighborhoods.

Write a definition or synonym:

227a

c

e lon gate (i lông′ gāt, i long′ gāt)

Gradually each side of the bridge seemed to **elongate**.

Write a definition or synonym:

251c

c

fic ti tious (fik tish′əs), *adj.*   1 not real; imaginary; made-up: *Characters in novels are usually fictitious.*   2 assumed in order to deceive; false: *a fictitious name.* —**fic ti′- tious ly,** *adv.* —**fic ti′tious ness,** *n.*

Which of the following are **fictitious**?
- __a. fairy tale
- __b. alias
- __c. autobiography
- __d. fable
- __e. lie
- __f. history textbook

276c

c

dupe (düp, dyüp), *n., v.,* **duped, dup ing.** —*n.* 1 person easily deceived or tricked. 2 one who is being deluded or tricked. —*v.t.* deceive or trick. [< French] —**dup′- er,** *n.*

In which of the following can **dupe(d)** be substituted for the italicized word?
- __a. He was easily *fooled* by the clever magician.
- __b. Watch the dog do the *trick*.
- __c. I cannot *solve* the puzzle.
- __d. She was *deceived* by his flattering promises.

25a

feign (fān)

Connie took the stand early in the trial. The prosecutor, Franklin Ferter, was sure Connie's lack of intelligence was **feigned**.

Write a definition or synonym:

b, c

50b

The discarded bones and bits of hair and clothing were **strewn** carelessly over the countryside. They appeared to have been dropped from a great height.

"If this is a dream," Peggy said, gasping in terror, "you can wake me anytime!"

Another word for **strewn** is:
—**a.** spattered
—**b.** thrown
—**c.** scattered
—**d.** placed

75b

A crowd of peasant women approached the manor house. They fell down on their knees and began offering prayers and earnest appeals to **invoke** Wanda's aid.

The meaning of **invoke** is:
—**a.** demand
—**b.** receive
—**c.** beg for
—**d.** question

100c

d

stig ma (stig′mə), *n., pl.* **-mas** or **-ma ta.**
1 mark of disgrace; stain or reproach on one's reputation. 2 a distinguishing mark or sign. 3 an abnormal spot or mark in the skin, especially one that bleeds or turns red. 4 the part of the pistil of a plant that receives the pollen. See **pistil** for diagram. 5 **stigmata,** *pl.* marks or wounds like the five wounds on the crucified body of Christ, in the hands, feet, and side, said to appear supernaturally on the bodies of certain persons. 6 ARCHAIC. a special mark burned on a slave or criminal. [< Latin < Greek, mark, puncture < *stizein* to mark, tattoo]

Check the sentence(s) in which **stigma** is used correctly.
—**a.** His unmarked face showed the stigma that led to his arrest.
—**b.** The girl was identified by a stigma on her left hand.
—**c.** Stigma is a familiar word to horticulturists.
—**d.** The children bore the stigma of their father's crimes.

125c

b

cha grin (shə grin′), *n.* a feeling of disappointment, failure, or humiliation. —*v.t.* cause to feel chagrin. [< French, apparently < *chat* cat + *grigner* to purse (the lips)]

In which of the following situations would you be most likely to feel **chagrin**?
—**a.** receiving a straight-A report card
—**b.** hitting 4 home runs in a baseball game
—**c.** striking out 4 times in a baseball game
—**d.** sewing up a dress on the wrong side
—**e.** being elected class president

b

LESSON 16

One-Man Show

Pablo Lucasto and Sonia Chase had been close friends since their graduation from art school. While Sonia had been sensible and taken a job as a designer for a clothing manufacturer, Pablo continued to believe he was an exceptionally talented artist. He was. But until he could put together his first one-man show, no one would ever know it.

276b

People who are well-bred and who would never dream of doing anything disreputable are often easy **dupes** for dishonest salespersons.

A **dupe** is a:
—a. stupid person
—b. person with latent criminal tendencies
—c. person who is easily tricked
—d. person who pretends to be someone else

251b

By using **fictitious** names, Maria keeps her real identity secret.

Fictitious means:
—a. foreign
—b. abbreviated
—c. made-up
—d. international

226c

hy drau lic (hī drô/lik), *adj.* 1 having to do with water or other liquids at rest or in motion. 2 operated by the pressure of water or other liquids in motion, especially when forced through an opening or openings: a *hydraulic press.* 3 hardening under water: *hydraulic cement.* 4 having to do with hydraulics: *hydraulic engineering, hydraulic mining.* [< Latin *hydraulicus,* ultimately < Greek *hydōr* water + *aulos* pipe] —**hy drau'li cal ly,** *adv.*

d

Hydraulics is the science of:
—a. navigation
—b. purifying water
—c. fluids in motion
—d. powerboating

201c

au ra (ôr'ə), *n., pl.* **au ras, au rae** (ôr'ē). 1 something supposed to come from a person or thing and surround him or it as an atmosphere: *An aura of holiness enveloped the saint.* 2 a subtle emanation or exhalation from any substance, as the odor of flowers. [< Latin, breeze, breath < Greek]

c

Check the sentence(s) in which **aura** is used correctly.
—a. There was an aura of sap from the tree.
—b. There was an aura of mystery about the stranger.
—c. Their friendship created an aura of goodwill.
—d. She put on her best aura for the ceremonies.
—e. This restaurant is noted for its aura.

177a

cre den tial (kri den' shal)

When people write to me and offer a valuable stamp for sale, I always check their **credentials**.

a, c

Write a definition or synonym:

152a

fru gal (frü' gal)

Sonia had to be quite **frugal** when she made the arrangements for Pablo's show.

a, d

Write a definition or synonym:

25b

Ferter thought that no one could really be as dumb as Connie Craven seemed to be. She must be **feigning** stupidity. Ferter questioned Connie closely, trying to trap her and make her drop that mask of foolish innocence.

The meaning of **feign** is:
— **a.** ignore
— **b.** pretend
— **c.** be stupid
— **d.** be honest

50c

c

strew (strü), *v.t.*, **strewed, strewed** or **strewn, strew ing.** 1 scatter or sprinkle: *She strewed seeds in her garden.* 2 cover with something scattered or sprinkled. 3 be scattered or sprinkled over. [Old English *strēowian*]

Check the sentence(s) in which **strewn** is used correctly.
— **a.** When a dog has been after the chickens, there are feathers strewn all over the yard.
— **b.** An ear of corn, covered with butter and lightly strewn with salt, is delicious.
— **c.** He ate strewn prunes for breakfast.
— **d.** The burglars left the books strewn around the library.

75c

c

in voke (in vōk′), *v.t.*, **-voked, -vok ing.** 1 call on in prayer; appeal to for help or protection. 2 appeal to for confirmation or judgment: *invoke an authority.* 3 ask earnestly for; beg for: *The condemned criminal invoked the judge's mercy.* 4 call forth with magic words or charms. [< Latin *invocare* < *in-* on + *vocare* to call] —**in vok′er**, *n.*

Check the sentence(s) in which a form of **invoke** is used correctly.
— **a.** I invoked my father's leniency in punishing me for the foolish prank.
— **b.** She was invoked into murder.
— **c.** Cinderella invoked her fairy godmother's aid.
— **d.** She invoked the children for the prank.
— **e.** The ancient Greeks constantly invoked the aid of their deities.

LESSON 11

Mutiny on the Amazon

Lord and Lady Stanley were famous explorers of the Amazon River region. The natives who acted as their guides and bearers hated them both. Each outdid the other in cruel treatment of their workers. All of this changed on one memorable river trip.

126a

c, d

sil hou ette (sil′ ü et′)

An enemy soldier had caught just a glimpse of Lou's **silhouette.**

Write a definition or synonym:

151a

ben e fac tor (ben′ ə fak′ tər, ben′ ə fak′ tər)

Pablo was not fortunate enough to have a **benefactor.**

Write a definition or synonym:

151c

d

ben e fac tor (ben′ə fak′tər, ben′ə fak′tər),
n. person who has helped others, either by
gifts of money or by some kind act. [< Late
Latin < Latin *benefactum* befitted < *bene*
well + *facere* do]

Check the expression(s) that best describe(s) a
benefactor.
__a. "friend in need"
__b. "left in the lurch"
__c. "person of note"
__d. "good Samaritan"

176c

b

eth i cal (eth′ə kəl), *adj.* 1 having to do with
standards of right and wrong; of ethics or
morals. See **moral** for synonym study.
2 morally right: *ethical conduct.* 3 in ac-
cordance with formal or professional rules of
right and wrong: *It is not considered ethical
for a doctor to repeat a patient's confidences.*
4 (of drugs) that cannot be dispensed by a
pharmacist without a doctor's prescription.
—**eth′i cal ly,** *adv.*

Which of the following would *not* be **ethical**?
__a. giving out answers before a final examination
__b. helping one's colleague in biology laboratory
__c. keeping a $10 bill you found in the locker room
__d. beating your best friend at tennis

201b

The **aura** of glamor and excitement is especially
noticeable in the theater district in the early evening.
The sidewalks are filled with animated people,
chatting gaily in anticipation of a stimulating
performance.

Another word for **aura** is:
__a. heat
__b. sensation
__c. atmosphere
__d. speed

226b

Work was held up for several days when a water leak
developed in the feed line to the main cylinder of the
crane's **hydraulic** system.

Hydraulic means:
__a. powered by steam
__b. electrically operated
__c. generating power
__d. operated by water

251a

fic ti tious (fik tish′ əs)

Maria has five or six **fictitious** passports so she can
travel anywhere in the world in safety.

Write a definition or synonym:

276a

a, b,
c, d,
f

dupe (düp, dyüp)

Rhoda knew that unethical people can make **dupes** of
wealthy travelers.

Write a definition or synonym:

b

25c

feign (fān), *v.t.* 1 put on a false appearance of; make believe; pretend: *Some animals feign death when in danger.* 2 make up to deceive; invent falsely: *feign an excuse.* —*v.i.* make oneself appear; pretend (to be): *He isn't sick; he is only feigning.* [< Old French *feign-*, a form of *feindre* feign < Latin *fingere* to form] —**feign'er**, *n.*

In which of the following sentences is a form of **feign** used correctly?

__a. He feigned at me with his sword.
__b. A possum feigns sleep when in danger.
__c. Another feigned animal is the unicorn.
__d. She feigned anger at the embarrassing accusation.

Go back to page 1 and continue on frame 26a.

a, d

LESSON   The Slime Creature, Part 2

Tom and Peggy managed to get back to the bus in time for the return trip to the city. The next day, they heard that the monster of Gray Lake had been killed and transported to the laboratory of Dr. Roger Thornbill.

Go back to page 1 and continue on frame 51a.

a, c, e

76a

hum bug (hum' bug')

Today, of course, most people believe that witches and magic spells are **humbug**.

Write a definition or synonym:

Go back to page 1 and continue on frame 76b.

101a

tor rid (tôr' id, tor' id)

Along the banks of the mighty Amazon River, the climate is **torrid**.

Write a definition or synonym:

Go back to page 1 and continue on frame 101b.

126b

Lou made a perfect target for the enemy bullet when he was **silhouetted** against the moonlit sky. It was too dark to see his face or any other details. But Lou's general shape was clearly visible.

Silhouette means:
__a. outline
__b. outlying
__c. profile
__d. darkness

Go back to page 1 and continue on frame 126c.

151b

In a way, Sonia had been a **benefactor** to Pablo. She had not contributed money, but she had given a lot of time and energy when she helped Pablo set up his paintings for display.

A **benefactor** is a person who gives:
__a. comfort
__b. advice
__c. criticism
__d. help

Turn the book upside down and continue on frame 151c.

EDL WORD CLUES MASTERY TESTS*

Elinor H. Kinney
Rumson-Fair Haven (N.J.) Regional High School

When you finish each Word Clues lesson, how well do you re-member the meanings of the words you have studied? The Word Clues Mastery Tests will help you answer this question.

There is one test for each lesson in the book. Each test has ten questions, one on each word taught in the lesson. These target words are set in **boldface** type.

Five kinds of questions are used in the tests. Here are the di-rections for each kind.

Definitions in Context: Choose the best meaning of the tar-get word in each sentence.

Synonyms or Similar Meanings: Select the word or phrase that is closest in meaning to the target word.

Antonyms or Opposite Meanings: Select the word or phrase that is most nearly opposite in meaning to the target word.

Words in Context: Choose the word that best completes the sentence.

Analogies: Choose the word or phrase that best completes each analogy.

Answer all questions as directed by your instructor. Caution: Pay attention to the headings because the kinds of questions are not always in the same order.

---

*The authors of the Word Clues Mastery Tests for the various levels are as follows:

G	Carolyn A. Hill	K	Joseph J. Dignan
H	Marie H. Hughes	L	Paul A. Fuchs and
I	Margaret B. Holton		Mary Ellen Grassin
J	Elinor H. Kinney	M	William A. Speiser

NOTE: This edition of Word Clues J contains a final posttest. For this test, 25 words have been randomly chosen as representative of the total number of words taught. Students who score 80% or higher can move to the next higher book.

DEFINITIONS IN CONTEXT

11. **Scavengers** are quickly attracted to the kills of carnivorous animals.
    a. animals that feed on decaying matter
    b. animals that hunt smaller animals
    c. animals that kill their own kind
    d. animals that are vegetarians
    e. animals that see in the dark

12. The **intensity** of the cold soon numbed my nose and cheeks.
    a. increase
    b. great quantity
    c. temperature
    d. extreme strength
    e. persistence

SYNONYMS OR SIMILAR MEANINGS

13. **compile**
    a. identify   d. discover
    b. collect   e. expand
    c. analyze

14. **dilate**
    a. contract   d. close
    b. darken   e. lessen
    c. expand

ANTONYMS OR OPPOSITE MEANINGS

15. **exotic**
    a. foreign   d. different
    b. curious   e. ordinary
    c. unusual

WORDS IN CONTEXT

16. For greater protection, the crown jewels were kept in a(n) ____ part of the castle.
    a. dynamic   d. cryptic
    b. carnivorous   e. imperial
    c. inaccessible

17. Our cat's ____ instincts are quite obvious when he spots and stalks an unwary bird or squirrel.
    a. exotic   d. vegetarian
    b. listless   e. carnivorous
    c. canine

18. The gardener's ____ manner led the police to discover the body buried beneath the bluebells.
    a. listless   d. furtive
    b. dynamic   e. inaccessible
    c. carnivorous

ANALOGIES

19. curtail : increase :: maul :
    a. caress   d. dilate
    b. compile   e. seethe
    c. mangle

20. furtive : shifty :: listless :
    a. exotic   d. dynamic
    b. languid   e. inaccessible
    c. carnivorous

SYNONYMS OR SIMILAR MEANINGS

1. **dignitary**
   a. a government employee
   b. a person of high rank
   c. a member of a jury
   d. an elderly person
   e. a newspaper employee

2. **assess**
   a. organize anew
   b. estimate the value of
   c. be responsible for
   d. make like new
   e. change the meaning of

ANTONYMS OR OPPOSITE MEANINGS

3. **reorganize**
   a. antagonize   d. retain
   b. remodel   e. renew
   c. revise

DEFINITIONS IN CONTEXT

4. The sizable **appropriation** for a new swimming pool delighted the student body.
   a. reorganization   d. renovation
   b. ownership   e. allotment of money
   c. operation

5. A **dynamic** presentation often arouses audience response.
   a. destructive   d. forceful
   b. designated   e. seething
   c. powerless

6. Many workers were needed to **renovate** the colonial village.
   a. restore   d. assess
   b. rent   e. fill
   c. design

WORDS IN CONTEXT

7. In order to ____, the family limited its spending for luxuries.
   a. economize   d. revise
   b. evaluate   e. seethe
   c. assess

8. The general ____ the oil refinery as the primary target.
   a. induced   d. evaluated
   b. curtailed   e. designated
   c. segregated

ANALOGIES

9. renovate : renew :: seethe :
   a. talk   d. assess
   b. blush   e. reorganize
   c. boil

10. economize : cut expenses :: curtail :
    a. seethe   d. exchange
    b. reduce   e. function
    c. designate

WORD CLUES MASTERY TEST J-4

DEFINITIONS IN CONTEXT

31. Because of her experience and success in the courtroom, she was sought as a **consultant** by several law firms.
    a. client
    b. adviser
    c. laborer
    d. official
    e. dignitary

32. Federal law **necessitates** that citizens pay an income tax.
    a. allays
    b. urges
    c. compiles
    d. requires
    e. rules out.

SYNONYMS OR SIMILAR MEANINGS

33. **recuperate**
    a. transfuse   d. consult
    b. succumb   e. recover
    c. stand

34. **transfusion**
    a. transfer   d. clot
    b. removal   e. solution
    c. transaction

ANTONYMS OR OPPOSITE MEANINGS

35. **sterile**
    a. beneficial   d. unproductive
    b. avid   e. chronic
    c. fertile

36. **vigilant**
    a. oblivious   d. erect
    b. wary   e. alert
    c. tense

WORDS IN CONTEXT

37. Hurricane warnings made it ____ that residents evacuate their homes at once.
    a. chronic   d. imperative
    b. sterile   e. cryptic
    c. vigilant

38. His ____ lateness required strong disciplinary action.
    a. convalescent   d. imperative
    b. cryptic   e. dynamic
    c. chronic

ANALOGIES

39. **convalescent : recovering ::**
    a. vigilant : peaceful   d. imperative : unnecessary
    b. chronic : occasional   e. pertinent : related
    c. plausible : honest

40. **allay : relieve ::**
    a. necessitate : feign   d. maul : renovate
    b. curtail : lessen   e. recuperate : reorganize
    c. dilate : contract

WORD CLUES MASTERY TEST J-3

DEFINITIONS IN CONTEXT

21. The final report included information **gleaned** from many sources.
    a. gathered little by little
    b. slowly copied
    c. expanded slightly
    d. typed in duplicate
    e. quickly read

22. Whether to leap into the shark-filled waters or to cling to the rapidly burning boat: this was his **dilemma.**
    a. prejudiced opinion
    b. difficult choice
    c. main problem
    d. exotic dream
    e. serious circumstance

WORDS IN CONTEXT

23. The message taken from the spy was so ____ that it was no help to his captors.
    a. deadly   d. dynamic
    b. cryptic   e. diverse
    c. pertinent

24. Violent behavior is often evident in ____ persons.
    a. glib   d. plausible
    b. anonymous   e. demented
    c. listless

SYNONYMS OR SIMILAR MEANINGS

25. **plausible**
    a. true   d. natural
    b. honest   e. careless
    c. reasonable

26. **fallacy**
    a. weakness   d. intensity
    b. prejudice   e. falsity
    c. dilemma

ANTONYMS OR OPPOSITE MEANINGS

27. **glibly**
    a. smoothly   d. hesitantly
    b. plausibly   e. rapidly
    c. incessantly

28. **pertinent**
    a. impudent   d. important
    b. disrespectful   e. impolite
    c. inconsequential

ANALOGIES

29. **scavenger : feeds :: coroner :**
    a. economizes   d. investigates
    b. curtails   e. renovates
    c. feigns

30. **dilate : expand :: feign :**
    a. pretend   d. assess
    b. glean   e. compile
    c. maul

ANTONYMS OR OPPOSITE MEANINGS
51. vertebrate
   - **a.** having bones
   - **b.** having no backbone
   - **c.** having arms and legs
   - **d.** having a backbone
   - **e.** walking on hind legs

52. embryo
   - **a.** an untried idea
   - **b.** an unhatched chicken
   - **c.** developed plant or animal
   - **d.** central part of a thing
   - **e.** an organism with a backbone

SYNONYMS OR SIMILAR MEANINGS
53. incision
   - **a.** mark
   - **b.** scrape
   - **c.** bore
   - **d.** cut
   - **e.** scratch

54. nucleus
   - **a.** structure
   - **b.** brain
   - **c.** skeleton
   - **d.** embryo
   - **e.** center

DEFINITIONS IN CONTEXT
55. Organisms found in the sea may well be the food source of the future.
   - **a.** living bodies
   - **b.** undeveloped creatures
   - **c.** social groups
   - **d.** sea shells
   - **e.** sea weeds

56. Her interest in plants and her concern for animals seemed a natural result of her love for **biology.**
   - **a.** mutations
   - **b.** invertebrates
   - **c.** science of living matter
   - **d.** science of dissection
   - **e.** science of the universe

WORDS IN CONTEXT
57. Getting along well with one's _____ is basic to a compatible working relationship.
   - **a.** reveries
   - **b.** assessors
   - **c.** antagonists
   - **d.** colleagues
   - **e.** scavengers

58. Some very delicious fruits have been produced as a result of a(n) _____.
   - **a.** mutation
   - **b.** embryo
   - **c.** incision
   - **d.** organism
   - **e.** vertebrate

ANALOGIES
59. dissect : analyze ::
   - **a.** compile : seethe
   - **b.** curtail : dilate
   - **c.** feign : commend
   - **d.** glean : gather slowly
   - **e.** renovate : seclude

60. invertebrate : worm ::
   - **a.** dignitary : slave
   - **b.** fallacy : truth
   - **c.** convalescent : corpse
   - **d.** reverie : reality
   - **e.** scavenger : vulture

ANALOGIES
41. dulling : invigorating ::
   - **a.** stagnant : active
   - **b.** opaque : dark
   - **c.** chronic : habitual
   - **d.** imperative : urgent
   - **e.** secluded : withdrawn

42. urban : citified ::
   - **a.** suburban : town
   - **b.** country : farms
   - **c.** rural : countrified
   - **d.** populous : crowded
   - **e.** apartment house : town house

DEFINITIONS IN CONTEXT
43. Timid and shy, he became a dashing hero in his favorite **reverie.**
   - **a.** thoughtfulness
   - **b.** solitude
   - **c.** imagination
   - **d.** daydream
   - **e.** mire

44. Ravenous after their victory, the team devoured all the available refreshments.
   - **a.** overly anxious
   - **b.** very hungry
   - **c.** ferocious
   - **d.** angry
   - **e.** alone

SYNONYMS OR SIMILAR MEANINGS
45. secluded
   - **a.** chronic
   - **b.** dark
   - **c.** bracing
   - **d.** inhospitable
   - **e.** isolated

46. invigorating
   - **a.** withdrawn
   - **b.** listless
   - **c.** stimulating
   - **d.** desolate
   - **e.** rippling

ANTONYMS OR OPPOSITE MEANINGS
47. solitude
   - **a.** privacy
   - **b.** isolation
   - **c.** togetherness
   - **d.** daydream
   - **e.** intensity

48. opaque
   - **a.** dull
   - **b.** obscure
   - **c.** stupid
   - **d.** transparent
   - **e.** frightening

WORDS IN CONTEXT
49. After the storm, the streets were _____ with fallen branches, wires, and debris.
   - **a.** secluded
   - **b.** chronic
   - **c.** opaque
   - **d.** vigilant
   - **e.** strewn

50. Because of the unexpected rain, the hikers found themselves in _____ up to their knees.
   - **a.** solitude
   - **b.** mire
   - **c.** reverie
   - **d.** fallacy
   - **e.** dilemma

ANALOGIES

71. flail : grain ::
 a. assess : coroners
 b. renovate : deities
 c. delve : necessitate
 d. pulverize : grind
 e. compile : data

72. humbug : fraud ::
 a. biology : geology
 b. cryptic : crypt
 c. coroner : corpse
 d. colleague : associate
 e. dignitary : scavenger

DEFINITIONS IN CONTEXT

73. On long winter evenings, the grandfather **narrated** marvelous tales of mystery, adventure, and fantasy.
 a. related   d. suggested
 b. made up   e. uncovered
 c. acted out

74. The stormy sea was whipped into **froth** by the wind.
 a. peaks   d. edge
 b. tide   e. foam
 c. crest

SYNONYMS OR SIMILAR MEANINGS

75. ire
 a. curiosity   d. patience
 b. mire   e. doubt
 c. anger

76. inquisitive
 a. thirsty   d. sickly
 b. curious   e. angry
 c. restless

77. manor
 a. ranch   d. estate
 b. apartment   e. hotel
 c. farm

ANTONYMS OR OPPOSITE MEANINGS

78. dispel
 a. gather   d. strew
 b. disperse   e. relate
 c. repel

WORDS IN CONTEXT

79. The strange _____ left its victims weak, paralyzed, and near death.
 a. incision   d. humbug
 b. malady   e. manor
 c. froth

80. The starving peasants _____ their lord for food and supplies.
 a. narrated   d. dispelled
 b. flailed   e. pulverized
 c. invoked

DEFINITIONS IN CONTEXT

61. His many trips to study volcanoes and glaciers were a result of his deep interest in **geology.**
 a. study of the world
 b. study of natives
 c. study of treasures
 d. study of climate
 e. study of the earth's crust

62. Through the beautifully carved **portal,** one caught a glimpse of the distant castle.
 a. path
 b. entrance
 c. window
 d. corner
 e. banister

SYNONYMS OR SIMILAR MEANINGS

63. strata
 a. intelligence   d. civilization
 b. culture   e. customs
 c. levels

64. delve
 a. grind   d. search
 b. allay   e. hide
 c. dilate

ANTONYMS OR OPPOSITE MEANINGS

65. oblivion
 a. being forgotten   d. being well-remembered
 b. being buried   e. being dissected
 c. being convalescent

66. diligent
 a. industrious   d. furtive
 b. swift   e. lazy
 c. sober

WORDS IN CONTEXT

67. Outside Rome there are many _____ where early Christians were buried.
 a. crypts   d. tenements
 b. portals   e. hospitals
 c. amphitheaters

68. Fans crowded into the _____ to watch the athletic event of the season.
 a. exits   d. crypts
 b. amphitheater   e. cave
 c. strata

ANALOGIES

69. pulverize : demolish :: renovate :
 a. strew   d. renew
 b. allay   e. mire
 c. curtail

70. vertebrate : mammal :: deity :
 a. coroner   d. furtive
 b. colleague   e. chronic
 c. goddess

WORD CLUES MASTERY TEST J-10

ANALOGIES

91. **psychiatrist : mental disease ::**
    a. horticulturist : flowers
    b. deity : economize
    c. stagnant : sluggish
    d. dilate : contract
    e. malady : health

92. **narcotic : dulls ::**
    a. manor : fortress
    b. delve : dissect
    c. hybrid : pulverizes
    d. froth : ire
    e. sea breeze : invigorates

93. **stigma : mark ::**
    a. humbug : feign
    b. allay : glean
    c. dilemma : puzzle
    d. symmetry : solitude
    e. portal : urban

DEFINITIONS IN CONTEXT

94. Since the **jargon** of the actors was unfamiliar to her, she felt ill at ease at the gathering.
    a. foreign words
    b. special language
    c. baby talk
    d. falsehood
    e. pronunciation

95. The only witness was in a state of **hysteria** and could not be questioned.
    a. physical pain
    b. a contagious disease
    c. deep sleep
    d. stubborn silence
    e. nervous disorder

SYNONYMS OR SIMILAR MEANINGS

96. **induce**
    a. lessen
    b. prevent
    c. curtail
    d. persuade
    e. allay

97. **eradicate**
    a. eliminate
    b. heal
    c. control
    d. relieve
    e. help

ANTONYMS OR OPPOSITE MEANINGS

98. **despondent**
    a. melancholic
    b. elated
    c. anxious
    d. dejected
    e. furtive

WORDS IN CONTEXT

99. Her knowledge of _____ helped her understand the emotionally disturbed child.
    a. stigma
    b. jargon
    c. narcotics
    d. psychology
    e. horticulture

100. The _____ of mentally disturbed persons is hastened if they can live and work with normal persons.
    a. rehabilitation
    b. hysteria
    c. eradication
    d. symmetry
    e. psychology

WORD CLUES MASTERY TEST J-9

DEFINITIONS IN CONTEXT

81. Her evident dedication as well as her long years of service accounted for her **prestige** among her colleagues.
    a. pride
    b. knowledge
    c. reputation
    d. talent
    e. honesty

82. Pills and capsules represent an advance over medicines that are dispensed in **soluble** form.
    a. able to be hardened
    b. able to be crushed
    c. able to be injected
    d. able to be ripened
    e. able to be dissolved

SYNONYMS OR SIMILAR MEANINGS

83. **germinate**
    a. ripen
    b. sprout
    c. fertilize
    d. mature
    e. die

84. **horticulture**
    a. gardening
    b. agriculture
    c. farming
    d. blooming
    e. reaping

ANTONYMS OR OPPOSITE MEANINGS

85. **deficient**
    a. superior
    b. faulty
    c. glib
    d. opaque
    e. incomplete

86. **enhance**
    a. enlarge
    b. increase
    c. scent
    d. augment
    e. detract

WORDS IN CONTEXT

87. Unidentified flying objects are part of the _____ of our age.
    a. dignitary
    b. symmetry
    c. phenomena
    d. prestige
    e. oblivion

88. The precise _____ of the sculpture was marred by a slight chip on the right ear.
    a. dignitary
    b. horticulture
    c. phenomenon
    d. seclusion
    e. symmetry

ANALOGIES

89. **hybrid : mule ::**
    a. dilemma : solution
    b. convalescent : corpse
    c. carnivorous : vegetable
    d. invertebrate : worm
    e. urban : country

90. **immature : ripe ::**
    a. humbug : feign
    b. vigilant : alert
    c. opaque : transparent
    d. curtail : economize
    e. inquisitive : prying

DEFINITIONS IN CONTEXT

111. The sound of an approaching plane **bolstered** the survivors' hopes for an early rescue.
    a. changed
    b. lessened
    c. corrected
    d. curtailed
    e. supported

112. Her **superlative** performance brought the cheering audience to its feet.
    a. pleasing
    b. charming
    c. supreme
    d. dramatic
    e. exaggerated

SYNONYMS OR SIMILAR MEANINGS

113. **proficient**
    a. adept
    b. desirable
    c. satisfactory
    d. aggressive
    e. acceptable

114. **exuberant**
    a. moderate
    b. overflowing
    c. hysterical
    d. shrewd
    e. immature

ANTONYMS OR OPPOSITE MEANINGS

115. **vitality**
    a. listlessness
    b. enthusiasm
    c. hysteria
    d. difficulty
    e. popularity

116. **adept**
    a. expert
    b. difficult
    c. unusual
    d. strong
    e. unskilled

WORDS IN CONTEXT

117. The formerly _____ Yankees were stunned by the defeat.
    a. adept
    b. proficient
    c. exuberant
    d. invincible
    e. bereaved

118. The _____ of the avalanche completely destroyed the tiny village in its path.
    a. stance
    b. pinnacle
    c. proficiency
    d. oblivion
    e. momentum

ANALOGIES

119. **stance : feet ::**
    a. mire : swamp
    b. dilemma : mind
    c. delve : dig
    d. bauble : valuable
    e. deficient : lacking

120. **pinnacle : acme ::**
    a. torrid : cool
    b. pertinent : brash
    c. symmetry : balance
    d. diligent : lazy
    e. enhance : lessen

DEFINITIONS IN CONTEXT

101. The heavy rains flooded the **tributaries** which in turn caused the river to overflow its banks.
    a. steep banks
    b. high waterfalls
    c. backyard pools
    d. small streams flowing into larger bodies of water
    e. wooden barrels

102. Despite complaints about the food, the students behaved like **gluttons** in the cafeteria.
    a. dainty eaters
    b. angry customers
    c. greedy eaters
    d. tired shoppers
    e. hysterical critics

SYNONYMS OR SIMILAR MEANINGS

103. **torrid**
    a. quiet
    b. hot
    c. dull
    d. slow
    e. easy

104. **stupefy**
    a. alert
    b. melt
    c. heat
    d. cleanse
    e. stun

ANTONYMS OR OPPOSITE MEANINGS

105. **slothful**
    a. listless
    b. indulgent
    c. oblivious
    d. energetic
    e. furtive

WORDS IN CONTEXT

106. For months after the tragic accident, the _____ woman led a secluded life.
    a. slothful
    b. bereaved
    c. gluttonous
    d. inquisitive
    e. glib

107. The doctors were not immediately able to determine the extent of the injuries to the _____ woman's unborn child.
    a. bereaved
    b. secluded
    c. pregnant
    d. diligent
    e. plausible

ANALOGIES

108. **waif : homeless ::**
    a. nucleus : mutation
    b. humbug : fraud
    c. convalescent : recuperating
    d. psychiatrist : stigma
    e. humbug : deceives

109. **bauble : trinket ::**
    a. symmetry : triangle
    b. crypt : vault
    c. psychiatrist : psychology
    d. urban : rustic
    e. plausible : excuse

110. **dirge : funeral ::**
    a. hum : whistle
    b. burial : birth
    c. tune : pitch
    d. ballad : concert
    e. hide : bury

ANALOGIES

131. **satellite : moon ::**
   a. vertebrate : worm
   b. devastate : destroy
   c. urban : countrified
   d. scavenger : vulture
   e. invincible : Superman

132. **canine : dog-like ::**
   a. silhouetted : outlined
   b. valley : peak
   c. vertebrate : spineless
   d. induce : reduce
   e. bolster : undermine

DEFINITIONS IN CONTEXT

133. In mid-race, a sudden muscle **spasm** brought the runner to an unexpected halt.
   a. contraction
   b. relaxation
   c. itch
   d. tickle
   e. weakening

134. **Culled** from many and varied sources, the completed report was a masterpiece of thorough research.
   a. reported
   b. selected
   c. located
   d. written
   e. outlined

SYNONYMS OR SIMILAR MEANINGS

135. **disintegrate**
   a. slip
   b. fall
   c. break up
   d. disappear
   e. fade

136. **components**
   a. mechanisms
   b. items
   c. wires
   d. parts
   e. cases

ANTONYMS OR OPPOSITE MEANINGS

137. **tolerable**
   a. unbearable
   b. mediocre
   c. fair
   d. supportable
   e. plausible

WORDS IN CONTEXT

138. His work in space research made him keenly sensitive to ___ problems.
   a. canine
   b. tolerable
   c. exuberant
   d. exotic
   e. cosmic

139. Mathematical ___ are behind much successful space exploration.
   a. satellites
   b. components
   c. theorems
   d. spasms
   e. canines

140. A careful ___ of election results enabled each candidate to see where she or he had lost or gained support.
   a. theorem
   b. tabulation
   c. spasm
   d. disintegration
   e. component

DEFINITIONS IN CONTEXT

121. Successful **guerrilla** raids on supply trains depleted the enemy's ammunition reserves.
   a. mountain animal
   b. criminal
   c. army officer
   d. independent fighter
   e. helicopter

122. During the Civil War, border **skirmishes** between slave and free states were a frequent occurrence.
   a. slight fights
   b. delaying actions
   c. ambushes
   d. massacres
   e. great debates

SYNONYMS OR SIMILAR MEANINGS

123. **devastate**
   a. burn
   b. hesitate
   c. consider
   d. demolish
   e. argue

124. **encampment**
   a. dormitory
   b. village
   c. tent
   d. ranch
   e. camp

ANTONYMS OR OPPOSITE MEANINGS

125. **demolition**
   a. destruction
   b. explosion
   c. surprise
   d. design
   e. creation

126. **frustrate**
   a. thwart
   b. fulfill
   c. frame
   d. feign
   e. induce

WORDS IN CONTEXT

127. Hurricane ___ often totals millions of dollars.
   a. intensity
   b. income
   c. havoc
   d. pinnacle
   e. hysteria

128. With a quick ___, he restored the humor of the group.
   a. sally
   b. fallacy
   c. chagrin
   d. flail
   e. skirmish

ANALOGIES

129. **silhouette : outline ::**
   a. malady : cure
   b. cryptic : puzzling
   c. exotic : ordinary
   d. induce : eradicate
   e. hybrid : mix

130. **chagrin : delight ::**
   a. stigma : stain
   b. nucleus : center
   c. invigorating : dulling
   d. devastation : creation
   e. allay : relieve

DEFINITIONS IN CONTEXT

151. After being **scrutinized** by three jewelers, the gem was still considered practically flawless.
    a. polished
    b. chipped into small stones
    c. closely examined
    d. weighed and measured
    e. placed in several acids

152. Location as well as price sometimes determines the type of **clientele** a store attracts.
    a. employees
    b. employers
    c. advertisers
    d. security
    e. customers

SYNONYMS OR SIMILAR MEANINGS

153. **patron**
    a. rival
    b. artist
    c. neighbor
    d. sponsor
    e. dignitary

154. **evaluate**
    a. perfect
    b. improve
    c. estimate
    d. establish
    e. esteem

ANTONYMS OR OPPOSITE MEANINGS

155. **frugal**
    a. saving
    b. wasteful
    c. hungry
    d. empty
    e. poor

156. **benefactor**
    a. friend
    b. relative
    c. neighbor
    d. patron
    e. enemy

WORDS IN CONTEXT

157. Her keen ____ of persons and their problems was a result of her ability to observe and to listen.
    a. scrutiny
    b. clientele
    c. eccentric
    d. tolerance
    e. perception

158. His extremely strange appearance, habits, and speech led neighbors to think of him as a(n) ____.
    a. eccentric
    b. patron
    c. benefactor
    d. economist
    e. clientele

ANALOGIES

159. **pigment : paint ::**
    a. convalescent : recuperates
    b. ingredient : recipe
    c. silhouette : landscape
    d. enthrall : captivate
    e. diligent : careless

160. **crucial : critical ::**
    a. bauble : trinket
    b. allay : increase
    c. pertinent : unimportant
    d. feign : pretend
    e. plausible : reasonable

DEFINITIONS IN CONTEXT

141. Winning a seat on a crowded bus often involves a brief **scrimmage**.
    a. handshake
    b. rough struggle
    c. delay
    d. conversation
    e. exchange of greetings

142. **Spontaneous** ideas are sometimes more effective than long-range and carefully plotted programs.
    a. clever
    b. ripe
    c. unplanned
    d. skillful
    e. happy

WORDS IN CONTEXT

143. Although he had been a star in high school athletics, he found ____ competition much more demanding.
    a. collegiate
    b. secondary
    c. illustrious
    d. appalling
    e. invigorating

144. Her failure to get a basket on her eighteenth try seemed ____ proof that basketball was not the extracurricular sport for her.
    a. mediocre
    b. conclusive
    c. inevitable
    d. spontaneous
    e. premature

SYNONYMS OR SIMILAR MEANINGS

145. **enthrall**
    a. destroy
    b. hesitate
    c. plan
    d. rage
    e. captivate

146. **bedlam**
    a. rage
    b. chagrin
    c. spasm
    d. uproar
    e. stance

ANTONYMS OR OPPOSITE MEANINGS

147. **illustrious**
    a. inaccessible
    b. glib
    c. unknown
    d. inappropriate
    e. imperative

148. **mediocre**
    a. average
    b. false
    c. secluded
    d. indifferent
    e. extraordinary

ANALOGIES

149. **premature : overdue ::**
    a. tolerable : unendurable
    b. superlative : supreme
    c. chagrin : embarrassment
    d. express : expand
    e. embryo : tadpole

150. **diaphragm : midriff ::**
    a. silhouette : figure
    b. nucleus : center
    c. dissect : analyze
    d. opaque : transparent
    e. exotic : native

WORD CLUES MASTERY TEST **J-18**

DEFINITIONS IN CONTEXT

171. Because she was so **preoccupied** with her own worries, she could not follow the conversation properly.
    a. slowly numbering
    b. in a trance
    c. bored with
    d. happily thinking of
    e. taken up with

172. The building of a sewage plant caused nearby property to **depreciate** rapidly.
    a. break into small lots
    b. increase in value
    c. lessen in value
    d. acquire a strong smell
    e. tilt toward the river

WORDS IN CONTEXT

173. Oscar would ____ out his clean clothes from among the piles of laundry scattered about his room.
    a. ferret
    b. cater
    c. liquidate
    d. preoccupy
    e. depreciate

174. Ignoring pleas for identification, the desperate caller remained ____.
    a. humdrum
    b. anonymous
    c. bogus
    d. ethical
    e. preoccupied

SYNONYMS OR SIMILAR MEANINGS

175. **ethical**
    a. shy
    b. polite
    c. moral
    d. eternal
    e. valuable

176. **bogus**
    a. ridiculous
    b. monotonous
    c. frightening
    d. counterfeit
    e. ordinary

ANTONYMS OR OPPOSITE MEANINGS

177. **humdrum**
    a. loud
    b. rainy
    c. commonplace
    d. horrible
    e. exciting

178. **cater**
    a. provide
    b. withhold
    c. release
    d. give
    e. hurry

ANALOGIES

179. **credentials : references ::**
    a. dynamic : forceful
    b. bolster : support
    c. enhance : heighten
    d. inducements : incentives
    e. employers : evaluations

180. **liquidate : debt ::**
    a. dilate : expand
    b. bolster : bauble
    c. allay : pain
    d. deficient : funds
    e. budget : economize

WORD CLUES MASTERY TEST **J-17**

ANALOGIES

161. **decay : putrid ::**
    a. bauble : glitters
    b. frustrate : foil
    c. spontaneous : voluntary
    d. fugitive : furtive
    e. colleague : enemy

162. **segregate : isolate ::**
    a. eradicate : removal
    b. evaluate : estimate
    c. disintegrate : create
    d. chagrin : frustration
    e. dilate : contract

SYNONYMS OR SIMILAR MEANINGS

163. **inducement**
    a. salary
    b. prize
    c. incentive
    d. conspiracy
    e. penalty

164. **populate**
    a. inhabit
    b. attend
    c. count
    d. supply
    e. organize

ANTONYMS OR OPPOSITE MEANINGS

165. **futile**
    a. careless
    b. difficult
    c. trifling
    d. useful
    e. trivial

166. **hovel**
    a. shed
    b. poverty
    c. mansion
    d. tent
    e. hut

WORDS IN CONTEXT

167. The child's whining had ____ the baby-sitter to the point of tears.
    a. enthralled
    b. scrutinized
    c. appalled
    d. segregated
    e. exasperated

168. So great was her belief in planetary influence that she would make no major decisions without close study of her ____.
    a. psychology
    b. horoscope
    c. heritage
    d. geology
    e. satellite

DEFINITIONS IN CONTEXT

169. She was grateful to her grandmother for a rich **heritage** of cooking, weaving, and sewing skills.
    a. inheritance
    b. story
    c. characteristic
    d. handbook
    e. pattern

170. The brutal murders were especially **appalling** to neighbors of the victims.
    a. confusing
    b. exciting
    c. mystifying
    d. fascinating
    e. horrifying

WORD CLUES MASTERY TEST **J-20**

ANALOGIES

191. **transcribe : to record ::**
   a. enhance : to heighten
   b. dilemma : to decide
   c. ferret : a weasel
   d. adept : skillful
   e. stigma : a mark

192. **enraptured : delighted ::**
   a. premature : late
   b. demented : secluded
   c. bereaved : superimposed
   d. spasm : fit
   e. catered : supplied

DEFINITIONS IN CONTEXT

193. Having won three gold medals at the Olympics, he felt he had reached the **apex** of his career.
   a. bottom
   b. midpoint
   c. pinnacle
   d. beginning
   e. turning point

194. By wearing dark colors and extremely well-cut clothes, she diminished the impression of her **portly** figure.
   a. tall
   b. short
   c. skinny
   d. stout
   e. elderly

SYNONYMS OR SIMILAR MEANINGS

195. **ardor**
   a. disease
   b. ability
   c. sloth
   d. jargon
   e. enthusiasm

196. **qualm**
   a. chill
   b. daydream
   c. storm
   d. doubt
   e. shiver

ANTONYMS OR OPPOSITE MEANINGS

197. **subside**
   a. increase
   b. dwindle
   c. abate
   d. settle
   e. sink

198. **finale**
   a. termination
   b. inauguration
   c. finish
   d. conclusion
   e. exception

WORDS IN CONTEXT

199. The lights dimmed, the audience settled down, and the first delightful notes of the _____ began.
   a. strata
   b. finale
   c. overture
   d. ardor
   e. dirge

200. The audience responded to the splendid performance of both chorus and orchestra by giving a standing ovation to the entire _____.
   a. panorama
   b. overture
   c. tributary
   d. ensemble
   e. qualm

WORD CLUES MASTERY TEST **J-19**

ANALOGIES

181. **conveyance : cab ::**
   a. bogus : false
   b. ferret : search
   c. credentials : benefactors
   d. futile : useful
   e. canine : poodle

182. **girth : circumference ::**
   a. humdrum : ordinary
   b. heritage : inheritance
   c. populate : population
   d. clientele : symmetry
   e. depreciate : increase

DEFINITIONS IN CONTEXT

183. With new problems **superimposed** on her existing worries, Jan felt smothered by an overwhelming burden.
   a. removed
   b. colored
   c. cut out
   d. added to
   e. darkened

184. It was difficult to believe that the **petite** cheerleader, who weighed only 100 pounds, was the twin sister of the 185-pound quarterback.
   a. pretty
   b. lively
   c. shy
   d. young
   e. tiny

SYNONYMS OR SIMILAR MEANINGS

185. **bane**
   a. burn
   b. ruin
   c. noise
   d. excitement
   e. blessing

186. **esteem**
   a. please
   b. hope
   c. respect
   d. thank
   e. weigh

ANTONYMS OR OPPOSITE MEANINGS

187. **demure**
   a. modest
   b. coy
   c. humble
   d. forward
   e. sober

188. **deft**
   a. clumsy
   b. skillful
   c. small
   d. sharp
   e. stubborn

WORDS IN CONTEXT

189. From the peak we stared down at the _____ of the valley spread before us.
   a. bane
   b. conveyance
   c. girth
   d. esteem
   e. panorama

190. The emperor's entire household took particular pride in the rare beauty of the _____ gardens.
   a. humdrum
   b. bogus
   c. demure
   d. imperial
   e. putrid

WORD CLUES MASTERY TEST **J-22**

DEFINITIONS IN CONTEXT

211. The pioneers **hewed** their way through forests to make roads and settlements.
    a. cut
    b. burned
    c. beat
    d. dug
    e. dynamited

212. One wonders who first phrased such **axioms** as, "An ounce of prevention is worth a pound of cure."
    a. stories with morals
    b. established principles
    c. rumors
    d. fictitious statements
    e. statements denied by most people

SYNONYMS OR SIMILAR MEANINGS

213. **saturate**
    a. soak
    b. cover
    c. touch
    d. color
    e. exhaust

214. **vigil**
    a. worry
    b. watch
    c. fear
    d. warning
    e. anxiety

ANTONYMS OR OPPOSITE MEANINGS

215. **turbulent**
    a. violent
    b. cold
    c. calm
    d. revolving
    e. portly

216. **bland**
    a. smooth
    b. suave
    c. equal
    d. even
    e. irritating

WORDS IN CONTEXT

217. Dangerous driving conditions led to the ____ of our skiing trip.
    a. vigil
    b. axiom
    c. prelude
    d. overture
    e. cancellation

218. His ____ attitude soon depressed even his usually cheerful companions.
    a. turbulent
    b. bland
    c. pessimistic
    d. vigilant
    e. naïve

ANALOGIES

219. **buttress : support ::**
    a. precinct : voter
    b. cater : supply
    c. anonymous : named
    d. subside : increase
    e. clientele : employers

220. **prelude : introduction ::**
    a. putrid : foul
    b. ferret : search
    c. exasperate : satisfy
    d. hovel : mansion
    e. finale : conclusion

WORD CLUES MASTERY TEST **J-21**

DEFINITIONS IN CONTEXT

201. The price of a precious stone is directly related to its **carats.**
    a. degree of hardness
    b. measure of sparkle
    c. units of weight
    d. color content
    e. design

202. Following her coming-out party, the **debutante** was caught in a whirl of social activities.
    a. college freshman
    b. girl having her first season in society
    c. a very wealthy woman
    d. juvenile actress
    e. a girl renowned for her beauty

SYNONYMS OR SIMILAR MEANINGS

203. **ordinance**
    a. request
    b. refusal
    c. peculiarity
    d. regulation
    e. discrimination

204. **aura**
    a. atmosphere
    b. circle
    c. odor
    d. rumor
    e. speed

ANTONYMS OR OPPOSITE MEANINGS

205. **naïve**
    a. artless
    b. sophisticated
    c. stupid
    d. unrefined
    e. stubborn

206. **diverse**
    a. varied
    b. different
    c. similar
    d. demure
    e. petite

WORDS IN CONTEXT

207. So ____ was he in his views that he spoke of and read only neighborhood news.
    a. diverse
    b. naïve
    c. portly
    d. imperial
    e. parochial

208. Every year the students staged a(n) ____ which made fun of the faculty.
    a. bauble
    b. humbug
    c. revue
    d. ordinance
    e. skirmish

ANALOGIES

209. **precinct : district ::**
    a. deity : dirge
    b. portly : large
    c. appropriation : allotment
    d. patron : enemy
    e. subside : increase

210. **dialect : region ::**
    a. pinnacle : bottom
    b. petite : tiny
    c. enrapture : enthrall
    d. credentials : references
    e. clientele : store

DEFINITIONS IN CONTEXT

231. His inability to follow directions may well have been the result of his **auditory** difficulty.
    a. nervous
    b. having to do with sight
    c. emotional
    d. having to do with speech
    e. having to do with hearing

232. **Simultaneous** action by both fire and police departments saved many lives.
    a. sudden
    b. at the same time
    c. clever
    d. scientific
    e. orderly

SYNONYMS OR SIMILAR MEANINGS

233. **environment**
    a. countryside
    b. appearance
    c. heredity
    d. surroundings
    e. residence

234. **pictorial**
    a. auditory
    b. illustrative
    c. oral
    d. accurate
    e. motionless

ANTONYMS OR OPPOSITE MEANINGS

235. **enlighten**
    a. entertain
    b. brighten
    c. educate
    d. illuminate
    e. obscure

236. **exploit**
    a. brave act
    b. humdrum activity
    c. courageous adventure
    d. daring deed
    e. narrow escape

WORDS IN CONTEXT

237. Since the delay was the airline's fault, I was ____ for my two-day stopover in Detroit.
    a. revoked
    b. enlightened
    c. reimbursed
    d. embossed
    e. exploited

238. Although ____ has increased the efficiency of manufacturing, it has eliminated many jobs.
    a. mainstay
    b. environment
    c. exploit
    d. automation
    e. frontage

ANALOGIES

239. **mainstay : support ::**
    a. deft : clumsy
    b. subside : rise
    c. naïve : sophisticated
    d. compulsion : segment
    e. ordinance : regulation

240. **revoke : issue ::**
    a. finale : overture
    b. buttress : weaken
    c. portly : thin
    d. saturate : soak
    e. proficient : adept

DEFINITIONS IN CONTEXT

221. The more **frontage**, the higher the price of a property.
    a. legal requirements
    b. building permits
    c. windows and doors
    d. land facing street or river
    e. electric outlets

222. The **embossed** stationery lent a touch of elegance to the invitation.
    a. with raised design
    b. with colored pictures
    c. tinted
    d. perfumed
    e. heavy

SYNONYMS OR SIMILAR MEANINGS

223. **reputable**
    a. similar
    b. respected
    c. plausible
    d. organized
    e. pertinent

224. **stability**
    a. intensity
    b. diversity
    c. eagerness
    d. steadiness
    e. deftness

ANTONYMS OR OPPOSITE MEANINGS

225. **laborious**
    a. easy
    b. industrious
    c. weariness
    d. impossible
    e. repetitious

226. **elongate**
    a. force
    b. lengthen
    c. age
    d. improve
    e. shorten

WORDS IN CONTEXT

227. Unable to control his ____ to gamble, he lost his job and alienated his family.
    a. stability
    b. frontage
    c. compulsion
    d. segment
    e. labor

228. The ____ power generated by dams often stimulates the growth of industry in nearby cities.
    a. hydraulic
    b. lateral
    c. reputable
    d. laborious
    e. elongated

ANALOGIES

229. **segment : whole ::**
    a. finale : overture
    b. portly : thin
    c. pit : leaf
    d. chapter : book
    e. boil : broil

230. **lateral : side ::**
    a. prelude : ending
    b. urban : country
    c. cosmic : universe
    d. auditory : visual
    e. hew : cut

DEFINITIONS IN CONTEXT
251. Her **discretion** in keeping private matters confidential made her an excellent secretary.
   a. sense of humor
   b. organization
   c. speed
   d. filing
   e. good judgment

252. When sweetness, stubbornness, and threats failed, the child's **ultimate** weapon was a tantrum.
   a. important
   b. certain
   c. hidden
   d. final
   e. silent

SYNONYMS OR SIMILAR MEANINGS
253. **fraught**
   a. confused   d. excited
   b. decorated   e. filled
   c. angered

254. **foible**
   a. crime   d. illness
   b. weakness   e. secret
   c. attack

ANTONYMS OR OPPOSITE MEANINGS
255. **fictitious**
   a. imaginary   d. amazing
   b. puzzling   e. amusing
   c. real

256. **obituary**
   a. want ad   d. birth announcement
   b. singing telegram e. party invitation
   c. for sale sign

WORDS IN CONTEXT
257. After all the careful scientific investigation, it is often a police officer's ____ which solves a case.
   a. foibles   d. oratory
   b. spinster   e. intuition
   c. obituary

258. While bachelor is a positive term, it is unfortunate that ____ has negative connotations.
   a. obituary   d. spinster
   b. discretion   e. foible
   c. intuition

ANALOGIES
259. **evidence : incriminates ::**
   a. narcotic : dulls   d. rabbit : embosses
   b. finale : overture   e. ferret : buttresses
   c. dormant : lively

260. **inkling : hint ::**
   a. colleague : enemy   d. scrutiny : glance
   b. qualm : doubt   e. revoke : issue
   c. diverse : same

DEFINITIONS IN CONTEXT
241. Her **droll** humor occasionally lightened a dull lecture.
   a. quaintly amusing
   b. sarcastic
   c. loud
   d. unpleasant
   e. silly

242. She was the type who **reveled** in being first with the worst.
   a. waited anxiously
   b. took great pleasure in
   c. relaxed in
   d. concentrated on
   e. revolted against

SYNONYMS OR SIMILAR MEANINGS
243. **artisan**
   a. skilled worker   d. speaker
   b. magician   e. acrobat
   c. apprentice

244. **gala**
   a. pictorial   d. large
   b. musical   e. silly
   c. festive

ANTONYMS OR OPPOSITE MEANINGS
245. **dormant**
   a. dead   d. active
   b. closed   e. foggy
   c. stubborn

246. **provident**
   a. lucky   d. grateful
   b. prudent   e. wasteful
   c. intelligent

WORDS IN CONTEXT
247. Since it was the second ____ of the town's founding, none of the original settlers were alive.
   a. artisan   d. appropriation
   b. centennial   e. event
   c. gala

248. Only the finest actor is able to hold his or her audience with a(n)____.
   a. revel   d. animation
   b. jargon   e. oratory
   c. monologue

ANALOGIES
249. **provincial : local ::**
   a. revoke : issue   d. spontaneous : unplanned
   b. segment : whole   e. bland : spicy
   c. turbulent : calm

250. **oratory : solemn ::**
   a. horticulture : garden d. malady : cure
   b. parochial : limited   e. celebration : jubilant
   c. dissect : frog

DEFINITIONS IN CONTEXT

271. Out-of-towners often find the **allure** of city excitement and entertainment irresistible.
   a. idea
   b. sensation
   c. suggestion
   d. truth
   e. fascination

272. Led **astray** by clever advertising, the obese couple acquired a large collection of diet foods, diet pills, and diet books.
   a. beyond exercise
   b. into the health food store
   c. away from snacks
   d. in the wrong direction
   e. into the mail-order catalog

SYNONYMS OR SIMILAR MEANINGS

273. **genteel**
   a. firm
   b. young
   c. refined
   d. gentle
   e. smooth

274. **disillusion**
   a. excite
   b. darken
   c. delay
   d. confuse
   e. disenchant

ANTONYMS OR OPPOSITE MEANINGS

275. **expressly**
   a. unintentionally
   b. plainly
   c. definitely
   d. rapidly
   e. slowly

276. **infidel**
   a. foreigner
   b. believer
   c. traitor
   d. colleague
   e. spinster

WORDS IN CONTEXT

277. Having indulged in double portions of everything, he was feeling somewhat _____.
   a. indisposed
   b. ravenous
   c. disillusioned
   d. inaccessible
   e. intolerable

278. With the stereo playing at full volume, I found the noise level was _____.
   a. communicable
   b. intolerable
   c. genteel
   d. alluring
   e. imperial

ANALOGIES

279. **dupe : deceive ::**
   a. incriminate : pardon
   b. dormant : active
   c. visualize : picture mentally
   d. segment : whole
   e. droll : humorous

280. **disease : communicable ::**
   a. revel : mourn
   b. belated : early
   c. annihilate : create
   d. cat : canine
   e. myth : fictitious

ANALOGIES

261. **eloquent : speaker ::**
   a. bland : mild
   b. fictitious : story
   c. petite : hippopotamus
   d. cater : supply
   e. liquidate : remove

262. **grotesque : bizarre ::**
   a. turbulent : calm
   b. foible : weakness
   c. invincible : unconquerable
   d. elongate : lengthen
   e. saturate : soak

SYNONYMS OR SIMILAR MEANINGS

263. **visualize**
   a. picture mentally
   b. make a list of
   c. explore thoroughly
   d. analyze in detail
   e. say aloud

264. **befall**
   a. upset
   b. knock down
   c. trip
   d. befit
   e. happen to

ANTONYMS OR OPPOSITE MEANINGS

265. **belated**
   a. delayed
   b. reduced
   c. early
   d. wished
   e. incorrect

266. **inevitable**
   a. curable
   b. avoidable
   c. conquerable
   d. stable
   e. available

WORDS IN CONTEXT

267. Clothing styles once considered _____ are favored by many fashionable young people.
   a. belated
   b. grotesque
   c. eloquent
   d. passé
   e. maternal

268. Greedy hunters have almost _____ some beautiful and rare species of animals.
   a. annihilated
   b. befallen
   c. visualized
   d. incriminated
   e. revoked

DEFINITIONS IN CONTEXT

269. He made his fortune through a series of small, **illegitimate** business deals.
   a. licensed
   b. cruel
   c. illegal
   d. clever
   e. careful

270. To protect one's young is a natural **maternal** instinct.
   a. fatherly
   b. parental
   c. sisterly
   d. motherly
   e. brotherly

SYNONYMS OR SIMILAR MEANINGS

291. **namesake**
   a. person having the same name as another
   b. niece or nephew
   c. relative
   d. family friend
   e. adopted child

292. **infatuate**
   a. become convinced of something
   b. make aware of
   c. become involved in criminal activity
   d. inspire with a foolish passion
   e. have a trick played upon oneself

ANTONYMS OR OPPOSITE MEANINGS

293. **rift**
   a. incision   d. flight
   b. break   e. joining
   c. stream

294. **betroth**
   a. promise to marry   d. plan a wedding
   b. plan to divorce   e. select a best man
   c. announce an engagement

DEFINITIONS IN CONTEXT

295. The director's **searing** criticism left the players' faces red with embarrassment.
   a. drooping   d. lengthy
   b. lively   e. sudden
   c. burning

296. Lonely people often have a **doting** relationship with their pets.
   a. being concerned about   d. being adept with
   b. being in debt to   e. being demure with
   c. being too fond of

WORDS IN CONTEXT

297. The scissors sharpener was last seen moving rapidly out of the range of angry housewives ____ bent knives and broken scissors.
   a. feigning   d. brandishing
   b. invoking   e. searing
   c. doting

298. A ____ to the birthplace of the founder is often an essential element of many Eastern religions.
   a. ritual   d. betrothal
   b. pilgrimage   e. foible
   c. namesake

ANALOGIES

299. **infernal : hell ::**
   a. conclusive : theory   d. disillusion : disenchant
   b. deity : servant   e. boisterous : rally
   c. artisan : author

300. **baptism : ritual ::**
   a. fallacy : truth   d. revoke : issue
   b. humility : pride   e. expressly : specially
   c. monologue : speech

DEFINITIONS IN CONTEXT

281. Continued **disuse** left the lawn tools cobweb-covered.
   a. care
   b. washing
   c. mowing
   d. lack of use
   e. search

282. For me, learning to play the violin was a triumph of **perseverance.**
   a. strength
   b. courage
   c. persistence
   d. loyalty
   e. annoyance

ANALOGIES

283. **revel : boisterous ::**
   a. measles : communicable   d. dupe : deceive
   b. infidel : believer   e. beauty : grotesque
   c. allure : fascinate

284. **debts : liability ::**
   a. salesmen : glib   d. auditory : visual
   b. obituary : birth   e. decisions : dilemma
      announcement
   c. enlighten : obscure

SYNONYMS OR SIMILAR MEANINGS

285. **comparative**
   a. obvious   d. increasing
   b. relative   e. impolite
   c. superficial

286. **torso**
   a. physique   d. toes
   b. head   e. trunk
   c. neck

ANTONYMS OR OPPOSITE MEANINGS

287. **animation**
   a. liveliness   d. dullness
   b. health   e. existence
   c. lightheartedness

288. **humility**
   a. conceit   d. weakness
   b. modesty   e. stability
   c. chagrin

WORDS IN CONTEXT

289. His lack of ____ certainly hastened his death.
   a. animation   d. humility
   b. temperance   e. torso
   c. liability

290. Her ____ efforts to overcome illness, poverty, and prejudice were surely rewarded when she accepted her Olympic medal.
   a. comparative   d. dogged
   b. temperate   e. humble
   c. boisterous

1 When the finance committee *economized* to such a great extent, no money was allowed for anything but essential operations.

The best meaning for *economize* is:
a. spend money
b. cut expenses
c. revise laws
d. stop spending

2 While a person is fully conscious, the psychiatrist may have difficulty in *inducing* him to talk freely. For this reason, hypnosis and drugs are sometimes used.

Another word for *induce* is:
a. persuade   c. help
b. prevent   d. force

3 Viewing Japan from the air, one sees a *panorama* of green rice paddies, terraces of tea plants, crowded cities, and smoking factories.

The best meaning for *panorama* is:
a. cultural pattern
b. natural history
c. wide view
d. geography

4 The *intensity* of the heat often causes sunstroke or heat exhaustion in those who are not accustomed to it.

Another meaning for *intensity* is:
a. extreme degree
b. violence
c. temperature
d. great quantity

5 In an operation, everything must be *sterile* in order to prevent infection.

Sterile means:
a. germ-free   c. shining
b. boiled   d. anesthetic

6 An acquaintance of ours became extremely *despondent* as a result of a series of misfortunes. We arranged a party in hopes that it would accomplish some good.

Despondent means:
a. rejected
b. overlooked
c. neglected
d. dejected

7 The *axiom* that in a hurricane it is better to be safe than sorry has been proved many times over.

An *axiom* is:
a. a story with a moral
b. a wise precaution
c. an established principle
d. a fictitious statement

8 Though the younger tennis player was becoming better known each day, he had not yet reached the *pinnacle* of his career.

Another word for *pinnacle* is:
a. peak
b. middle
c. bottom
d. perfection

9 An archaeologist is most likely to find treasures of metal since they do not *pulverize* as readily as pottery. Many pieces of pottery are so *pulverized* that it is impossible to restore them.

Pulverize means:
a. crash; shatter
b. crack
c. wear out
d. become dust

10 Some taxes are *assessed* according to individual income. Though most people object to taxes, the amount they are required to pay is usually fair.

The best meaning for *assess* is:
a. fix the amount of
b. underestimate the value of
c. judge to be
d. demand a fine

11 Sometimes a talent may lie *dormant* for years before it is awakened. Putting such a talent to use is like discovering unknown riches.

Another meaning for *dormant* is:
a. in a window
b. awake
c. forgotten
d. inactive

12 We found articles of all types buried with some of the skeletons. Often we could determine the social *strata* of individuals by the articles that were buried with them.

Strata means:
a. levels
b. minds
c. cultures
d. civilizations

13 In olden times, all stories were *narrated*. Many stories were hundreds of years old before they were written down.

Narrate means:
a. read
b. relate
c. unfold
d. relive

14 At the first meeting, the *nucleus* of the group was formed. Through the efforts of these few people, a giant organization developed.

The best synonym for *nucleus* is:
a. core   c. skeleton
b. shape   d. structure

15 The most important *dignitary* I met was the president of a new African nation. He was making a speaking tour through our country.

The best meaning for *dignitary* is:
a. government employee
b. member of a royal family
c. member of the armed forces
d. person of high rank

16 After the sultry air of the city, the bracing country air was very *invigorating*. It restored the energy I had lost in my urban home.

The best synonym for *invigorating* is:
a. exciting   c. lusty
b. vital   d. stimulating

17 For many years the public seemed indifferent to the fact that the buffalo was becoming extinct. *Eloquent* appeals from conservationists finally moved the government to take action.

Another meaning for *eloquent* is:
a. humorous
b. persistent
c. expressive
d. very angry

18 The armies of the enemy had created *havoc* in the surrounding area. Hardly a village was left standing.

Havoc means:
a. great destruction
b. good will
c. impatience
d. shortage of materials

19 It was a serious *dilemma*. The two individuals suspected of the crime were outstanding citizens of the town. Both had sound alibis. The evidence, however, indicated that one of them was the murderer.

Dilemma means:
a. serious circumstances
b. prejudiced jury
c. difficult choice
d. impossible decision

20 The fully developed blossom will not last as long as the *immature* one.

The best synonym for *immature* is:
a. unripe   c. rare
b. fresh   d. embryonic

21 The *fallacy* in the man's story finally appeared. After claiming he had not seen the victim that night, he accidentally mentioned the clothing she had worn.

Another word for *fallacy* is:
a. weakness
b. prejudice
c. trick
d. falsity

22 It was interesting to observe the progress of our *dynamic* Congressman in Washington affairs. Through his activity, he became well known in a short time.

The best synonym for *dynamic* is:
a. powerless
b. forceful
c. athletic
d. pleasing

23 A clear sparkling pool that held the sunlight would have been more beautiful than the *opaque* waters of the pond near our home. In our pond I could imagine all kinds of creatures lurking beneath the surface.

The best meaning for *opaque* is:
a. full of light
b. not transparent
c. not moving
d. black and brown

24 The victorious tennis player expressed his *exuberant* feelings by throwing his racket high in the air and leaping over the net to shake his opponent's hand.

The best synonym for *exuberant* is:
a. moderate
b. overflowing
c. exciting
d. hysterical

25 After a hurricane sweeps through with heavy rains, the ground is *saturated* with water.

The best synonym for *saturate* is:
a. wet
b. touch
c. soak
d. cover

Check your answers with the key in the front of this book. If you have 20 or more correct answers, proceed to the next level.